Highest Praise for Caitlin Rother and Her Nonfiction Thrillers

THEN NO ONE CAN HAVE HER

"I honestly could not stop reading Caitlin Rother's new book, THEN NO ONE CAN HAVE HER. It is riveting, revealing, and insightful . . . . The way she unfolded the mystery of who did it was accomplished with perfect pacing. And her closing chapters, written in first person, made my eyes water. What a fabulous, fabulous book!"

—**Suzy Spencer,** *New York Times* bestselling author of
Secret Sex Lives

"From the first page, Caitlin Rother makes the hair stand up on the back of your neck with this thorough, unforgettable account of greed, flawed love, and homicide. It's all here: a true, modern murder mystery, told with a reporter's perceptiveness and a storyteller's sensibilities."

—**Ron Franscell,** bestselling author of *The Darkest Night* and
Delivered from Evil

"It's exciting to see a reporter's reporter like Caitlin Rother, churning out journalism built around sharp prose, while getting to the core of a compelling crime story. Her latest, *Then No One Can Have Her*, equals and maybe surpasses anything she's done to date. It's a dark, twisty, riveting true story that will leave readers' jaws on their bellies while they burn through."

—**M. William Phelps,** *New York Times* bestselling author and
TV host

"Tightly written, meticulously researched, Rother has hammered out a riveting new true crime from a complicated and fascinating case."

—**Steve Jackson,** *New York Times* bestselling author of
Monster

"Prepare to be hooked by Rother's absorbing narrative of greed, desperation, and twisty relationships in her latest spellbinder, *Then No One Can Have Her.* Between lies, financial shenanigans, shady legal maneuverings, and divided families, this tale sounds like fiction, but it's all true. And very dark."

—**Katherine Ramsland,** forensic psychologist and author

I'LL TAKE CARE OF YOU

"Rother has written another 'ripped from the headlines' page-turner. Journalistic and thorough, this title is sure to be popular. Purchase for public libraries with large true crime collections."
  —**Library Journal**

"Riveting . . . a story that will haunt you. . . . Rother presents a fascinating study of one woman's evil and greed—that ultimately leads to the murder of a kind-hearted millionaire. The compassion the author shows for the victim and the victim's family makes this book an emotional and gripping tale from beginning to end."
  —**Aphrodite Jones,** *New York Times* best-selling author of
    A Perfect Husband

"Once again Caitlin Rother gets to the heart of a very compelling story, with an eye for detail. A must-read for true crime fans."
  —**Robert Scott,** *New York Times* best-selling author of
    Shattered Innocence

"Caitlin Rother hooks you from the prologue on in *I'll Take Care of You.* With the keen eye of a veteran journalist, Rother objectively details the murder and shocking investigation of Newport Beach, Calif., millionaire Bill McLaughlin—a crime that took nearly 20 years for police and prosecutors to convict his greedy, live-in lover, Nanette Johnston, and her former NFL-playing, ne'er-do-well boyfriend, Eric Naposki."
  —**Suzy Spencer,** *New York Times* best-selling author of
    Wasted and *Secret Sex Lives*

"*I'll Take Care of You* is a chilling account of murder and its aftermath by an author at the top of her game. Caitlin Rother's background as an investigative reporter, plus her skill as a storyteller, combine to create a book that is impossible to put down."
  —**Fred Rosen,** author of *Lobster Boy*

LOST GIRLS

"A close look at a killer . . . a deeply reported, dispassionately written attempt to determine what created a monster and predator . . . a cautionary tale and a horror story, done superbly by a writer who knows how to burrow into a complex case."
  —**Los Angeles Times**

DEAD RECKONING

"Well researched and a quick, engrossing read, this should be popular with true crime readers, especially the Ann Rule crowd."
   —*Library Journal,* **Starred Review**

"Rother's investigative journalist's tenacity and eye for detail and her knack for telling a good detective story that reads like a novel set this book above most in the genre. This was one of those true crime tales that gave me chills, and that's not easy to do."
   —**Steve Jackson**

"With this headline-grabbing case of multiple murder, Rother skillfully tells a breathless tale of unthinkable events that no true crime fan should miss."
   —**Katherine Ramsland**

"Rother digs deep into the story of this horrible murder—unearthing never-before-told details of the crime, the investigation and the twisted mind of the man who set it all into motion."
   —**Susan Leibowitz,** producer of *Dateline*'s "The Last Voyage"

"Gripping . . . Rother gives readers compelling insight to an unthinkable American nightmare. The book is frank and frightening, and it sizzles."
   —**Aphrodite Jones**

"Impressively reported in a forthright narrative . . . a pitch-perfect study of avarice, compulsion and pure California illusion."
   —**Ron Franscell**

"We've finally found the next Ann Rule! Caitlin Rother writes with heart and suspense. *Dead Reckoning* is a chilling read by a writer at the top of her game."
   —**Gregg Olsen**

"Gripping, brutal, riveting—once again, Rother delivers a thrilling account of murder and mayhem."
   —**M. William Phelps**

"A true-crime triumph . . . . Rother solidifies her star status."
   —*The San Diego Union-Tribune*

"Rother is at her best. . . . This gruesome story is fast-paced and will grip any lover of the true crime genre."
   —*North County Times*

"Rother brings a journalist's careful attention to detail in this chilling look into the mind of a psychopath."
   —*Coronado Life Magazine*

"A mesmerizing story."
   —*Orange Coast Magazine*

POISONED LOVE

"A true-crime thriller that will keep you on the edge of your seat."
   —**Aphrodite Jones**

"A gripping and chilling book. A tawdry and twisted story of sex and drugs, deception and murder. And here's the scariest part—it's all true."
   —**Tom Murray,** producer for *Court TV*'s "Pretty Poison"

"Absorbing and impeccably researched . . . a classic California noir story of passion and betrayal and death, with a beautiful, scheming adulteress at the center of the web."
   —**John Taylor**

"With integrity, class and skill, Rother weaves this complex story seamlessly in the page-turning fashion of a suspenseful novel."
   —**M. William Phelps**

"Chilling . . . Rother paints a portrait of the culture that raised Kristin, hired her, was lured by her beauty, and now must share in the dire consequences."
   —**Kevin Barry,** producer for Oxygen Network's *The Kristin Rossum Story*

"A lively and immaculately researched book."
   —**Carol Anne Davis**

"A devastating portrait . . . an unwavering look at how one young woman fantasized herself into murder."
   —*The San Diego Union-Tribune*

"A page-turner."
　　—*San Diego Metropolitan*

"A gripping account."
　　—*San Diego Magazine*

"An absorbing page-turner, driven by well-drawn characters and a dynamic investigation."
　　—**Crimemagazine.com**

"A concise and riveting account of one of the most challenging but fascinating investigations of my police career."
　　—**Laurie Agnew,** San Diego Police Department homicide detective

"A riveting and detailed view of a cold, calculated homicide romantically staged as a suicide. I couldn't put it down."
　　—**Bob Petrachek,** Regional Computer Forensic Laboratory examiner

BODY PARTS

"A must read . . . well-written, extremely intense; a book that I could not put down."
　　—**Kim Cantrell,** *True Crime Book Reviews*

"Excellent, well researched, well written."
　　—**Don Bauder,** *San Diego Reader*

"Page-turning excitement and blood curdling terror . . . riveting, fast-paced, and sure to keep you up at night."
　　—**M. William Phelps**

"Rother paints every page with all the violent colors of a malignant sociopath's fever. This kind of frightening and fascinating glimpse into a killer's mind is rare."
　　—**Ron Franscell**

"A superior study of the formation of a serial killer and his lost and lonely victims."
　　—**Carol Anne Davis**

"Shocking, chilling, fast-paced . . . a book crime aficionados will be loath to put down."
　　—**Simon Read**

Also by Caitlin Rother

I'll Take Care of You

Naked Addiction

Lost Girls

Poisoned Love

My Life, Deleted
(By Scott and Joan Bolzan and Caitlin Rother)

Dead Reckoning

Where Hope Begins/Deadly Devotion
(By Alysia Sofios with Caitlin Rother)

Body Parts

Twisted Triangle
(By Caitlin Rother with John Hess)

*Available from Kensington Publishing Corp.
and Pinnacle Books

THEN NO ONE CAN HAVE HER

CAITLIN ROTHER

PINNACLE BOOKS
Kensington Publishing Corp.
http://www.kensingtonbooks.com

Some names have been changed to protect the privacy of individuals connected to this story.

PINNACLE BOOKS are published by

Kensington Publishing Corp.
119 West 40th Street
New York, NY 10018

All Kensington Titles, Imprints, and Distributed Lines are available at special quantity discounts for bulk purchases for sales promotions, premiums, fund-raising, and educational or institutional use. Special book excerpts or customized printings can also be created to fit specific needs. For details, write or phone the office of the Kensington special sales manager: Kensington Publishing Corp., 119 West 40th Street, New York, NY 10018, attn: Special Sales Department, Phone: 1-800-221-2647.

Pinnacle and the P logo Reg. U.S. Pat. & TM Off.

ISBN-13: 978-0-7860-3257-0
ISBN-10: 0-7860-3257-X
First Kensington Mass Market Edition: November 2015

eISBN-13: 978-0-7860-3258-7
eISBN-10: 0-7860-3258-8

10 9 8 7 6 5 4 3 2 1

Printed in the United States of America

CHAPTER 1

A thunderstorm hit the quiet town of Prescott that first Tuesday in July 2008, drenching the thirsty pines, manzanita and scrub oak in this rural enclave, nestled at the foot of Granite Mountain. Even at 5,400 feet, summertime is sweltering in Arizona, and monsoon season always provides a welcome reprieve.

But these particular showers brought an emotional cleansing as well, helping to wash away the tensions that had developed between Carol Kennedy and her daughter Charlotte during the divorce battle with the girl's father, Steve DeMocker.

Sixteen-year-old Charlotte, who had always been more of a daddy's girl than her older sister, Katie, accused her mother of unfairly prolonging the divorce by refusing to accept Steve's settlement offers. Carol, who saw it as quite the other way around, got so upset during an argument that she jumped out of the car in the middle of an intersection and walked away.

At one point relations between mother and daughter grew so strained that Charlotte moved into Steve's condo near the Hassayampa golf course. Still angry, though,

Charlotte complained that if Carol continued to reject Steve's offers, there would be no money left for her to study premed at her out-of-state dream college and become a neurosurgeon.

Not only is the paying of your bills hurting and restricting my immediate life, but now, my future and the quality of my education and degree is in jeopardy, Charlotte wrote her mother. *It's hard to realize that my Mom, someone who I unconditionally have loved all my life, may damage the rest of my life.*

After Charlotte said she was unwilling to spend time with her mother until the divorce was resolved, Carol cried to her friends that Steve had turned their daughter against her.

But since the divorce had been finalized in late May, a new and more comfortable family dynamic had begun to emerge. Carol and Charlotte were making amends, and things also seemed better—and calmer—between Carol and Steve as well.

As a result, they were all able to gather at the Phoenix airport in late June, just days before the storm, to give Katie an intimate send-off to a study-abroad program in South Africa. Making an emotional scene near the security gate, they told each other tearfully that they still appreciated one another, even if they weren't the family they once were.

"There was nothing but expressions of love and gratitude and happiness," Katie recalled later. "We spent about twenty minutes, all talking about that, and crying and giving big group family hugs."

As Katie walked toward the gate, she turned to see Steve, with his arms around Carol and Charlotte, all of them waving good-bye.

A few nights later, on Wednesday, July 2, the recent

rainstorm gave Carol and Charlotte a chance to bond even further by talking about such mundane topics as the weather.

Howd ya like that boomin storm yesterday? Carol texted Charlotte that evening at seven-fourteen.

It was "awesome," Charlotte responded, saying she loved the showers so much she only wished there had been more of them.

Carol texted back in capital letters that she LOVED her daughter, to which Charlotte responded at 7:39 P.M. with the same high emotion.

Later, these last healing moments would seem so poignant and yet so bittersweet, exchanged just before a far more tumultuous storm—that no one saw coming—tore this family apart forever.

Carol was a gentle, loving and openhearted soul, a devoted mother, a gifted teacher, therapist and artist, a role model and a mentor. Often described as lighting up a room with her benevolent life force, she was a spiritual being who emanated compassion. Carol taught courses such as "Yoga Psychology," "Painting From the Heart," and "Dream Work" for eleven years at Prescott College, where many students saw her as a guru who not only changed their lives, but also became a faithful friend.

These days she was working as a therapist at Pia's Place, an extended-care treatment facility run by women for women in the outskirts of downtown Prescott. Pia's billed its services as "empowering" women in recovery, treating them also for depression, PTSD, sexual trauma, codependence, and love/sex addiction. The goal was to help them get in touch with the issues that had caused them to turn to drugs and booze.

Although Carol had no personal problems with drugs or alcohol, she did have extensive counseling and life experience with love and sex addiction from which to draw. She'd met Steve, her charming, intelligent and athletic husband-to-be, in her late twenties after a short-lived, failed first marriage. Deeming each other a soul mate, they were married in 1982. But after a promising start, their marriage devolved into a bumpy roller-coaster ride of Steve's multiplying affairs. In 2003, the couple separated and, reaching her limit, Carol finally filed for divorce in March 2007.

As the oldest of nine children, Steve was also a mentor and role model, especially among his siblings. In his educated and accomplished family, Steve stood out for his ability and willingness to perform death-defying rescues—scaling a steep cliff to save one injured woman and flipping his own kayak to pull another woman out of churning white-water rapids.

In 1995, he switched careers from academics to investment brokering, saying he wanted to continue to help people, just in a different way. The more money he made, however, the more friends he lost as he became more materialistic and manipulative, his personality, tastes and spending habits changing as his annual income shot up to $500,000.

After Carol and Steve separated, the couple fought over who could and should spend what, how to divide their assets and sizable credit card debt. Nonetheless, Steve continued to spend and take out loans, even borrowing tens of thousands of dollars from his elderly parents to pay bills. As the battle grew more contentious and stressful for Carol, some of her friends worried she might take her own life.

But now that the divorce papers had been signed and she had a new boyfriend—whom she was flying to Maine to visit in just a few days—Carol was doing much better. Finally feeling free of Steve's hold over her, she was optimistic, as if she could really move on with her life.

That relief was bolstered by the fact that she'd been tested recently and had managed to hang tough. Carol said as much in a call after work that Wednesday to her longtime friend Katherine Dean Warnett, who, coincidentally, was about to go through her own divorce the next morning.

Carol said she'd declined Steve's offer to drive together to see Katie off at the airport in Phoenix on Saturday, so they went separately, which made her feel even stronger. During a family dinner Steve and Carol took snapshots of each other with the girls. Then, as they were waving goodbye to Katie at the terminal, Steve put his hand on Carol's shoulder.

"For the first time in a really long time, I didn't get totally creeped out," Carol told Katherine on the phone as she was driving home Wednesday evening. "It was okay. It was just okay."

And then in the next sentence, Carol said, "Of course he had to ruin it. He asked if I wanted to meet him for coffee. We just got divorced. Why is he asking to have coffee?" But it wasn't just that, she said. "He had the audacity to come over."

Carol said Steve came to the house to plead with her to get back together. Katherine could visualize Carol shaking her head as she said, "That he would have the audacity to even propose that we should start dating again and then get married—"

"Whaaat?" Katherine asked, dumbfounded.

"Yes, yes," Carol said insistently. "And for him to think that I would actually do that."

In the past Carol had received some rather erratic

push-pull e-mails from Steve, first accusing her of being a terrible mother and then expressing his love for her. More recently, Carol had told friends that Steve had broken into her house, that she was convinced he'd been hacking into her e-mails, and that she feared for her personal safety. And even though she still considered him the love of her life, she told a coworker at Pia's that she'd refused his most recent offer to "forget this whole thing" and get back together.

The sunshine returned that Wednesday, reaching a searing high of ninety-six degrees. A couple of hours before she left work, Carol and Steve exchanged texts about Katie's BMW, which was parked in Carol's garage: I need to come pick up the X3, he texted, asking when he could collect the keys.

You may come out to pick up katies car this evening if ud like, Carol replied, adding that she assumed he had a spare key to get into the car, where Katie had left her set.

As Carol and a coworker closed the Pia's office around 4:30 P.M., her financial struggles were nagging at her. Although she'd agreed to the final settlement with Steve, she'd come to realize that the agreement would likely cost her the dream home she and her now–ex-husband had custom built. The home where they'd raised their girls together, the four of them sleeping in the same bed or at least in the same room, back in the days when their future had seemed more hopeful.

Given the lopsided share of liabilities she'd inherited in the split, she realized she couldn't afford the mortgage payments on her own, especially after Steve had taken out a second mortgage and equity line without her knowledge. The annual $24,000 she earned from her counseling, odd jobs and selling her artwork, just wasn't enough. She still had to cover taxes on the chunk of money she'd gotten in the divorce, and pay off Steve's credit card debts. Soon she would be completely underwater.

While she was talking to Katherine on the drive home, Carol stopped at the animal hospital to buy special food for her two dogs. Ike, a Boston terrier, had urinary problems after being disemboweled by a wild boar, known as a javelina, and Daisy, a fluffy bichon frise that looked like a white teddy bear, kept throwing up. Carol also stopped at Safeway to buy some groceries for herself. A vegetarian for most of her life, she frequently ate salads for dinner.

After pulling up to her sage-green house, she went inside and checked her e-mails from her home office, forwarding one to her tenant and close friend, Jim Knapp, who was living in the guesthouse out back. The two of them had known each other for years—from when their kids had gone to school together. For the past several months, they'd been supporting each other through their respective divorces, often sharing wine and conversation in the evenings before they went to their separate bedrooms.

Next, Carol chatted briefly with her accountant about the horribly bad, upside-down deal she felt she'd gotten in the divorce. She'd been talking about reporting Steve to the IRS for tax fraud, and she was stressed from arguing with him over some loose ends, which she thought she might go back to court to tie up.

Perhaps inspired by that conversation, Carol e-mailed Steve to dispute his claim that she owed him $8,300, refusing to give him a check so he could cover his $6,000 overdue alimony payment to her. Steve had suggested they trade checks that night.

Your assertion and information here is inaccurate and incorrect, she wrote to Steve at 6:30 P.M.

Done with that unpleasant bit of business, she put on a lavender tank top, blue shorts and a pair of running shoes and went on her usual half-hour, three-mile stint on the trails through the ranch land behind her house. During her run Carol usually left the side door unlocked, which led out to the backyard and down some steps to the garage, where she parked her car.

As she was heading east on the trail, she bumped into two neighbors, Lila Farr and Marge Powell, on horseback. Carol stopped for five minutes to chat and pet Lila's horse before heading on. It was warm that evening, not as warm as some days, but the horses, just like Carol, preferred to exercise when it was cooler.

Back at the house, Carol texted Steve again, at 7:06 P.M., after seeing no response to her message about Katie's car.

You never replied to let me know if u were coming to get it, she texted.

It was unlike Steve not to respond quickly. He always had his cell phone with him, and a spare battery or two as well.

Carol switched gears and texted Charlotte at 7:12 P.M. How was ur day darlin? she wrote, asking Charlotte if she'd started her new job yet.

Charlotte replied that she still had to finish training, but was set to start work the next day.

At 7:36 P.M., Carol used her cordless landline to make her usual call to her eighty-three-year-old mother, Ruth Kennedy, in Nashville, Tennessee. Carol had checked in with her mother most every night since her father had died in March 2006. With the two-hour time difference, Carol always called before 8 P.M., her time, before she ate dinner and her mother went to bed. As she chatted with Ruth, Carol also texted Charlotte about the rain.

"Mom, the dogs are fed and the doors are locked," Carol told Ruth, proactively answering her mother's usual questions.

Ruth worried about her daughter, living in a relatively isolated area known as Williamson Valley, about half an hour's drive from downtown Prescott. Carol's mother found it odd that she never seemed concerned or scared about leaving her doors unlocked. To Ruth, locking doors always "seemed paramount to safety." But when she questioned her daughter about it, Carol would say, "Oh, Mom."

Still, it wasn't a complete nonissue. Carol did change the locks after filing for divorce; she also suspected that Steve had been climbing in through a back window. Steve's name was still on the title, and he'd been paying the mortgage during the separation, but she gave spare keys only to her daughters.

Ruth could hear the water running in the background as Carol washed her salad ingredients and they discussed the companies Carol could use to send Katie her belongings. Rather than pay for extra bags on the flight, Carol was going to pack some boxes, then ship the items to her daughter. In fact, just ten minutes before she'd called Ruth, she texted Steve to follow up on the DHL shipping information. But again, no response.

The sun set at 7:46 P.M., as Carol told her mother that she and Steve were still arguing about money. Typically, Carol didn't complain about her problems to Ruth, she usually tried to solve them on her own. But this time she seemed extremely worried.

"You know, Mom, this is July second, and there's been no [alimony] payment made into my account," she said.

Because Ruth stopped hearing the water running, she later wondered if her daughter might have walked with the cordless phone down the hallway near the laundry room, where she kept the dogs' crates and food, and toward the back bedroom. Carol had been using that room as her office since Charlotte had moved out. Had Carol heard a noise?

After Ike's javelina incident he was still barking at wild animals—and strangers, when they came to the door. But as Ruth thought about it later, she didn't recall hearing any barking in the background that night.

"I suppose I will call my lawyer tomorrow," Carol said, sighing. *"Welllll,"* she said, drawing out the word, as if she had run out of things to say.

It was 7:59 P.M., when Ruth heard her daughter utter these last two words: "Oh, no."

Although Ruth reported to police that night that Carol had screamed these words, Ruth said later that she'd misspoken because she was anxious, and that she was referring to her own emotions. The tone Carol used, she said, was not one of fear but of surprise and dismay, as if she were saying, *"Oh, no, not again."*

Then there was no sound at all. Ruth didn't hear the phone drop on the floor. Not even a click. Nothing but raw silence on the other end.

Carol had never hung up on her mother before. She always said, "I love you, Mama," and Ruth responded in kind before they hung up simultaneously.

"Carol, are you okay?" Ruth asked. "What's the matter?"

But the line had gone dead.

CHAPTER 2

Carol's number was programmed into Ruth's phone, so she tried calling back several times, but the line just rang and rang. The answering machine didn't pick up, either. Ruth knew something was wrong, but she felt helpless, being so far away. Still, she had to do something, try to reach someone, to find out what had happened.

Ruth called Steve DeMocker's condo and left a message on his answering machine, asking him to check on Carol. Charlotte heard the phone ring and looked at the caller ID, but she and her boyfriend were too busy playing video games to pick up, so she let it go to voice mail.

After getting no answer on Steve's landline, Ruth tried his cell phone. When the call went straight to voice mail, she left a message as her anxiety escalated.

"Steve, this is Ruth Kennedy in Nashville. I was on the phone with Carol and she screamed and said, 'Oh, no,' and I can't get her to answer me back. I—I wonder if you could see what . . . you can find out, and let me know something."

Ruth had chatted briefly by phone with Carol's tenant, Jim Knapp, and thought she would try to reach him next, but directory assistance had no listing for him. She didn't know that Jim shared Carol's landline.

By this point Ruth didn't know what else to do but call the police for help. However, because Carol's house was outside the jurisdiction of the Prescott Police Department (PPD), the dispatcher said Ruth needed to call the Yavapai County Sheriff's Office (YCSO) and gave her the number.

"How can I help you?" the dispatcher said when Ruth called on the recorded emergency line at 8:14 P.M.

Explaining that she was calling from Nashville, Ruth recounted what had happened during her aborted call with Carol. "Is there anything you can do? Can you go check?" she asked. "I'm just at my wit's end."

"Now, did you call her, or did she call you and this occurred?" the dispatcher asked.

"She called me tonight and we—she calls me every night because I'm eighty-three and she worries about me."

"Uh-huh."

"I haven't been able to get her to answer the phone back. So I'm, you know, afraid that something bad's happened."

"Who does your daughter live with?"

"She's recently divorced. She's alone."

"Do you believe that there's any reason that she would be concerned if her husband—ex-husband—came back?"

"Oh, I don't think so," Ruth said. "I don't think it's that kind of a thing."

"All right, we will send somebody out to check on her. And we'll have them give you a call."

Clearly anxious, Ruth encouraged the dispatcher to send someone out right away. "If you happen to get a hold of her and she is okay, could you call us back and let us know?"

"I sure will."

Ruth then called Carol's brother, John, who lived seven miles away in the town of Old Hickory, Tennessee. Although he and Carol weren't close after high school, they'd been writing letters to each other and talking more often lately, every six weeks or so, in the past five years.

Figuring they could get further if they both made calls, John and Ruth each kept trying Carol and Steve, leaving messages to call them as soon as possible. They tried the sheriff's office again as well.

"The deputy in charge is not here" was the standard reply.

They heard nothing that evening from Carol, and nothing from the sheriff's office as they sat, waiting and worrying. Why wasn't she answering her phone?

Something really bad has happened. I don't know what, and I can't do anything about it, Ruth thought. *I'm trying to do what I can, but it's not enough.*

CHAPTER 3

The call for a welfare check at Carol Kennedy's house in the 7400 block of Bridle Path went out on the police radio just after her mother's emergency call. The sheriff's deputies on duty heard Matthew Taintor get dispatched, and they also heard him arrive at the house thirty-eight minutes later, at 8:52 P.M.

"They have a huge, huge area to cover. For a simple 'check welfare,' thirty-eight minutes is actually a decent [response] time," said Mike Sechez, who retired as an investigator for the Yavapai County Attorney's Office in 2014, after working this case for nearly five years.

However, as defense attorney Craig Williams noted later, Deputy Taintor's arrival was delayed because he'd pulled over a car in front of him, which was traveling the same direction on Williamson Valley Road toward Carol's house, and ran a check on the two occupants' driver's licenses.

In terms of square miles, Yavapai County spans about the same area as the state of Massachusetts, although Yavapai's population of 211,000 is much more geographically dispersed across its vast expanses of open land. At one time the capital of the Arizona Territory, Prescott is now the county seat, with nearly forty thousand residents. Carol's neighborhood, which is on the outskirts of town in an unincorporated area, is home to many horse owners.

The week of July 4 has always been a hectic one for Prescott area residents, because every year since 1888, Prescott has spent this week hosting the "World's Oldest Rodeo." People come from all over to participate in these annual festivities, drawing nearly fifty thousand to this small town, where celebrations spill into the streets with water fights breaking out between giant squirt guns on trucks. The event in 2008 was even bigger than usual because it marked the volunteer organizing committee's induction into the Pro Rodeo Hall of Fame in Colorado.

"The whole vibe of the community changes from the sleepy town to just madness, total madness," said Carol's friend Katherine, who goes by her married name of Morris today. Katherine wondered whether Carol's killer chose this particular weekend on purpose, knowing that it would be rife with the usual chaos on Whiskey Row, the line of bars across from the courthouse that gets "lit up with all kinds of gunslinging cowboys."

When Deputy Taintor pulled into Carol's driveway, the night sky was so dark he couldn't see anything that wasn't illuminated by the beam of his flashlight. No lights were on in the house, either, except for a tiny faint blue flashing light, which he assumed was the computer router.

Approaching the front door, he knocked several times, but got no response other than the dogs barking inside. As he shined his flashlight through the front windows and doors, all he could see was darkness.

As he walked around toward the rear of the house, he

peered into the dining-room window. He could see the two small dogs now, which were looking back at him and yapping like crazy.

Seeing a detached building in back, which he thought was a garage, he checked its front door and found it unlocked. Drawing his gun, he announced himself, then did a walk-though, realizing it was a guesthouse. No one home there, either.

Returning to the main house, he checked the double French patio glass doors that led to the dining room, and found them unlocked as well. But not wanting to search the big house on his own, he continued walking around the perimeter, peering through windows. He saw nothing suspicious until he reached the last set of windows on the east side.

That's when he saw the woman inside—five feet eight inches tall, weighing 122 pounds, and lying with her feet toward him. Given the amount of blood pooled around her head, she appeared to be dead. Unsure whether the killer was still inside, waiting to jump him, Taintor didn't feel safe going in alone with just a gun and a flashlight to protect him.

As he retraced his steps to his patrol car, he heard the dispatcher checking on him over the radio. He also heard Sergeant Candice Acton requesting his location and saying she was heading his way.

Taintor radioed in a "code four" to notify them that he was okay, then called Acton on her cell phone to report an apparent homicide, a pretty unusual crime in their picturesque little mountain town.

Because homicides were so rare here, and the YCSO knew this was going to be a massive undertaking, it was all hands on deck. Investigators from the county attorney's office, who were trained detectives, were called later that night to come to an early-morning briefing on the case.

"It gets pretty intense and pretty chaotic at first, because there's a million things to get done and you have to prioritize," said Mike Sechez, the now-retired investigator, who left a detective's job with the Phoenix Police Department to work in Prescott.

The sheriff's deputies started to arrive at Bridle Path, one by one, Sergeant Acton being the first, at 9:10 P.M.

As she and Taintor stood at the top of the driveway, waiting for their colleagues, a white Ford Ranger truck pulled up with a license plate that read *STOKAGE*. The driver, in his early fifties, introduced himself as Jim Knapp, and said he lived in Carol's guesthouse.

Asked if Carol had been home when he left earlier that day, Jim said no. She'd already left for work. "She should be home now," he said. "I could call her and have her come out."

"No," Acton said, choosing not to tell him about the woman's body inside, given that they hadn't entered the house yet to confirm her identity or condition. "What is your relationship with Carol Kennedy?"

"Best friends," Jim said, adding that they'd been commiserating as they'd both recently gone through nasty divorces; hers had only just been finalized.

Acton asked Jim for his driver's license, then ran his name through dispatch to see if he had any outstanding warrants. In the meantime Acton told him they didn't know what was going on yet, and that he needed to stay in his truck and out of the crime scene.

As other deputies began to arrive, they came up with a plan to determine if the killer was still on the property, then to enter the house. Deputy Mark Boan was assigned to stay with Jim and his truck.

"What's going on?" Jim asked.

"We're investigating a suspicious incident," Boan replied.

Understandably concerned and impatient, Jim ignored the sergeant's instructions and took it upon himself to call Carol's cell phone. He left her a message at 9:37 P.M., expressing concern for her welfare, saying something like, "Are you all right? The sheriff's office is here." His tone indicated that he was concerned she wasn't at home and might freak out if she pulled up to see all the police cars.

While the other deputies went inside, Boan talked to Jim through his driver's-side window, asking about his whereabouts earlier that day. Jim said he'd been at the Bridle Path house till about 1 or 2 P.M., when he went into town to meet with his sons, ages thirteen and eleven, at his ex-wife's house.

While his ex took their older son, Jay, to hockey practice, Jim stayed with Alex, their younger son, and watched a movie that he'd gotten at the Hastings Entertainment video store. Jim said he headed home once his ex-wife, Ann Saxerud, got back from practice around 8:30 or 8:45 P.M. On his way, he said, he stopped off at Safeway for some cherries and wine.

Jim said he'd last seen Carol the night before, when she'd come to the guesthouse to say good night, around eight or nine o'clock. That morning she'd left him a sweet note on his truck window, which he retrieved from the vehicle to show investigators.

Thinking of you all day, it said.

Carol often left notes like this for him since he'd moved in about four or five months earlier, he said. The idea was to provide moral support to each other and for him to keep an eye out for her because she'd been living alone.

"Carol has wanted a man on the property for years, ever since Steve, her husband, moved out," Jim said, describing Steve "as a very sneaky, manipulative man."

"If anything happened to her, you should be looking at him."

The deputies cleared the guesthouse again, then proceeded on to the main house. As they stood on the back patio, the dogs continued to bark, jumping up and pawing the glass door. The glass patio door was unlocked, so the deputies entered the house there, walking into the dining room and kitchen as the dogs ran outside.

Going from room to room, they approached Carol in the back bedroom, where she was lying facedown, her right arm under her body. To enter the room, they had to duck under a wooden ladder that was leaning against the wall above the doorway. A great deal of blood was spattered around the room, but it was primarily on and around the desk leg, and pooled around Carol's head. A bookcase was toppled over next to her body. The side of the desk had blood on it as well, and someone had left a bloody smudge, maybe a handprint, on the beige carpet, where a bottle of stain remover was sitting nearby.

Acton put on some gloves and checked Carol for a pulse, but found none. Her skin felt cool to the touch. Although she appeared to have been dead for a while, the deputies called for the paramedics. The ambulance crew arrived around 9:40 P.M., and assessed Carol's condition to confirm that she'd passed away.

* * *

When the paramedics left less than ten minutes later, it didn't take long for Jim to figure out that something was seriously wrong.

"Is she dead?" he asked Deputy Boan.

"Yes," said Boan, who had only just learned this fact himself.

Jim, still sitting in his truck, broke down crying and remained visibly upset for quite some time.

After this emotional scene, Boan's superiors told him to record his conversation with Jim Knapp, going back over the same questions the deputy had asked earlier, to get the answers on tape. Boan put a small microcassette recorder into his shirt pocket, but as it rustled against the cloth it distorted the sound quality and the recording was later deemed "inaudible."

Once Jim recovered from the news and got out of his truck, Boan tried to casually look him over with a flashlight, searching for any injuries or sign of blood on his clothes, but saw none. He also peeked inside Jim's truck and saw nothing overtly suspicious. Jim's speech didn't seem slurred; his eyes didn't look bloodshot or watery, or his pupils dilated or constricted. Other than being very upset about the death of his best friend, Jim didn't seem impaired in any way.

Later, when Boan was called to testify about that night, the defense asked him how Jim could have known enough about all the blood at the crime scene to describe it to a woman at Safeway the next day. Boan said he didn't know. He didn't talk to Jim about the blood, he said, nor did he recall Jim mentioning the bloody scene to him. They'd both been standing outside the house the entire time.

* * *

Sheriff's Detective Doug Brown was at home brushing his teeth and getting ready for bed when he got a call from his supervisor, Sergeant Luis Huante, around 10 P.M., telling him to head over to the crime scene on Bridle Path.

Brown had started working in the jails for the sheriff's department in 2001, then moved to patrol. He had only just transferred to the Prescott sheriff's station about ten days earlier, after a year and a half investigating child-related sex offenses for the Criminal Investigations Unit (CIU). This would be his first homicide investigation, of which he was about to become the case agent—without any homicide training.

Brown was the first detective to arrive at the crime scene at 10:35 P.M. Walking through the house with Sergeant Huante he examined the position of Carol's body, the ladder and the overturned bookcase, and the pattern of blood spattered around them.

At first, Brown, Huante and Lieutenant Dave Rhodes thought Carol could have fallen off the ladder, injuring her head as a result. The cordless phone, on which she'd been speaking to her mother, lay on the carpet between the swivel desk chair and the north wall.

But as they viewed the blood spatter pattern more closely, they realized pretty quickly that the killer had moved the bookshelf and ladder *after* the savage assault, staging the scene to look like an accident. The degree of trauma to Carol's head, not to mention the dense collection of blood on the desk corner, was too severe to have come from a simple fall.

The ladder was positioned with the rungs going the wrong way for her to have climbed it, and it had no fingerprints or blood on it, even though blood was spattered on the wall behind it. Blood had also dried on the bookshelf unit in a way that would have defied gravity if it had been at that angle during the attack.

It wasn't until they moved Carol into the body bag that Brown was able to see the trauma not only to the left side of her head, but to the right as well.

"It was obvious, things that didn't make sense," Brown testified later. "So you've got the damage to her skull and then the [blood on the] desk. I thought at that time that, you know, she was slammed against the desk."

After checking the track lighting in the dark laundry room, they discovered that one of the bulbs was missing and three had been partially unscrewed. It seemed as if the killer wanted to keep Carol in the dark about his presence until he was ready to attack.

CHAPTER 4

After dating Charlotte DeMocker for six months, her boyfriend Jacob "Jake" Janusek moved in with her and her father the day before the murder—on Tuesday, July 1, 2008.

Jake, who was also sixteen, had occasionally stayed the night with Charlotte at Steve's condo at Alpine Meadows. And after Jake's parents kicked him out, Steve agreed to let him stay there temporarily. Back in February, before Jim Knapp moved in at Bridle Path, Carol had also offered Jake the guesthouse.

On Wednesday, July 2, Jake and Charlotte had lunch together, then stopped off at Safeway to pick up some cookies, which they delivered to Steve at his office in response to his plea for a sweet treat.

Finished for the day at his investment broker job at UBS (formerly the United Bank of Switzerland) Financial Services in Prescott, Steve logged off his computer at 4:38 P.M. UBS was fanatical about having its employees log off—but not necessarily turn off—their computers before leaving the office, fearing that someone might break in and hack into the international system.

Steve drove home from the office, which was about a half mile away, and used his remote control at 4:52 P.M. to open the gate to his condo complex, where Charlotte and Jake were hanging out.

Dressed in his usual suit, Steve immediately changed into workout clothes, informing the teenagers that he was going to go for a long bike ride. Jake later told investigators that he thought Steve went on the loop trail around the nearby fitness center, where he often went running, followed by an upper-body workout with weights. They expected him to be gone a couple of hours.

Steve left the condo just after five o'clock, and unbeknownst to Charlotte and Jake, he turned off his phone at 5:36 P.M.

While he was gone, the teenagers played video games, then went for a swim at the fitness center pool around six o'clock, but they didn't see Steve's car there. As the sun was setting they came back to the condo to play more video games and wait for Steve to return so they could start dinner.

In the meantime Charlotte texted with her mother about the rain, and let her grandmother's subsequent call on the landline go to voice mail.

When Steve still wasn't home by dark, they started wondering where he was. Charlotte tried texting and calling him, but got no answer. She also tried calling his girlfriend, Renee Girard, to find out where he'd gone riding, however Renee was unsure. There was some confusion later about who said what, but Jake told investigators that Renee said she didn't know whether Steve had gone to the Granite Basin Trail, the Granite Mountain Trail, or the trail by the fitness center, which was about six to eight miles long.

Still waiting, Charlotte and Jake fell asleep, and woke up around 9:40 P.M.

"Wow, your dad has been gone a really long time," Jake said.

Charlotte tried twice more to reach Steve on his cell, at 9:40 and 9:52 P.M., leaving him a voice mail. They tended to eat dinner later because of Steve's summer evening workout schedule, but this seemed like a much longer workout than usual. He also had his phone with him virtually all the time, and it was unlike him to be out of reach for so many hours.

By ten o'clock, the teenagers decided they were too hungry to wait any longer, so they drove to Safeway to buy ingredients for Chinese stir-fry. On the quick five-minute sprint over there, Jake thought he saw Steve's car—a four-door silver BMW—as they stopped at an intersection.

At 10:08 P.M., Steve DeMocker turned his phone back on. During the four and a half hours it had been off, he'd missed eleven calls and three text messages, but he never listened to the voice mails or responded to the texts. The forensic examiners who went through them later could tell that they were the first to hear the messages.

Steve's first call was to Charlotte, who was at the same Safeway where her mother and Jim Knapp had stopped in earlier—separately—that evening. Charlotte was captured on the store's surveillance video, talking on her cell phone, presumably telling her father that she was buying food for dinner. He told her that he'd been on a bike ride, gotten a flat tire, and his cell phone had died. He was thinking of working out at the fitness center, which was about a half mile from the condo, but once he learned that she and Jake hadn't eaten yet, he said he'd come home and join them.

Within sixty seconds of the call to Charlotte, Steve used his remote control to enter the condo's security gate at 10:09 P.M.

A minute later he called Renee and proceeded to list all the reasons he couldn't come over to her house. "I'm tired. I'm dehydrated. I just need a shower," he said. "I just want to go home, get some food, and go to bed."

"Okay, great, go," Renee said, feeling angry and annoyed that he was making excuses when she wasn't even expecting him to come over that night. Her three-year-old grandson was staying with her and she'd been gearing up to break up with Steve anyway. She suspected that he'd been with another woman that night, because he hadn't answered his phone.

What he said next surprised her. "I'm bleeding," he said.

"What?"

"Well, I scraped my leg on a branch and got a deep gash. I've got to get home," he said, explaining that he'd run into a bush on his bike, snagging his leg on a twig that was sticking out into the trail.

A week or so later, he even took her to the trail to show her the twig. He said he also got scratches on his arm when he got off his bike, hiked down into a gulley and up on a hill to look down on the lot that he and Carol used to own. To Renee, Steve had always seemed like a pretty sentimental guy, so it didn't seem strange to her that he would go back to that area to look around.

At 10:16 P.M., seven minutes after Steve got home, Charlotte used her separate code to enter the security gate and pulled her white BMW into the condo garage next to

Steve's. The interior lights of his car were still on—the ones that stay on briefly after the ignition goes off, or if the door is accidentally left open.

As she and Jake walked up the stairs and into the condo, they heard the shower running in Steve's bedroom, which was just off the dining room.

Carol's brother, John Kennedy, finally reached Steve on his cell phone around 10:30 P.M. to personally relay his and Ruth's concerns about Carol in a three-minute call. But John barely had a chance to say anything before Steve interrupted.

"Hey, look, I'm standing here dripping wet. Just stepped out of the shower," he said, adding that he'd been out on his mountain bike for a long ride.

John tried to explain what had happened during Ruth's call with Carol, and asked if Steve would please go out to the house and check on his ex-wife. But Steve refused without hesitation.

"No, I will not," he said.

John tried modifying his request, explaining that he and Ruth thought something bad might have happened to Carol. "Why don't you just drive by and see if everything looks okay?" he suggested.

It didn't make any difference. Steve said no, absolutely not, because she might have a date over. He didn't feel comfortable stopping by at this late hour and infringing on her privacy.

As soon as they hung up, Steve sent Carol a text at 10:35 P.M., then called her cell phone three minutes later to leave a voice mail with essentially the same message: "Carol, I just left a message on your—out at Bridle Path. Would you give us a call? Your brother called me and he was worried because your mom was talking to you and all of a sudden you guys got disconnected. She said that you exclaimed something and hung up and then they haven't been able to get a hold of you. So people are a little worried, and they just want to know you are okay. Would you call," he said, pausing, "excuse me, call us, call your mom. Bye."

As Steve emerged from his bedroom wearing a towel, he asked what Charlotte and Jake were making for dinner.

"Stir fry, rice and vegetables," his daughter replied as she was cooking.

Steve asked if they had anything for the laundry, then started the washing machine. It was a small load—just Steve's workout socks, underwear, shorts and shirt. He told investigators later that he normally did a load of clothes every day.

Noticing some fresh scratches on Steve's left arm and leg, which were bleeding, Jake commented that the wounds looked pretty bad. "Are you okay?" he asked.

"I'm fine," Steve said, "just really tired. It was a really long ride." He mentioned that because of the flat tire, he'd had to walk his bike four miles back to the car and had gotten scratched by some bushes on the trail.

After Steve finished getting dressed, he came out of his bedroom wearing shorts and a T-shirt. He joined the kids at the table, where he talked about the stock market and made general conversation as they ate.

"When was the last time you heard from your mother?" he asked.

Charlotte replied that they'd been texting earlier in the evening. Steve mentioned that he'd gotten a call from

Carol's brother about the line suddenly going dead while she was on the phone with Ruth, and that Ruth was worried about her.

That comment concerned Charlotte as well, so she texted her mother at 10:48 P.M., asking if she was okay: I'm worried about you.

She also tried calling Carol's cell and home phones, around 11 P.M., and left a message: "If you want to text me back or call me or something just to let me know that you're okay and that everything is okay—otherwise I might drive out to your house to see if you are all right. I love you very much. Bye, Mom."

But there was still no response. Charlotte thought that maybe her mother had fallen asleep and just wasn't answering her cell. However, she also knew that the ringer on the landline was so loud that Carol usually answered it.

Steve wasn't sitting down long before he told them that he'd gotten a call from a coworker, alerting him that he'd left his computer logged on at the office, and he needed to go back and log off. Besides, he said, he also realized that he'd left something that he needed. He put on his flip-flops and left the condo. It seemed to Jake that Steve was gone for no more than five minutes.

Curiously, Steve used his security code to come back through the gate and into the condo three times between 11 P.M. and midnight: first at 11:04, then at 11:21 and finally at 11:51 P.M. (The gate opened on its own when cars leaving the complex approached, so a code or remote activation was only needed to open it when entering the complex.)

After dinner, Jake and Charlotte started up the video games again while Steve made some calls, pacing back and forth between the living room and his bedroom. To

Jake, Steve seemed unusually restless that night, moving around, and getting up and down. Typically, Steve was pretty calm.

As Charlotte grew increasingly worried about her mom, she and Jake started calling emergency rooms in Prescott and Prescott Valley to see if any patients had come in under the name of Carol Kennedy or Jim Knapp. Maybe something had happened to Carol's tenant, they thought, and she'd had to take him to the hospital. But there was no trace of either one of them.

Charlotte and Jake thought someone should go to Carol's house to check on her, but Steve told them the same thing he'd already told Carol's brother. Steve felt uncomfortable going there because they'd only just gotten divorced. He'd been dating, so she might be, too, and he didn't want to intrude. Everything was probably fine, he said. She was either out with someone, didn't hear the phone, or wasn't able to get to it in time.

Steve did come up with a plan for Charlotte to go, however. She could go to the house with Jake, but a half mile before she got there, she had to call Steve and stay on the phone with him as she was pulling up. If the house was dark, if she saw an unfamiliar car in the driveway or if one of the doors was open, they were not to go inside to look for Carol. The implication was that a robbery or home invasion could be under way. Once she got there, they would decide what she should do.

Charlotte agreed, but Jake was worried. One, they were heading to a remote area that was not well lit at night, and two, he was concerned that he might not be able to prevent his strong-willed girlfriend from going into her mother's house if she sensed something was wrong. As she and Jake were about to head out, Steve reiterated that he didn't want them going inside Carol's house.

Jake overheard Steve leaving Carol a message as they walked out the door: "People are really worried. If you wouldn't mind calling . . . I mean, if you're on a date or whatever, it is totally okay. I just—we don't want to intrude, but you're not answering anybody's calls. . . . I'm sure everything is fine, but if you could just even text us and let us know that you are okay, that would be great. I think your mom and John are up, back east, worried and waiting to hear. So please call somebody. Bye."

Carol's brother, John, heard back from Steve briefly around 11:30 P.M., which was 1:30 A.M., Nashville time, probably right after Charlotte and Jake had left for Carol's house.

"Have you heard anything?" Steve asked.

John said no. He and Ruth had called the sheriff's office again to check in, but were told, "We're kind of busy."

As Charlotte and Jake drove toward Williamson Valley, she continued to try to reach her mother on her cell phone. Once they reached Carol's neighborhood at 11:55 P.M., Charlotte called Steve, as instructed, and told him they were down the street, approaching the house. Staying on the phone with him, she described what she saw as they got closer: a whole slew of red and blue lights moving against the darkness.

"I see flashing lights," she said.

"Oh, no," Steve said.

Closer still, they saw a number of sheriff's cruisers and yellow crime scene tape blocking the driveway, all signs that something was very, very wrong. Even the driveway, which they would normally pull into, was blocked off with yellow tape.

Several detectives from the CIU were standing in the road, discussing whom to contact next, when one of them stuck out his hand to stop Charlotte's approaching car. As she pulled up, still holding the phone with her dad on the line, the officers walked over to stand on each side of the car.

Rolling down her window to talk to Lieutenant Dave Rhodes, Charlotte said, "This is my mom's house. What's going on?" Speaking quickly, she said she was worried because her mother hadn't been answering the phone.

When Rhodes told Charlotte that her mother had passed away, she dropped her phone onto the car floor and burst into tears.

CHAPTER 5

Jake immediately grabbed the phone, got out of the car, relayed to Steve what the lieutenant had just said, and told him that he needed to come down and be with Charlotte.

Hearing the news, Steve started breathing heavily and sounded like he was crying. He paused, then asked to speak to an officer.

Jake handed the phone to Detective Doug Brown, who was standing next to the car, while Sergeant Luis Huante pulled Jake aside to talk to him.

In all the commotion Jake tried to figure out what was going on. "What I've been told is possibly an accident, possible foul play," he said to Huante, who confirmed that they were investigating Carol's death and foul play was, indeed, a possibility.

Asked if Charlotte had mentioned Carol being in fear, Jake answered, "To my knowledge, no," although Carol had invited him and Charlotte to stay at the house that coming Saturday.

On the phone with Brown, Steve asked to whom he was speaking. "What's happened?" Steve asked after Brown identified himself.

"Carol, uh, I'm not really sure what's going on," Brown replied. "She's passed away."

After Steve sighed heavily again, the detective said, "I guess she had spoken with her mom and—"

"Yeah, we've been trying to call her. What happened?" Steve asked again.

"I'm not really sure, and I really don't have any information right now, so we're just kind of playing everything by ear. Some kind of possible fall or something. That's all we know right now."

"She's dead?" Steve asked, explaining that she was his ex-wife.

Brown said he'd been talking to the man who lived on the property, and had been about to try to contact Steve, but they didn't know how to get hold of him.

"Can I come out? I—I mean, my daughter—" Steve said. "She hasn't—she hasn't—what kind of state is the body in? She hasn't seen Carol, has she?"

"No, no, no," Brown said.

"Can I come out?"

"Yeah, if you'd like to," Brown said. "That'd be fine. I can talk to you outside or—"

"Well, I want to be with Charlotte," Steve said, explaining that her boyfriend didn't have a license and his daughter would be in no condition to drive home. "I'll be right out."

Steve called Charlotte right back, but she told him she was talking to the deputies and had to go.

Immediately calling Renee, Steve talked to her for about four minutes. "Carol is dead, Charlotte is out there and I need to get out there. Will you go with me?"

But Renee was still watching her grandson. "No, I can't go," she said. "I can't leave him."

Steve described the voice mail Carol's mother had left on his answering machine, which he'd checked just before leaving the house. Charlotte had gotten upset hearing it, he said, and wanted to go out right away. After pleading with him for an hour to go, he said, he'd finally let her.

Between calls to and from Steve that night, John Kennedy continued to call his sister's house, hoping she would pick up. But there was still no answer.

John got the last call back from Steve at 2:11 A.M., or 12:11 A.M., Prescott time. He thought he could hear gravel crunching, as if Steve was walking and talking.

Steve's tone was flat. Monotone. Emotionless. He offered no preamble or lead-in to soften the news. "John, you need to call your mom and tell her that Carol is gone," he said abruptly.

Not injured, not dead, just *gone*. John thought Steve's tone was so casual that he could have been informing him that Albertsons had some good ripe melons on sale.

Although John tried to press his brother-in-law for more information, Steve gave him very little. "She's gone," Steve repeated. "She's dead."

"What happened?" John asked.

"Apparently, she suffered a fall."

As soon as they hung up, John woke his wife, told her what was going on, and said they needed to make the short drive over to his mother's house to deliver the news in person.

When they arrived at Ruth's house and knocked on her back door, she was just hanging up with the chaplain from the Metropolitan Nashville Police Department, who was on his way over. The chaplain didn't say why, but Ruth knew what was coming.

After John confirmed Ruth's fears about what had happened to Carol, Ruth's knees collapsed out from under her. Her body crumpled, but John caught her and helped her into a chair before she could fall to the floor. Still in shock, she didn't cry. Not yet anyway.

The chaplain arrived shortly thereafter to deliver the bad news again. After he left, John stayed the rest of the night with his mother as they tried to console each other.

CHAPTER 6

Steve tried calling his longtime assistant, Barbara "Barb" O'Non, at 12:14 A.M., but she didn't answer, already asleep for the night.

Renee called Steve back a few minutes later and they talked briefly before he pulled up to Carol's house at 12:23 A.M. Seeing Charlotte talking to one of the detectives, he immediately went to hug and comfort his sobbing daughter.

Scott Mascher, one of two commanders who worked directly under the sheriff, had only just arrived a couple of minutes earlier. He'd been home in bed when he'd gotten the call of a possible homicide from Lieutenant Rhodes, who said they were short-handed.

"I'll be happy to come out and help," said Mascher, who didn't wear his three-star uniform that night—just a T-shirt and jeans.

Touring the house briefly with Rhodes, Mascher agreed that the crime scene seemed very suspicious. "Yeah, that just doesn't seem right," he said.

Heading back outside, Mascher waited until Steve had finished consoling Charlotte, then introduced himself. As they were talking, Mascher shined a flashlight on Steve's legs, illuminating the cuts and scratches on his left arm and leg. They were so fresh they glistened in the light. The cut on his left leg, just above his ankle, was bleeding quite a bit. He also had two thin, horizontal and parallel scratches above his left knee. The scratches and cuts on his forearm varied in length, depth and severity—a tiny one and two medium, deep but narrow gashes. They looked as if they could have been made at different times, maybe in different places.

"What happened?" Steve asked again.

Mascher explained that they wouldn't be sure until the medical examiner (ME) was able to examine Carol's body sometime in the morning.

"Am I a suspect?" Steve asked.

Surprised by the question and knowing that Steve's comments might be important later, Mascher led him over to Sergeant Huante and Detective Brown, indicating that they should record the conversation.

Brown took the opportunity to probe Steve, who said he'd been planning to come pick up Katie's car earlier that evening, but had decided that he would just have Charlotte come get it, instead. He said the divorce had been tense, but things had gotten better between him and Carol since it was finalized. In fact, he said, they'd just met for coffee on Sunday.

"We were talking about starting to date again," he said.

It had been quite a while since he'd been at the house—long enough that he couldn't recall when, he said. Within a few minutes, however, he mentioned that he'd come over a week or so earlier to drop off some art and pick up a grill. He said he'd spoken with the tenant, Jim Knapp, while he was there, but then left without the grill. He claimed he hadn't been inside the house in probably six months.

After he got home from his bike ride that night, he said, he checked his messages and that's when he saw the voice mails from Ruth and John Kennedy and learned what was going on. (He later said he didn't listen to them and that the call from John was his first knowledge of what had happened. He also said later, as he'd told Renee, that he listened to Ruth's message on his home answering machine when he saw the red light blinking—after Charlotte and Jake had left, and just before he left for Carol's house.)

Because of poor cell reception in the Granite Mountain area, Steve said, he'd left his phone in the car during his long bike ride, which would have been two to two and a half hours, but had turned into four because of a flat tire. He didn't turn the cell phone back on until he finished his ride.

As Brown continued to probe him about his phone and the text messages he and Carol had exchanged that day, Steve asked if they really had to go through this now. Brown explained that they were trying to find out when she'd sent the messages to build a timeline for the night. Steve conceded, saying he realized why they might be questioning him, given that he and Carol hadn't been on great terms.

Sergeant Huante asked if they could go down to the sheriff's station to ask Steve some more questions and take a closer look at his phone.

"So I'm a suspect?" Steve asked rhetorically this time.

"No, no, no, no," Huante said, reiterating Brown's comments about the need to build a timeline. "It's kind of hard to read in the dark out here."

Steve started to tell them about the garage sale Carol

had been planning, then stopped midsentence. "I'm sorry," he said. "This is just not real."

When Brown questioned him about the neighborhood area, Steve said the girls claimed that Carol's house, where both daughters had been living during the separation, had been broken into twice. "That's one of the reasons why Charlotte was so worried," he said.

About a year ago, he added, some money was taken from Katie's room, and they found the rear bedroom door ajar. "That happened another time, stuff was out of place. There was no evidence of anything being taken, but the girls were convinced somebody had been there. I don't know."

Steve expressed regret for allowing Charlotte to go to the house that night, given what John Kennedy had told him about Carol's aborted call with Ruth. "I shouldn't have let her come out here."

But Carol tended to screen her calls and didn't pick up sometimes, he said, especially when he was calling, and he didn't think he should show up there at midnight.

Mascher reiterated that it would be best if they took these questions down to the station to gather some more basic information. Afterward, they could bring Steve, Charlotte and Jake back for their cars.

"Pardon me, but, you know, I mean, if I'm—am I being questioned as a suspect?" Steve asked again. He said he wanted to cooperate, but wondered if he should have an attorney present.

"Well, right now, we don't really know what's going on, so you're free to leave at any time," Mascher said. "We just need to ask questions."

Mascher added that they would be talking to neighbors, family and friends, including Jim Knapp.

In fact, Detective Brown had interviewed Jim outside

the house that night, and the sound quality of their taped conversation was much clearer than Deputy Boan's. Brown and other detectives subsequently conducted several other taped interviews with Carol's tenant.

At 1:05 A.M., Lieutenant Rhodes took Charlotte in his car, Mascher took Jake and Steve got into Detective Brown's car.

After Brown pulled away from the house, Steve asked if it was necessary for them to drive together, because it would be easier for him to get some sleep before work if he could drive himself to the sheriff's office. Brown said that would be okay, turned around, dropped Steve at his car and let Steve follow him to the station.

Renee's son came back to her house after a night out and picked up her grandson, so she was eventually able to drive to the crime scene as Steve had requested, albeit a little late. By the time she got there, she saw several sheriff's vehicles pulling out, and was told that Steve, Charlotte and Jake were heading down to the station.

That said, at 1:07 A.M., Renee was surprised to get yet another call from Steve as he was driving behind Brown and she was following behind the cruisers, hoping to bring Charlotte home from the station. Renee and Steve spoke several more times over the next forty minutes.

When she arrived at the station, she saw Charlotte and Jake going inside. She went in after them and gave Charlotte a hug just before the teenager was whisked into an interview room.

The deputies told Renee to go home and wait, but instead she headed over to Steve's condo, where she tried to sleep on the couch between his calls during breaks in the interrogation. Steve arrived at the station at one-thirty in the morning, and his calls stopped once his cell phone was confiscated, sometime after 3:20 A.M.

Later that night Jim Knapp asked Deputy Boan if he could go into the crime scene. He was going to find a hotel room, but first he needed to get his medications. Boan told him he could only go into the guesthouse, into which the deputy escorted Jim, signing the crime scene log at 1:04 A.M.

When Jim started walking toward the kitchen area, Boan asked him what he was doing. Jim replied that he wanted to get a plastic grocery bag to carry his medications.

"Do you need anything else?" Boan asked, thinking he might need toiletries, a shaving kit or something from the bathroom.

Jim said no, he would be fine, and they signed out eight minutes later.

Boan told Jim not to talk to anyone about the case and asked him where he was staying, in case they needed to reach him. Jim said he was going to try the Marriott in Prescott.

At 1:19 A.M., Jim called his brother, Bobby, in Hawaii and told him the devastating news that Carol was dead.

Boan didn't bother to mention in his initial investigative reports that he'd searched Jim's truck that night. It wasn't until August that he did so, after another investigator pointed out the omission.

The delay in including these details didn't look too good—as if the officers had made a mistake—but this sort of thing happened a number of times, and they figured it was better to include the information late than not at all. However, it was these types of mistakes and omissions that became fodder for defense attorneys later as they accused the sheriff's department of failing to thoroughly investigate Jim as a suspect, especially when they had interrogated Steve all night and even photographed him in his underwear.

The defense questioned, for example, why investigators didn't ask why it took Jim Knapp so long to settle in for the night—it was ninety minutes before he finally checked into the Marriott Springhill Suites at 2:42 A.M. And how did he know about all the blood in the house if he wasn't allowed into the crime scene that night?

Responding to these criticisms, Mike Sechez, the former prosecution investigator, countered that the sheriff's team did look at Jim that night. They "searched his guesthouse, just like it was part of the crime scene, and they searched his truck and they interviewed him."

And the blood? Brown later testified that when Jim called him the next day to ask if he could return to the guesthouse, Brown warned him about all the blood in the house. "I didn't want to have anybody walk into it and not to be expecting something that wasn't pretty," Brown said.

CHAPTER 7

Around 1:30 A.M. on July 3, the detectives began a series of recorded interviews in separate rooms at the sheriff's station. Detective Brown and Sergeant Huante talked to Steve; Lieutenant Rhodes took Charlotte; and Commander Mascher spoke with Jake, trying to establish a timeline of everyone's whereabouts and activities that day.

At the start of Steve's interview, he said he would really rather talk to the detectives the next day. "I want to help you—"

"Right, I know, and—"

"Charlotte—we just—it's kind of a shock. I'd prefer not to be up all night."

"I'd prefer not to be up all night, either," Brown said, proceeding with his questions.

Steve asked for some water, then Brown started going through the text messages that had come into Steve's cell phone while it was turned off. The first was one from Barb at 8:46 P.M.

"Who is Barb?"

"Barb is a—a former partner. . . . She and I have been working together for a long, long time. . . . We were really involved for years and we are both business partners, and, uh, um—"

"Here's one from Carol," Steve said, referring to the one she sent at 7:27 P.M. about shipping Katie's things. Steve said it had gotten stored on his phone while it was off, and it didn't come in until 10:08 P.M.

"Is that when you turned it on, then?"

"That's when I—I remembered I had a, um, spare battery."

"So your phone was dead?"

"It was, yeah."

Throughout the course of the night, Steve's story about his cell phone changed. There wasn't a good signal where he'd been riding. His phone battery died and he didn't remember he had a spare until he got back to town. He didn't get a chance to put it in until 10 P.M.

From there, Brown moved on to the details of Steve's bike ride.

"I don't really mountain bike very often," Steve said, adding that he'd been mostly trail running lately.

But that night, Steve said, he drove to the top of a hill near Granite Mountain to ride on a trail off Love Lane, near where he and Carol had once owned property, off Rainmaker. He said he parked near there and rode down the hill to the trailhead. The trail is relatively flat, he said, which made it popular with mountain bikers and horse riders. However, he didn't see anyone else on the trail that night, and he didn't think anyone could prove where he was.

He was right. As Mike Sechez, the prosecution investigator, said later, "We never found a single person who saw his car parked anywhere." Sechez added that Steve also never gave the detectives a reason why he picked that particular trail other than he wanted some exercise.

The trail area that Steve described was about a mile from Carol's house, across Williamson Valley Road, about a twenty- or twenty-five-minute drive from Steve's condo. Asked to draw a map on the dry-erase board and to show detectives where he'd parked his car and ridden his bike, Steve did so, indicating that the trail was on the south side of Love Lane.

"Did you happen to get those scratches there?" Huante asked.

"Up higher in the basin, where it starts to get—"

"You've got a lot of scratches. I was watching your legs—"

"—brushed by something on the left," Steve finished, agreeing with Huante that the bushes can be thorny and scratchy if you ride too close to them.

Steve said he started his ride around six-thirty, and thought he got back to the car around 9 P.M. He then had to break down the bike to get it to fit into his car. He'd driven back into town before he realized that he had a spare battery to put into his phone.

Moving on to Steve's relationship with Carol, Brown asked if she was a "confrontational person."

"She's not a diplomat. She doesn't connect particularly well," Steve replied. "She doesn't have a lot of—she doesn't socialize a lot. She can have some sort of rough edges."

"Has she ever been aggressive or violent toward you or her daughters?"

"Not violent, but she was pretty inappropriate," Steve said. "She got a little angry at Charlotte. She's gotten really angry enough to be very dramatic with me during the worst of the divorce process." But he added that he didn't think Carol would ever get physical during a confrontation. "She just argues or, you know, gets verbal."

Asked if his daughters ever mentioned Jim Knapp and

Carol arguing, Steve started yawning and apologized, which, looking back later, seemed like a telling response, as if he didn't perceive Jim as posing any danger.

"I'm really tired," Steve said. "I'm really sorry."

At this point, when Steve said more forcefully that he wanted to leave, Brown said they weren't finished asking questions. He then read Steve his Miranda rights, saying they still weren't clear on some points and needed him to go over them again.

Asked what he'd been wearing on his bike ride, Steve said he'd had on some gray Patagonia shorts, a white Lycra Nike top, ankle socks, a helmet and red Lake clip-in shoes. No gloves that day.

"Is there any reason why your blood or anything would be at the residence?" Brown asked.

"No. I haven't been at the house."

"Or DNA or your fingerprints?"

"No, okay, well, I mean, I don't know how long finger-prints are around."

"Any reason why your bicycle tracks would be on the property?" Brown asked.

"Or on the trail behind the property?" Huante chimed in.

"I haven't been there."

The detectives told Steve that although they'd initially thought Carol might have accidentally fallen and hit her head, other evidence had now contradicted that theory. They told him they'd found blood in the house and, noting Steve's bleeding scratches, gave him a chance to admit that he'd been there. They were going to serve a search warrant and collect blood, fingerprints and DNA samples, they said, and they would eventually find out anyway.

"I'm happy to give you blood, saliva," Steve said, "anything you need. . . . I wasn't there. I wouldn't do that. . . .

What do you need from me? I mean, so now I get an attorney?"

"There's nothing in there at all that's going to tie you to this at all?"

"There is nothing that I'm aware of, 'cause I know what I was doing," Steve replied in yet another curious answer.

Brown and Huante tried to give Steve another chance to confess. "Now would be the time to say, 'You know what? I went over and we argued, and she threw this at me and I got upset, and I—'"

But Steve remained firm. "No," he said. "I was not there."

Told Jake's story that Steve had mentioned going riding on the trail around the fitness center, Steve said that was wrong, he'd never said such a thing. Asked to go over the information again about the trail he *had* taken off Love Lane, given its close proximity to the murder scene, Steve said, "Wish I'd chosen a different trail."

"I wish you had chosen a different trail also," Brown said.

"Of course if I had done it, I probably would have chosen something—I wouldn't have chosen to be right near the scene of what sounds like [it] may be a crime."

Steve asked why the detectives initially thought Carol had died from a fall. Brown told him that at first the ladder's position made it look as if she'd fallen from it, and that all the other stuff in the room had come "tumbling down." But the blood patterns and the position of Carol's body did not fit with that theory.

"There's blood in the room and, like I said, a very traumatic injury to her head. Very traumatic . . . It looks like something was possibly covered up after the fact."

* * *

During one of the breaks during that long night of questioning, Steve called his divorce attorney, Anna Young, and asked her to come down to the station. Young showed up and stayed with Steve until the search warrants had been written and executed. But knowing she did not have the experience necessary to defend a homicide suspect, Young referred him to criminal defense attorney John Sears.

Sears, in turn, called in private investigator Rich Robertson, a former investigative journalist and editor at the *Arizona Republic,* who had edited three separate stories that were Pulitzer Prize finalists.

Steve's sister Susan DeMocker was subsequently brought in as Sears's legal assistant for a time, which kept costs down and also allowed her to brief Steve's parents on the case regularly.

Outside Steve's interview room, Huante and Brown conferred.

"He thinks he's smart," Huante said. "That gouge he has on his leg—"

"A barbed-wire fence," Brown added.

"We got to check that area really good," Huante said, adding that as they'd already told Charlotte that "there were inconsistencies with her father's story and we're going to be doing a search on the house."

That's when they learned that Renee Girard had already arrived at Steve's condo—before the deputy who had been sent there to secure it and keep people from entering and moving or discarding evidence. In fact, one of the deputies noted, Renee had also been at the crime scene.

"Then we really need to search her and search her car. She might have taken shit to the car already. Her car."

* * *

Sheriff's investigators asked Steve to remove his shirt and shorts so they could photograph the numerous cuts on his body. In addition to the ones they'd seen earlier on his left arm and leg, they also found some that had been hidden under his clothes: a horizontal abrasion along his left side at the bottom of his rib cage, along with two narrow thin scratches under his underwear. They also found blood on the left side of his underwear's waistband.

Some of the scratches were very thin and some were deeper gashes. Several looked as if they could have been gouged by the barbed-wire fence that ran along the ranch land behind Carol's house. Investigators took DNA swab samples along that fence later in the week, and although Sorenson Forensics did find a mix of human DNA there, the results were inconclusive.

Meanwhile, as Commander Scott Mascher talked with Jake, and Rhodes spoke with Charlotte, neither teenager was very precise with times. For example, Charlotte first said that she and Jake had gone to the pool around sixish, coming back a half hour later, as the sun was setting. However, the sun didn't set until seven forty-six that night.

Charlotte was very emotional, speaking so softly at times that her words were unintelligible on the tape. She had just lost her mother, after all.

As she recounted how she'd dropped the phone when she learned that her mother was dead, Rhodes said gently, "Well, it's hard. It's hard for everybody."

Charlotte wasn't too precise on specific details, either. She said that once he got home, her father didn't go out again, while both Jake and Steve said that he went to the office for about five minutes.

After the teenagers were interviewed separately, Mascher and Rhodes talked to them together for about fifteen more minutes, starting around 2:30 A.M.

Asked if Steve would go riding on the trails behind the Bridle Path house, Charlotte said no, that wouldn't be very good bike riding, and Jake agreed. As far as trails go, he said, they were really short and narrow. Besides, Charlotte added, she didn't think Steve had even been out to the house since last year to get some tools.

During these sessions Charlotte said a few things that were interesting on their own or conflicted with what Steve told investigators.

One, she said he normally rode the loop trail around the Hassayampa workout center, from which he'd told her he was calling her after working out there that night. Jake said the same thing.

Two, she said Steve had been going for late three-hour trail runs recently, but this was nearly five hours and it was a bike ride.

And three, she said Steve told her that he had to "push his bike all the way back . . . through sand, he was telling us . . . 'cause you can't ride a flat tire through sand." She added that the loop trail at Hassayampa "is probably like gravel or sand."

But for that matter, so was the trail behind Carol's house. Decomposed granite sand, which, as Charlotte pointed out, would be pretty difficult terrain to ride—versus walk—a mountain bike.

Investigators kept Jake and Charlotte at the station until about five in the morning on July 3, when Renee Girard picked them up in her car and took them to her house. Detectives held Steve for questioning until ten o'clock, while they searched his office and condo.

The kids called in to their jobs to say they wouldn't be in, then they phoned Katie to break the bad news and tell her to come home. Katie heard the news just as her plane was taxiing into London's Heathrow Airport.

Jake spent the day consoling Charlotte, as Renee came in and out of the room to check on them. Steve came by later in the day, then left.

They stayed at Renee's until 4 P.M., when they were told that the condo search was over and they could return there. After Renee drove them back, Charlotte and Jake stayed alone for a while and made a snack before Steve came back briefly, then said he was going for a walk.

After finishing his interviews early that morning, Commander Scott Mascher headed over to the Hassayampa fitness center to check out the loop trail that Steve and the teenagers had described, and to search for any signs that Steve had been there that night.

Heading into the darkness around 3 A.M. with his flashlight, Mascher walked around the trailhead near the gym, searching for bike tracks or footprints, but found none. He also looked along the side of the roads for trash cans or discarded evidence. Coming up empty, he returned to the station to wait for sunrise. Once it was light enough, he made the same rounds with Lieutenant Rhodes before heading back to Bridle Path.

Meanwhile, around 4:30 A.M., following the map that Steve had drawn, Detectives Brown and Alex Jamarillo drove out to Love Lane to try to find the trailhead and bike tracks Steve had described. Brown didn't know this area very well from a professional standpoint. Even though he'd hiked Granite Mountain many times, he'd only been working out of the sheriff's Prescott office a very short time.

They drove down Love Lane, which coursed through a residential area, and stopped at several sections. But not seeing where a trail would even start, let alone any trailhead or car and bicycle tracks, they headed back to the office.

By the time Brown returned with better directions on July 13 to look again for the trail where Steve said he'd been riding, it had already rained, wiping out any chance of proving—or disproving—Steve's story.

CHAPTER 8

Assigned to canvass Carol's neighborhood in the hours after the murder, Deputy Taintor spoke with Ron and Jody Drake, who lived a few doors down on Bridle Path. Ron said he'd heard Carol coughing earlier that night and he'd also heard a male voice he didn't recognize near the trail to the east of their house.

Although that trail was on private ranch land, he explained, residents were allowed to use it. He said people sometimes walked through Carol's property to access the trail behind her house, using some wooden steps to climb over the barbed-wire fence.

Taintor and Sergeant Acton checked the map for a trailhead close to Carol's house, and noted that the nearest one was at the end of Glenshandra Drive. Taintor recalled seeing an entrance to the ranch land there during past patrols of the area.

Driving to the end of Glenshandra, they parked on the pavement near the turnaround, which was made of dirt and crushed rock and was a few hundred feet from the trailhead. There, they were able to identify fresh tracks that had been left by a car and a mountain bike.

The metal-pipe gate to the trail was closed, locked and surrounded by the barbed-wire fence that ran along the ranch land toward Carol's house, so Taintor had to climb over the east side of the fence. As he inspected the coarse, decomposed granite sand trail with his flashlight, he was able to make out some fresh tracks made by athletic shoes, horses and bike tires. Careful to step around them, he traced the bike tracks from the loose sandy trail to the dirt parking area and onto the road pavement.

After returning to Carol's house to report their findings, Taintor and Acton learned that Steve had mentioned riding his bike on a trail about a mile from the Bridle Path house earlier in the evening. So they wasted no time in heading back to the Glenshandra trailhead to string up crime scene tape and to take photos of the shoe prints and tire tracks they'd just found, using a flashlight and other techniques to illuminate the prints in the darkness.

"I tried several different things, and the photographs just didn't turn out very well," Taintor testified later. "They were just blurry, fuzzy."

The timing of the rainfall—and, as a result, the investigators' ability to identify and differentiate between fresh and preexisting shoe prints and bike tire tracks—became a matter of debate.

Carol and Charlotte's text messages referred to rainstorms in Prescott on Tuesday, July 1. And Curtis James, a meteorologist who testified as an expert for the defense, testified that a rain gauge at his home in Williamson Valley, about three-quarters of a mile from Carol's house, measured three-hundreds of an inch of rainfall between 5:00 and 5:20 P.M. that same day.

Commander Scott Mascher, however, testified that he

remembered having to use his windshield wipers when it started raining in the midafternoon of Wednesday, July 2, as he drove down Williamson Valley Road to his house in Chino Valley. And when he'd been called out around eleven o'clock that same night to Bridle Path, he brought an umbrella.

Because Mascher also testified that the monsoon showers he encountered fell as usual in isolated areas, both scenarios seem possible. Either way, Mascher said the recent rainfall allowed him to differentiate between the newer and older tracks at the Glenshandra trailhead, where he joined Detective Theresa Kennedy and Lieutenant Rhodes in the early afternoon of July 3 as they examined the tracks their fellow investigators had identified the night before.

As an experienced tracker, Mascher said he knew the rain would have made the newer tracks stand out from those left by previous hikers and bikers, which were not so clearly delineated, and looked older and more smoothed over than the fresh ones.

Mascher and Rhodes followed these bike tire tracks and shoe prints—which were side by side, as if someone were walking a bicycle—for about one hundred yards, where the bike tracks stopped at a bush. From there, the shoe prints continued toward Carol's house and milled around an area of brush behind it, a vantage point from which Mascher could see into the back window and into the curtainless room where Carol's body was found.

Inbound, those prints crossed over the barbed-wire fence at the back of Carol's property and headed onto her rear patio. Outbound, they went back in the other direction, over the fence, circled around the thick, heavy bush, where the bike tracks had stopped, and circled out toward the trailhead again. The detectives thought that these bushes could have caused the deep cuts on Steve's legs, as could have the barbed-wire fence.

Judging by the prints, the detectives believed that the killer had tried to find the least resistance between the thickest and scratchiest brush on the ranch-land side of the barbed wire on the way to and from the house. And coming and going, the killer had apparently lifted his bike over the locked gate at the Glenshandra trailhead.

Detective Kennedy had already gone over these same tracks that morning, starting at the back of Carol's house and working her way toward Glenshandra. Using her GPS, she recorded and marked the waypoints and directions of the inbound and outbound tracks, using orange triangle markers and pink flags. She also took photos using her flashlight as a reference to measure the size of the shoe prints.

The detectives were all surprised to learn what a short distance it was from the trailhead to the rear of Carol's property—only a few hundred yards, maybe a quarter mile—when a drive on the streets between the two points measured 3.1 miles. They figured that whoever had made those shoe and bike tracks must have had intimate knowledge of this shortcut, because Carol's house wasn't visible from the trail until a person got fairly close. The suspect also must have known the area well enough to know exactly where to turn in the thick brush to reach the house.

Kennedy had also tracked a different set of shoe prints from the ones that started at the trailhead. These other prints had a pattern of "three Z's"—ultimately determined to be "similar" to Carol's shoes—starting from the house, leading out to the trail and back again.

Mascher found one area where the Glenshandra set of shoe prints tracked right over the three Z prints—indicating they came later in time—as the suspect's outbound prints headed back toward the trailhead.

The detectives rolled Steve's front and rear bike tires, which had different tread patterns, in the sandy dirt next to the suspected killer's tire tracks to compare them. They looked "identical," at least to the naked eye, investigator Mike Sechez said.

The defense, however, claimed that the tracks identified as Steve's could have been older and left by any numerous hikers who had used the trail. The brand of tire and tread pattern—the VelociRaptor—was not uncommon; it was the number-one-selling mountain bike tire for a time.

Criticizing law enforcement for failing to preserve these shoe prints and bike tracks before the subsequent rainstorm washed them away, the defense underscored this point by demonstrating that plaster castings could have been made.

The court ultimately ruled that because dirt on the trail consisted of crushed granite, the sand was too coarse for investigators to properly recognize flaws in the tire tracks from photographs alone, and this prevented the prosecution from claiming that Steve's and the killer's tracks were an exact or "identical" match. They were only allowed to say that Steve's tire tracks were "similar" to the killer's.

Regardless of the fact that the bicycle tires were a common brand, the shoes were not. As the judge stated rhetorically later in court, what was the chance of finding both the tire treads and shoe prints together—both similar to Steve's—behind Carol's house, where he had lived for many years?

While one set of investigators was processing the Bridle Path crime scene, another team headed over to Steve's UBS office on West Plaza Drive. There they executed a search warrant around eight in the morning, when Steve's coworker John Farmer arrived and let them in.

The team, which included Detective Brown and Sergeant Huante, looked around and photographed Steve's office, bathrooms and common areas. But because the building had no security cameras, they couldn't collect any video to determine whether Steve had come back to log off the night before, as he'd claimed.

Steve had recruited John, whom he'd met at Prescott College in the late 1980s, to work at UBS. John was the one who had allegedly called to alert him about his computer.

John said Steve usually started work at 6:30 or 7:30 A.M. and left between 2 and 3 P.M., although he sometimes stayed late depending on client needs. UBS told them to shut down their terminals at the end of the day, he said, or they wouldn't get daily updates.

When investigators checked John's computer, it was shut down and powered off. Steve's computer, however, was still powered on, but it was logged off.

John later told investigators that he'd made no such call to Steve, which was easily confirmed through Steve's cell phone records. He said he never went into Steve's office to look at his computer because it was none of his business. But even if he had, the computer goes to a blank screen and he wouldn't have been able to tell if Steve had logged off or not.

They also learned that Steve had not, in fact, logged off his computer since doing so at 4:38 P.M. on July 2, and he did not do so again until July 7.

Around seven forty-five that same morning, another set of detectives served a search warrant at Steve's condo, where they photographed the clean and orderly two-story town house and seized a number of items, including his passport. They found a cell phone battery on the windowsill in Steve's office there, and another one in his computer bag. A third battery, in his cell phone, was working fine.

They also took photos in the garage, including a set of left-handed Cleveland golf clubs and a head cover for a Callaway Steelhead III #7 club, which was sitting on the third shelf from the bottom in a rolling unit of vertically stacked shelves. Steve typically stored his bike riding gear—such as his clip-in bike shoes, helmet and gloves— on the same unit.

Because Steve said he'd showered right after his bike ride and washed the clothes he'd been wearing, investigators seized the clothes he'd described, which were still in the dryer. Taking no chances, they dismantled the entire washer to check for any blood or DNA evidence tying him to Carol's murder. They also searched his drains and dryer as well. But in the end they found no blood or DNA there linking him to the crime scene.

They did, however, take note of a box of rubber gloves in the laundry room.

When investigators inspected Steve's mountain bike tires more closely, the rear flat tire's valve stem appeared to have been rotted for quite some time. This indicated to them that it probably couldn't have held any air, and was likely already flat the day Steve took that ride. It was as if he had walked in the bike, laid it down in the heavy brush and walked it out again.

CHAPTER 9

Around eleven o'clock that morning, Deputy Pam Edgerton was assigned to examine Carol's dogs, which had been taken to her neighbor Janet Drake's house, around the corner on Jockey Path.

Edgerton was able to pick up Daisy, the white dog, but Ike wouldn't let her. The deputy didn't see any sign of blood or stains on Daisy, which matched with the evidence—a lack of bloody paw prints—in Carol's house.

Janet said she hadn't washed the dogs, although Daisy had run through the sprinkler. Between the peeing and puking dogs, Carol often had to treat the rugs with spot cleaner, she said, and also had to put up gates around the house to keep them off the carpets.

Telling Janet that they were investigating Carol's death as a homicide, Edgerton asked if anyone might want to hurt Carol.

"Her ex-husband," Janet said immediately.

"Why do you think he might have done something like this?"

"He is the biggest creep ever," Janet replied, noting that he'd had at least thirteen affairs during the marriage.

Asked if she suspected Steve just because he was a creep, Janet admitted that certainly was part of it, but she also thought that he was capable of doing the deed. Carol was a very sweet person with no enemies, she said, but Steve might have been so used to women giving in to him that he couldn't handle it when Carol had rejected him this last time.

"He took everything else from her," she said, adding that during the protracted divorce period "he wouldn't give her a red cent" toward her bills.

Janet said Carol told her that Steve had asked her within the past week to try to work on their relationship and to get back together again. Aghast, Carol said no, and reminded him that he was already dating Renee.

"She means nothing to me," Steve told Carol, and continued to try to persuade her to reconcile.

But Carol, Janet said, told him she wasn't interested.

At three forty-five that afternoon, the county ME, Dr. Philip Keen, began the autopsy of Carol's body. He determined that she'd been struck at least ten times with a blunt-force object, including seven or more times in the head.

When Keen testified about his findings at a hearing on November 12, 2008, he explained that any one of the head blows would have rendered her unconscious and helpless. Calling it an "exceptionally vicious attack," he said the later blows were "beyond what was necessary to render one unconscious or even deceased."

Keen noted several of what appeared to be defensive

contusions on her right hand and forearm, two of which were long, thin and parallel to each other. She also had a broken nose and a bruised lip.

Based on the linear nature of her arm bruises, the curved scalp lacerations and the skull fractures beneath them, he thought a golf club, probably a wooden driver, not an iron, was the most likely murder weapon. A club's rodlike shaft and contoured head could cause both types of injuries he saw, and the club's head was dense enough to wield the force and momentum necessary to cause such deep skull fractures.

In addition to the defensive injuries on her right forearm, Keen also found that a fingernail on her right hand was fractured down to the quick, all indications of a struggle. He noted some brown material under the fingernails of her left hand, which was tagged and labeled as evidence number 603, and was later determined to contain male DNA. That unknown mystery man came to be known as "Mr. 603." Noting that her right hand was thick with blood, Keen also retrieved some hair from it, but it proved not to be human.

One of the detectives observing the autopsy remembered seeing a set of golf clubs and an empty golf head cover in Steve's condo garage, so they decided to run back and get it. However, because the first team had already finished its search there at 3:55 P.M., and they'd called Steve to let him know he could return, they had to obtain a second warrant.

Meanwhile, Steve reentered the gate to his condo complex at 4:06 P.M., and immediately began to clean up the garage.

* * *

When the detectives returned to the condo with the second warrant at 6:40 P.M., they were looking to seize the set of golf clubs and a pair of athletic shoes that might match the shoe prints they found at the end of Glenshandra. They were able to seize the left-handed set of Cleveland clubs, but the Callaway head cover, which was featured in the photos taken during the earlier search, was nowhere to be found.

Renee's white Toyota Camry was in the garage. Noting the windows were rolled up, Detective Ross Diskin searched the car for shoes and golf clubs, but found none. He looked through the glove box and in and around the child's car seat in the back, but saw nothing unusual, and specifically not the missing golf club head cover. However, Diskin did not complete his report about this search until five months later, on December 16.

While the kids were in Steve's dining room, they heard noise in the garage and Jake went downstairs to see what was going on. He saw the garage door open and sheriff's deputies doing another search.

Jake recognized a couple of them from the sheriff's station the night before. He told them that Steve had gone for a walk after cleaning up the garage and before the investigators returned with the new warrant.

When they asked to speak to Steve, Jake went back upstairs to relay the message, then stayed with Charlotte while Steve talked with the investigators.

Steve came back inside and sat on the stairs while the detectives asked him, Charlotte and Jake some more questions, specifically if they had seen a golf head sock cover.

"No," Jake and Charlotte replied.

But Sergeant Huante didn't believe them. He kept asking the teenagers questions in an aggressive manner, yelling at them, in fact, as he accused them of knowing where the head cover was and keeping that information from the deputies.

Inside, the detectives went through Steve's rather extensive, but neatly organized, collection of shoes. His many pairs of dress shoes were stacked next to each other in a section of rectangular compartments, and the athletic shoes were stored in a separate vertical row of square compartments, each housing a single pair. They seized all of his athletic shoes, including a pair of La Sportiva Rajas.

After the sheriff's team left the condo again, Renee came back. Steve told her, Charlotte and Jake that he'd known the investigators were looking for the head cover, which he said he'd found in the backseat of Renee's car. It could have been blown there by the wind from somewhere in the garage, he said.

Once attorney John Sears arrived, Renee took the kids to Bridle Path to pick up Charlotte's car, leaving Sears alone with his client.

But Steve didn't turn over the head cover to authorities or to his attorney that day. Instead, he gave it to Sears for safekeeping two days later. His defense team later said that although Steve knew the investigators were looking for the head cover, it wasn't on the search warrant, and he didn't know why they wanted it. Not knowing what to do, Steve discussed the issue with Sears, who then called the bar association hotline for advice on how to proceed.

"It is important to know that suspects (and their attorneys) are not required by the Constitution to help law enforcement investigate, particularly when the investigation is targeting you," Rich Robertson, the defense's investigator, said later. "The burden is on the government. People should not be put in the position of having to guess what law enforcement is looking for or why."

When detectives interviewed Jake again, he told them that the last time he'd been to Carol's house was that last Sunday, the day after Katie had left on her trip. He and Charlotte had spent a couple of hours picking through Katie's clothes for those that Charlotte wanted to wear. Carol, who was happy to see them, was getting ready for her garage sale, for which Steve said he'd given her some artwork and a golf club.

Steve also had offered Jake's father a set of left-handed mixed-matched clubs that he didn't use, but like Jake, his dad was right-handed and couldn't use them, either.

Believing they had collected all the evidence they needed from the Bridal Path house, the team of investigators cleared the crime scene around 5:30 P.M. on July 3. Within ten minutes Detective Brown called Jim Knapp to tell him that he could return. In Brown's mind it was Jim's residence, he was the caretaker of the house and Carol's pets, and no one knew what else to do with the animals.

That's when Brown, who had been assigned to be the case agent by then, also gave Jim a heads-up about the large amount of blood in Carol's office.

Around six o'clock, right after this conversation, Jim mentioned this bit of information to the cashier at the Safeway on Willow Road, where he was buying some wine. A woman who knew Carol through Van Gogh's Ear, the art gallery where she'd worked, was nearby and overheard him say that his roommate had been murdered and there was "blood all around." Concerned, she reported this to Detective Brown and faxed him a copy of her Safeway receipt as documentation.

Later, when Brown was confronted on the stand about why the detectives hadn't brought Jim down to the station for questioning the night of the murder, let alone why he told Jim about all the blood and let him back into the crime scene on July 3, Brown responded that he wasn't truly in charge of the case.

"I was not delegating or directing people to make decisions," he testified. "My supervisors were doing that."

In the view of Steve's attorneys, authorities should have considered Jim Knapp as a suspect or person of interest, but they didn't.

"You chose to believe Mr. Knapp's alibi and chose to disbelieve Mr. DeMocker's alibi," defense attorney Craig Williams said.

Brown countered that Steve was the one who drew attention to himself at the crime scene the night of the murder by asking several times whether he was a suspect, which raised Commander Mascher's suspicions as well. Charlotte, Jake and Jim, on the other hand, did not raise the investigators' suspicions in the same way, and they also did not ask whether they were suspects. Jim *was* a person of interest, Brown said, he just wasn't taken down to the station.

For the next five years, Brown continued to work the investigation, but he traded his detective title for deputy because he was mostly working patrol as the case dragged on. Detective John McDormett, who typically worked homicides, replaced him as the lead detective and case agent in September 2008, followed by Lieutenant Dave Rhodes, who took over because of concerns over a personality clash between McDormett and prosecutor Joe Butner.

* * *

On July 8, after a case briefing at the Prescott sheriff's station, Sergeant Dan Winslow, who was a golfer, was asked to look through the seized assortment of Steve's left-handed clubs. Winslow compared the photo of the now-missing head cover with the Mizuno bag that contained two metal drivers, two fairway woods, four irons and a sixty-degree wedge, but saw no matching club.

Winslow then went to the High Desert Golf shop in Prescott and looked through its selection of used clubs. Learning that the staff kept no record of when or who had brought them in, he purchased a used left-handed Callaway club, because it was the same make and model as the missing head cover—a Big Bertha Steelhead III #7 wood, which investigators believed was the likely murder weapon. Winslow gave the used club to Detective Brown.

This used club was the same model as Steve's except that it was one inch shorter. Steve, they later learned, had had his club custom made by Callaway, which shipped it to him in October 2003. The club Winslow purchased was later known as the "exemplar" club, and was admitted in court as an example of the alleged murder weapon.

Subsequently the detectives also seized two more sets of the family's clubs, a right-handed set from one location and yet another set of clubs from a storage facility. But investigators were never able to find the club that went with the missing head cover.

The detectives returned to the Bridle Path house several times with new warrants that week, looking for additional evidence that came to light as the investigation progressed.

When Brown and his team came back on July 6, Jim Knapp was on the property, and they saw that he'd thrown a red blanket over the bloody area in the office. He told them he could see the red mess from the laundry room, and he couldn't stand to look at it. He didn't want Carol's daughters to see it, either.

As the investigators inspected the laundry room, they noticed that the lights still didn't go on, so Detective Jamarillo, wearing gloves, screwed two of the loose bulbs back in and they worked.

Jim asked if they'd put new bulbs in, noting that the lights usually functioned properly. Figuring this was no coincidence, investigators collected the bulbs to check them for prints and DNA, theorizing that the killer could have come into the house and unscrewed the bulbs while Carol was out running, then hidden in the dark laundry room, behind the door, while she was on the phone. Ultimately, the DNA results were inconclusive on two of the bulbs. The third had no DNA, but did have a fingerprint. However, it was not Steve's, whose prints were the only ones submitted for comparison.

The investigators noticed that a *Body & Soul* magazine, which had a stapled packet of paperwork tucked into it, had been moved from the kitchen counter since they'd last been there. The packet contained a UBS bank statement and a couple of very recent e-mails between Carol and Steve, pertaining to the divorce agreement and division of Steve's 401(k) account balance. Carol had apparently printed out the e-mails late on July 1 or early on July 2, highlighting some areas and scribbling notes about the math. She'd written *$186,667.31,* in the margin, for example, referring to their agreement that she would get the first $180,000 and they would split any additional amount.

The investigators collected this paperwork because Brown wanted to test a reddish substance for blood, but it came back negative. Jim handed the magazine to Brown, and the defense later made an issue of Jim's fingerprint being on one of the e-mail printouts.

Investigators checking the doors and other access points of the house that week found what appeared to be blood on the dead bolt to the door leading out of the den and into the garage. The detectives found no blood in the hallway proper, although they did find some spatters on plastic containers stored there. They also found a droplet on a section of the door frame near the wall, where ants were milling around, so they figured the killer had used that door to leave.

On the sidewalk outside that door, which was made mostly of glass and enabled someone to look inside, they found a single round drop of blood. They figured the drop had dripped down, off the suspect or murder weapon, as if he'd stopped to look through the glass at the body. The shape of the droplet indicated that the person or object was not moving.

"Both of those blood spots came back to Carol, so the suspect had [her] blood on his glove or hand," said Mike Sechez, the prosecution investigator.

In addition, they found what they thought was some blood on the passenger seat and on a red flashlight in Katie's BMW in the garage. They had the car towed to an impound yard for processing.

They seized the ladder, which had been specially made to lock over wheels on the loft in that bedroom, to document the absence of blood on it. There were no fingerprints on it, either, which supported the theory that the killer was wearing gloves when he repositioned the objects in Carol's office.

With the help of the Gilbert Police Department on July 8, investigators processed the house with Bluestar, a revealing agent that turns blue when it reacts with blood.

They started at the front door and worked their way through the kitchen and down the hallway to the office, looking for any hidden traces that had been wiped or washed off or were invisible to the naked eye. They also used the agent in the bathroom, including the sinks. No area turned fluorescent until they got to the threshold of the office.

Despite all this searching, they still were unable to find any of Steve's blood or DNA at the house. And despite the fresh bleeding cuts on his arm and leg, the only bit of blood they found on his bicycle was a spot on his pump. They wondered whether he'd wiped it off, but had missed that one spot.

Later the defense questioned why Jim Knapp had been allowed into the main house to move items around—such as the magazine, financial paperwork, and Carol's purse, keys and day planner—when the investigators hadn't finished collecting evidence. Jim said he'd kept Carol's planner because it contained phone numbers for friends he wanted to call.

"I know he was looking over the search warrant supplement returns, so I think he was being nosey, and he was looking to see what we had seized and what was still around the house," Brown testified later.

The defense also questioned how Jim came up with the theory that he told Brown during the July 6 search, that the killer "got a hold of her head and he smashed her head into the corner of that desk."

Similarly, the defense criticized investigators for failing to do a DNA test on the blood-spattered rimless glasses found on Carol's desk, which the defense claimed were Jim's, as featured hanging around his neck in various photos. Furthermore, they took detectives to task for failing to ask Jim about the binoculars he kept in the guesthouse, where he had a clear view into the windows of the main house.

CHAPTER 10

Katherine Morris's best friend called her about Carol's death on July 3. But that being the day of her own divorce, Katherine didn't even want to listen to voice mails, let alone talk to anyone.

After checking her voice mail the next morning, Katherine called her friend back around nine o'clock. When she learned that Carol had died, Katherine immediately visualized a car wreck. Her response was visceral, and unlike any she'd had before or since.

"No, no, no!" she screamed from the gut as she felt her knees go limp. After she composed herself, she asked how and when.

"They found her dead in her home," her friend said.

"Whaat?"

"It looked like she was murdered."

Katherine couldn't even comprehend how that could have happened to her peaceful, spiritual friend—someone who didn't have a violent bone in her body, had never hurt anyone and had shined light from every pore of her being.

She waited until a civilized hour—noon, her time in Georgia, three hours later than Prescott time—to call

Carol's house, hoping that someone would answer. When no one did, she called Steve, knowing that Charlotte was living with him.

When he answered, his voice sounded raspy and tired. He said he was exhausted and that he was sorry for her loss, knowing "how close and dear Carol and you were," a remark that struck her as odd. Not to compare losses, but he'd been married to Carol for twenty-five years and she was the mother of his children. Surely, his loss was worse than Katherine's.

The emotionless tone in which he talked about Carol's death was "stone cold and not grief-stricken at all," she recalled. "I would have thought he would be in tears, crying, and there was none of that." All of this raised a red flag for her. It also made her feel like he was trying to manipulate her and her perception of what had happened, as if he were grooming her to support him.

"When you have the loss of someone, you're not able to talk like he spoke. You're not talking about the details of how they were killed, or murdered, or who did it. For me, you're just in a great tidal wave of emotion. You're waiting to answer questions." Instead, she said, "He was telling me what he wanted me to hear."

Being a therapist, Katherine was trained to take notes during discussions like these. Also knowing she was feeling emotional, she wanted to make sure she remembered what she thought might later become an important discussion. So she wrote down all the details of their conversation.

As they discussed the circumstances of Carol's death, Steve said the detectives hadn't even categorized it as a homicide, noting that the ladder near the loft was upside down.

"My understanding is that they aren't certain it was murder," Steve said. "They think it was an accident."

"An accident?"

"Yeah, apparently, the ladder was toppled over and so were some other things in the room."

Carol had made a phone date with her friend Debbie Wren Hill for noon, eastern time, on July 5, so she could tell Debbie all about her new boyfriend, David Soule. When the phone rang early that morning, Debbie groaned, wishing Carol hadn't called before she was really awake.

Oh, Carol, she thought.

Debbie's husband answered the phone. "It's your mom," he said.

Picking up, Debbie waited to hear whatever was so important that her mother needed to call so early.

"I have some really bad news for you," her mom said.

Debbie wondered which family member had died. She was surprised and saddened to hear that it was not family, but her dear friend.

"Did she kill herself?" Debbie said, asking the first question that came to mind.

"No, she was murdered."

"Oh, my God," she said. "Steve."

Debbie immediately called Katherine and together they tried to piece together what might have happened.

Steve never returned Ruth Kennedy's phone messages from the night of the murder. They didn't talk until the following Tuesday, six days afterward, on July 8, and only because Ruth was on the phone with Katie.

Katie had planned to stop in Europe on her way to South Africa, where she'd planned to take political economics and an apartheid history class at the University of Cape Town, and also work at a child soldier rehabilitation center in Uganda. But she had to cut her trip short to fly home as soon as she got the news about her mother's murder.

"My dad wants to speak to you," Katie told her grandmother.

Steve's mother, Janice "Jan" DeMocker, had been quick to send condolences and flowers to Ruth after both her sister and husband had died. Ruth was now wondering why she hadn't heard from her daughter's typically caring mother-in-law, who was a minister.

"Steve, have you told your mother about Carol?" Ruth asked, already guessing the answer. She was right.

"No," he said, "I'm going to. I thought Jim [Steve's brother] told her."

CHAPTER 11

In the weeks after the murder, as the investigation into Carol's death proceeded, Ruth Kennedy received one call after another from investigators working the case. The worst one came from Dr. Laura Fulginiti, a forensic anthropologist who called to get permission to piece Carol's skull back together.

"At that time they were considering me next of kin," Ruth recalled. The image of her daughter's skull, shattered into so many pieces that it needed to be reconstructed like a puzzle, had always stuck in her mind, a concept "just so horrible to even contemplate."

Sheriff's Deputy Steve Surak had transported Carol's head from the medical examiner's office in Yavapai County to the one in Maricopa County, where it was to be delivered to Fulginiti for an expert examination, analysis and reconstruction.

Within two weeks Fulginiti concluded that it was one of the three worst cases she'd ever seen. The skull, which showed a minimum of seven blunt-force blows, and possibly many more, was broken into more than two hundred pieces, including at least fifty larger pieces that were held together only by tissue.

When she saw the curvilinear shape of the fracture line
in the right cranial vault, with a flatness on top, she testified later, "I thought to myself, 'Wow, that looks a lot like
a golf club. Particularly a wood.'"

She developed this theory without conferring with the
ME, Dr. Keen, or any other investigator, and she did, in
fact, determine that the injuries were "consistent" with
a golf club. Given the Callaway Big Bertha Steelhead exemplar club to examine, Fulginiti confirmed that it was
capable of creating Carol's injuries. Although she couldn't
say for sure that this particular model of club created the
trauma, she also said it couldn't be "ruled out."

*She suggested that other golf clubs and objects be tested
to show the difference in impact damage, but said the left-
handed club appeared to be consistent with the trauma,*
Detective Brown wrote in his report.

By some accounts Steve didn't offer much comfort to
his daughters during this trying time. About a week after
the murder, Renee saw one scene that disturbed her
enough that she told her Unitarian minister friend, Dan
Spencer, about it: Steve was busy doing something on his
laptop when Katie started to cry on the living-room floor.
She began sobbing, so upset that she went into the fetal
position, and yet Steve continued to type. Charlotte's boyfriend had to get down on the floor and hug her to try to
calm her down.

The first news brief about the case was posted on Prescott's *Daily Courier* website the night of July 3, calling
Carol's murder an "apparent homicide."

Sandy Moss, a local radio and TV host on KPPV/KQNA and AZTV who has lived in town for more than two decades, said Carol's death left the community at large in shock. Not much crime is committed in Prescott, and certainly not many homicides. But this particular murder victim, who was a "really decent, artistic, spiritually aware person," seemed so unlikely.

"I've never met a person who didn't think Carol was the cream of the crop, the cat's meow, a really fine and dear person," Moss said. "To have someone like that who was so seemingly undeserving of being slaughtered" was such a shame.

In fact, Moss couldn't remember any murder like this one in at least twenty years. "It was horrendous," she said. "It was even shocking for the parties who didn't know Carol."

Later that month, when *Courier* columnist Randall Amster wrote about Carol's death, he recalled that she'd been one of the first colleagues at Prescott College to welcome him seven years earlier:

If you read about her in the newspaper and didn't know her, you might have an impression of a New Age artist with a gentle, kind spirit. And she was this, yet she also possessed a strength of character that you might not suspect. She was forthright and outspoken, and will be sorely missed in this community.

Some Prescott residents wondered if they were safe, if this was a random killing by a madman on the loose, or if this was someone who had set out specifically to kill Carol.

By July 7, sheriff's officials said publicly that they'd already identified "at least one person of interest," and that area residents should not fear that a serial killer had committed the murder.

As people learned more details of the homicide scene, "they thought this was likely someone she knew," Moss said. "Generally a random slaughter wouldn't make it so personal. The people I talked to were outraged and broken-hearted."

"Her artist friends believed from the beginning that it was [Steve]," Moss said. "They had no doubt in their mind."

Prescott is not only home to the alternative Prescott College, it also has drawn an unusual number of rehab facilities, homeless people, alcoholics and addicts, some of whom Carol was treating at Pia's Place. That's because buyers at one point streamed into town to purchase cheap property for rehab facilities in residential neighborhoods. The town also provides feeding care stations for the homeless.

"It's been a real bone of contention here," Moss said.

But at the same time, she explained, Prescott is also culturally alive. And although some small towns may be populated with small-minded or uneducated people, that's not the case there. Prescott's half-a-dozen higher-education institutions and its performing-arts venues have drawn big-name artists such as Anne Murray and Bill Cosby, during his earlier days before his reputation became tarnished with date rape allegations.

"We have a much more sophisticated populace with opportunities for education, entertainment and growth," Moss said, adding that Prescott is also known for being a spiritual community with "a higher consciousness in terms of social responsibility and awareness."

The town's more temperate weather also draws residents

from the valley or flatlands of Phoenix, especially during the hottest months of the year.

The monsoons that start up at the end of June or beginning of July come at the best time of year. "It's just so refreshing and such a nice break," she said. "It rains for a couple of hours, then it goes away. The sun comes out, and there's often a rainbow."

More than half of Prescott's population is forty-five or older, and about a quarter of the town's residents are sixty-five or older, although the town still has its share of kids and schools. But for a single person like Carol was, it's hard to find someone to date, which is likely why she turned to online dating sites to find someone special.

"I have single friends, and it's really hard . . . to hook up with the right kind of single people or to find a variety of people that you might be interested in," Moss said. "Singles always feel excluded here, I know. . . . It's hard to find people who match up to other people."

A year or so before her murder, Carol had been seeing a man who lived in Malibu, California. Sometime after they broke up, she met David Soule on Match.com in April 2008. David was among the first people investigators interviewed.

David had a home in nearby Jerome, but he primarily lived on the coast of southern Maine in Lincoln County, where he was fixing up a sailboat for a long trip.

After they met, he and Carol got together ten times over the course of the next month before he left for Maine on May 6, and they communicated regularly by e-mail and phone until she died. Carol was preparing to fly east for a visit on July 12, to see his boat, and to spend some time together.

On July 3, a friend of David's saw the news brief about Carol's murder in the *Courier* and called him. David immediately phoned the sheriff's office, asking to speak to Detective Doug Brown, who, busy writing and carrying out search warrants and attending the autopsy that day, didn't get back to him until the next day.

When they talked, David was clearly shaken by the news. "He was at a loss, I think, for the most part," Brown recalled later.

David wondered if Carol had told Steve about the upcoming trip and he'd become angry. As far as he knew, Steve was not to go to the Bridle Path house. Carol told David that she'd been upset when Steve had shown up unannounced that past week, supposedly to pick up the barbecue grill. Luckily, Jim Knapp had intercepted him.

David had heard about the golf club being a possible murder weapon, noting that when Steve came over to pick up the grill, that may have been a good opportunity to plant a weapon. He didn't know Jim all that well, but he didn't think Carol's tenant had anything to do with the murder.

Asked about the golf shoes found in Carol's car, David said she'd mentioned taking some lessons in her Match.com dating profile, but he'd never seen any clubs at the house.

When Carol and David last spoke, on Tuesday, July 1, around 10 P.M., she told him she'd been crying after getting home from work that day. She wondered aloud whether she was sad about Katie leaving for South Africa.

Carol had been under a tremendous financial strain lately, he said. She was making only $24,000 a year, but was going to have to pay $12,000 to the IRS because of the divorce settlement, presumably taxes on her share of Steve's 401(k) account.

David was aware that Steve had tried to get back together

with Carol since the divorce, even after everything he'd put her through, with all his women.

Carol had told Soule of a $300 Viagra bill that Steven got and she suspected that he was banging everything in sight, Brown wrote in his report. *Soule thought that Steven had some type of sexual addiction.*

Soule thought that Steven was the type that wanted what he couldn't have and that he didn't want what he could, Brown wrote. *He thought that this may be the first time that someone has actually left him and refused him.*

In one of Carol's last e-mails to her boyfriend, she said Steve had been "exceedingly nice" around the time of Katie's airport send-off, which sent up red flags for her. *[She felt she was] caught in a toxic net and did not know how she would be able to get out,* Brown wrote.

David agreed to give a DNA swab to his local law enforcement to rule him out as a suspect in case he'd left any DNA at the house, but he said he'd been in Maine at the time of the murder.

Katie DeMocker flew home and arrived in Prescott on July 4. During dinner that night after Charlotte, Jake and Steve picked her up at the airport, they discussed Carol's possible killers.

Steve suggested that Barb O'Non—his former assistant, with whom he'd claimed to have been in love with for years and wanted to marry—could have hired someone to kill Carol. If he was arrested, he said, Barb could get his entire client book, worth $110 million, versus the 30 percent of the annual $750,000 she'd been earning before.

With that seed planted, Katie mentioned Barb as a possible suspect to Detective Brown in an interview on July 7.

But before they got to Barb, Brown asked her about

the nasty e-mails Jim Knapp had been sending, spouting hateful allegations against Steve, the latest of which had come in just the night before. Brown asked if Katie could think of any scenario—"from what your mom said, from what your dad said, from what anyone said"—where Jim would intentionally cause her mother's death.

"I don't know how to answer these questions because I can't imagine anybody wanting to do this to anyone," Katie said.

Before she had a chance to elaborate, Brown reminded her that she'd mentioned Jim was "romantically kind of interested" in Carol.

"Yeah, he was," she said, explaining that one night he was drunk and the two of them had to put him to bed. He playfully grabbed at Carol's clothes, but after they tucked him in, "that was the end of it."

Brown asked if she could see any reason why others, such as her sister or Jake, would want to hurt Carol. Katie said no.

"Your dad?"

"No," she said.

"Anytime that you've been alive that you've seen any type of physical abuse?"

"No, and my parents didn't even believe in spanking us," she said. "Both of them are probably two of the most unviolent people. . . . I was a terror child and my dad never even hit me."

"No spanking at all?"

"I mean my mom did it once and they both felt so bad about it when I was, like, three that they vowed never to do it again."

But when Brown tried to push harder on the nature of arguments between her parents, Katie shut down. "I don't feel comfortable talking about this right now," she said.

Moving on, Brown asked about obsessive or violent clients and "unwarranted" phone calls to Carol, which prompted Katie to bring up Barb.

"I mean, I suppose, of all people that I could think of, maybe, I mean she hated my mom. I think she had some sort of, like, thing. She lives down in Anthem or somewhere around there, but she had something at the guard gate thing that my mom wasn't to be allowed anywhere near her. . . . It was kind of a combination of the fact that she just thought my mom was crazy, that she thought my mom hated her for having the affair," she said. She added that Barb also wasn't very friendly with Steve at the moment. "Their business is flamed. It got split up today."

Katie explained that the Barb affair was hidden from Carol for a while, but then she knew and then the girls knew, and then their parents "would say that it had stopped, but it didn't . . . or it kept going back and forth. . . . It was kind of a confusing process, I think, for both my mom and Barb, but I think Barb was pretty convinced that, you know, if my dad got a divorce they would end up together, and they didn't. But she wanted him to get a divorce for a really long time."

Asked what motive Barb would have to kill Carol, Katie said she didn't want to say more for fear of saying the wrong thing. But she did say this: "I don't trust her is the bottom line. She's always been manipulative."

Overall, she said, her mom had "very, very few enemies. . . . Everyone that she met liked her. She was nice to almost every single person."

Brown asked how Charlotte was doing under the circumstances, and what her views were about all this.

"She's about the same place I am. She's scared and stressed that this is how it happened because, you know, we can't even really deal with the fact that we're sad that she's gone. We're stressed about who did it and, you know, I mean, we're just scared."

"Have you talked to your dad about all this?"

"He's really sad. When I first got home, he just broke down and was crying. . . . He's been trying to be supportive of us and reassuring, but I think he's stressed out."

Brown told Katie that the detectives were going to do everything they could "to find out the truth, not find out some made-up thing that we want just to fit. We want the truth, that's all we want."

But in the meantime he asked her to keep to herself any information he'd told her about the investigation, a concern that ultimately became a major victims' rights issue in this case.

"The fact that it seemed accidental, but was not accidental, kind of puts this in position that somebody did this and for whatever reason tried to cover it up," he said.

As he cited evidence to support that conclusion, Brown drew a diagram of the room where Carol's body was found, along with the position of the ladder and the bookshelves, one tipped over the other, almost propped up, "like it had been right there, pushed over."

"Someone set this up, okay, to make it look like she fell from the ladder and possibly hit her head on the desk," he said. "It looks like someone staged all that stuff."

Last time she saw the ladder, Katie said, it wasn't even in that bedroom, it was out in the hall. "I've come to the terms with the fact that somebody killed her," she said, promising that if she knew anything or "thought that anyone, no matter how much I cared about them, knew anything about this, I swear to you I would tell you."

Brown asked Katie to think carefully, and if she had any information, to share it with the detectives. If she didn't, she was "doing [her] mom a disservice, because what everyone has said . . . is she did not deserve to be killed."

"She didn't at all," Katie agreed.

Brown said some "Joe Blow off the street" could have been "walking around in the backyard, came into your house, your mom's house, killed your mom and then staged it to look like an accident." And although that was a possible scenario, he said, "is it probable, or does it make sense for somebody to do that, is the question."

"Most likely not," Katie agreed.

Because Carol didn't leave money lying around and no property was evidently missing or stolen, the probability of a stranger staging a scene in that situation "is so minute, it's almost just not even worth looking at," Brown said. "Someone, for whatever reason, killed your mom because of anger, frustration, whatever."

Brown asked if there was any reason she might have gotten blood on the passenger seat of her car, the black BMW that was parked in Carol's garage.

"Not that I can think of," she said.

"There was blood found in your car."

"Oh," she said, surprised.

"Is there any reason your mom's blood would be in the passenger seat that you know about?"

"Don't think so. Wow," she said. "That was a shock."

Walking a careful line to gain Katie's help with the investigation and yet not give her too much graphic detail as to be insensitive, or to prompt her to share it with Steve, Brown tried to help Katie understand that the killer had to be someone close to her, and that investigators needed her help to solve the crime.

Carol couldn't have hurt her head so severely in a fall, he said. The trauma showed that she was hit multiple times, and she had "defensive wounds, meaning she tried to protect herself." The murder weapon, he said, would be "something similar to a golf club, something similar to a very skinny stick."

The trauma to her head was caused by enough force to fracture her skull, and her blood was not only in that room but tracked outside as well. "That was the first indication that this can't be an accident," he said. Given the multiple "hits to the head, it's usually because of, they call it a passionate-type thing, you lose control for a brief moment. I believe that's what happened here."

But every time Brown brought the interview back to Steve, noting, for example, that a block of his time was "lost" and that didn't "make a lot of sense" given the rest of his bike-riding story, Katie backed away and said she didn't want to talk about it.

Shortly after the murder, Charlotte's boyfriend, Jake, was working at Barbudos, a Mexican restaurant in the Safeway shopping center on Iron Springs, when Jim Knapp came in. Jake overheard Jim telling a woman that he thought Steve DeMocker was the only person who could have killed Carol and that he might have had financial motives for doing it.

Jake immediately texted Charlotte, and she came right over, which seemed to catch Jim off guard. Jake went back to work while Jim and Charlotte went outside to talk. In Jake's view, Jim seemed "a little shady" and had strong feelings for Carol.

The DeMockers heard that Jim was also telling people that Steve had been violent with Carol in the past, dragging her around by the hair.

The family asked Jim to vacate the guesthouse, which he didn't want to do. After Steve's brother Jim finally evicted Jim Knapp in August, the tenant asked for $5,000 in damages to his personal belongings—rust on his washer and dryer, which he said the DeMockers had left outside for several weeks.

In an e-mail to Katie, he noted that he was in a "very precarious financial situation," living on unemployment, with possible surgery coming up. He said he wasn't sharing that information to gain sympathy, only to inform her of his circumstances.

Katie, I loved your mom deeply, he wrote. *She was my coach, my confidante, and my friend.* But he also noted that despite the rumors going around, they n*ever had a romantic involvement.* When Carol was killed, he wrote, he was really *at a loss of what to do, where to go, and how I would manage,* but he did his utmost to care for Carol's two dogs and her cat, Max.

As executor of Carol's estate, Katie and her attorney worked out a percentage of Jim Knapp's damage claim and paid him. Without waiting for her attorney's advice, she also wrote a check for about $20,000 to her father, who pressured her to pay the claim he submitted for the professional cleanup team that removed the blood at Bridle Path so they could sell the house.

CHAPTER 12

Some of Carol's closest longtime friends, including Debbie Wren Hill, Katherine Morris and Sally Butler, flew in to attend one or both of the celebrations of life that were held in Carol's memory.

Like Carol, Debbie and Katherine are both therapists. Debbie works with children, and Katherine with children and families. Sally, who had known Steve since college, also had worked with him in Outward Bound fifteen years before she met Carol in the late 1980s. The two women subsequently developed a close friendship.

The first memorial service was open to the public, just before Carol's birthday, on the afternoon of Thursday, July 24, at the Unity Church of Prescott, where Carol had sporadically attended services.

The second was a private service for about fifty family members, neighbors and close friends on Sunday, July 27, outside the L'Auberge resort in Sedona. The Reverend Dan Spencer, a Unitarian minister and close friend of Renee Girard, facilitated the ceremony. Steve later submitted a claim for the service costs to Carol's estate, which had assets valued around $284,000, including several bank accounts and furniture. Claims against the estate came in pretty close to that same amount.

Debbie flew up from Nashville for the second service in Sedona, as did Ruth and John Kennedy, and John's two kids. Steve's father picked up Carol's family at the airport and dropped them at a hotel. The Kennedy family rented a car, then drove to the service with Debbie.

As the Kennedys pulled up to a red light, they looked over and saw Steve, Katie and Charlotte in the car next to them.

Oh, God, I just don't want to see him there, Debbie thought, dreading the inevitable interaction at the service.

They pulled into the parking lot at the same time, and after getting out of their respective cars, Debbie hugged the girls.

"I'm really sorry for your loss," Steve told Debbie.

"Thanks," she replied, uttering the only words she could manage for the man she was already convinced had killed her dear friend.

David Higgs, one of Carol's college friends, showed up after saying he didn't think he could make it. When Ruth saw him, she was so touched that he'd come, after all, that she hugged him and burst into tears.

Katherine Morris and Ali Rappaport, another of Carol's former students and friends, gave eulogies during the service, as did Ruth, Katie, Charlotte, Steve and his mother.

Ali talked about "walking the labyrinth" with Carol—one of Carol's specialties, involving a spiritual meditation to find inner peace, knowledge and healing—and described the strong connection they had formed.

Charlotte mentioned that she'd gotten into a rollover car accident in Phoenix the day before in Carol's Acura, and felt like her mother had been with her as a guardian angel, helping to keep her safe.

Clearly in a lot of emotional pain, Katie and Charlotte's heartfelt speeches were very difficult to listen to, but Steve's speech was the one that some mourners found odd.

During his daughters' time at the microphone, Steve didn't show any emotion. Yet, after only a minute or two into his own eulogy, he was pushing away tears. The minister noticed the marked contrast in Steve's reactions and figured he was an emotional guy, after all.

But after listening to Steve's entire speech, Reverend Spencer was struck again. Rather than talking about Carol, "the whole thing was about him, and how much Carol still meant to him, and about their dating, and what their relationship was like, and how he'd gone to Colorado and put up some kind of reconciliation pin," the minister recalled later. "He was suggesting that he and Carol had pulled things together, which wasn't true."

"I think Renee's dating a sociopath," Reverend Spencer told his wife afterward, recalling that he'd also found it curious that Steve had made a point of telling him before the service that no one should be allowed to record the eulogies.

Debbie and her group also listened to Steve's speech with disbelief. First, they couldn't believe that he wore his sunglasses through his entire remarks, and second, that he was able to speak so beautifully and eloquently about losing Carol, the woman with whom he'd spent half his life, after they thought he'd killed her.

Debbie's impression was different from Reverend

Spencer's, though it was still negative. "He seemed so smooth as he gave the eulogy," Debbie said, "working the crowd, just being Steve, charismatic, charming Steve. . . . He painted this picture of a soul mate that he had loved dearly. He referenced the fact that they were no longer married, but made it sound like that didn't affect the love that they still shared with each other."

As she listened, Debbie couldn't understand how he could carry around what he'd done to Carol and yet say such wonderful things about her. It was confusing for her—not just as Carol's friend, but also as a licensed therapist who had previously experienced such behavior only in objective or academic textbook terms. At one point she turned to David Higgs and shared her feelings of conflict and ambivalence.

"Maybe he didn't [do it]," she said. "How could he get up here and say those things if he'd just brutally murdered her?"

Carol's mother shared with Debbie that she, too, had been sitting in disbelief as she listened to Steve's eulogy, wondering how he could stand six feet in front of her and say such things when they both knew that he'd killed her daughter. Where did he find such nerve?

It wasn't until later that Debbie realized, "This is what a narcissist can do. He wanted to get rid of Carol and he also wanted to create a favorable impression in front of her closest people and make himself look innocent."

At the reception in the shade by the creek afterward, Debbie was standing with David, expressing their common dread that Steve would come over to speak to them.

"I don't want to talk to him. I don't want to shake that man's hand. I hope he doesn't try to," David said just before Steve approached them and did just that. Not wanting to make a scene, David accepted the gesture and shook Steve's hand.

"I just really want to thank you guys for being with Carol after the divorce," Steve told them. "Every divorce has two sides and I really appreciate you guys being there for her."

Debbie and David were dumbfounded and almost speechless.

"It was just stupefying, having to interact with him, knowing what we thought we knew, to have that hand that we thought had brutally murdered Carol reach out to us," Debbie recalled.

Steve looked at Debbie as though he wasn't sure—and maybe with some apprehension—about what she was going to say. Debbie and Carol used to discuss each other's dreams, and Carol had inspired Debbie to chronicle them in a journal, a practice she continued for some thirty years.

"I think I'm going to get a dream that will let me know what happened," she told Steve.

One of the most difficult concepts for Debbie to process was that she'd known Steve and Carol when things were so good between them, when Steve had seemed so benevolent.

"There are some people you meet and you know, this is a really devious person, but it wasn't like that with Steve," she said recently. "He seemed like a very nice guy, very attentive, and engaged with Carol."

Ruth Kennedy found it odd that Steve didn't say a word to her, hug her or offer his sympathies to her at the service, or on any other occasion, frankly.

Her son John had never come to Arizona to visit while

his sister was alive, but being there now he wanted to find out more about what had happened to Carol.

Steve's girlfriend, Renee, introduced herself to John Kennedy at the reception, but every time he tried to talk to Steve about the murder, Steve moved away from him. John tried half-a-dozen times that day, but he could not get Steve's ear.

Right around the second service, Katie DeMocker arranged for some of her mother's friends to visit the Bridle Path house, where a strange scene played out.

When Katherine arrived with her sister and Sally Butler, she was stunned to see that Steve had brought Renee, which she saw as inappropriate. Steve's brother Jim and sister Susan were there as well, along with Katie and Carol's mother and brother.

Carol's office, where the murder had occurred, hadn't been cleaned yet, and the desk and carpet were still covered with her blood. Jim DeMocker was trying to keep her friends out, but Katherine was determined. It's not that she wanted to see the crime scene. She simply felt she needed to be in the place where Carol's soul last was.

"The door was shut and I went to go open it and Jim [DeMocker] intercepted me," blocking her from going in, she recalled. "Jim walked away, I looked at Katie, Katie gave me the nod, and I opened it up and went in."

Because Carol had been cremated, Katherine wasn't able to see her body, which is an important part of the grieving process—to fully realize and accept that a loved one is dead. As a result, viewing this room was something she felt she needed and wanted to do. Katherine also wanted to see if she could feel Carol or any part of her there, or if anything else came to her.

But as she stood in that room and looked around, she didn't feel her friend there. Carol was gone. Instead, what Katherine felt was deep grief as reality set in and a sense of shock at the gruesome nature of the scene—the pool of blood still on the floor, the blood spatters on the walls, the shelves and the desk, which still had strands of Carol's hair stuck to the corner.

"It became more real, the violence of her death," Katherine said. "It became more apparent the brutality of it, the animalistic state that someone would have to be in to do that."

As Katherine emerged from the room, crying, Steve was standing in the hallway with Katie. As Katherine stood with her right side toward the kitchen and laundry room, Steve put his arm around her and gave her a sideways hug.

"You just want to think that it was an accident," he said. "Things would be so much easier if it was an accident."

Steve was usually gregarious, but not that day. He was a man of few words. His remark and hug sent shivers down Katherine's body as she shook her head no.

Katie agreed. "Dad, they ruled that it was not an accident," she said.

Based on that exchange, as well as her earlier conversations with Steve, Katherine again felt like he was trying to "groom" her to take his side, to believe his accident claim.

Steve had been guarded with her at the service, and he still seemed so calm, detached and composed. But after seeing the crime scene, and talking with Carol's mother about the details of Carol's death, Katherine knew that it was a murder.

"It was not an accident," she told him.

* * *

When Ruth walked into the house that afternoon, she noticed a vase of dead flowers on the dining-room table, where Carol had always kept fresh blooms.

"Well, would you look at that, the dead flowers are still on the table," Ruth said.

Steve's sister Susan promptly ran out of the room with the withered flowers, and Ruth subsequently felt bad about her remark because she knew Susan was under a lot of strain.

Unlike Katherine, Ruth couldn't bear to go into the room where her daughter was killed. Ruth noted once again that Steve didn't try to comfort her at this difficult moment.

"I don't know why he didn't, if he was so innocent, [why] wouldn't he? Why wouldn't he come up to me and hug me, say, 'Ruth, I'm so sorry about this. I'm out of my mind about this'?" she said recently. "But to say nothing and to do nothing. I thought that was really strange."

That night Katie begged Ruth to come to dinner with the DeMockers, so she did, although her son, John, refused.

On her way out the door afterward, Ruth put one arm around Katie to say good-bye. When Steve came up and put his arm around Ruth's waist, she did the same to him, although it was more out of reflex than a purposeful hug on her part.

Debbie Wren Hill had never seen the Bridle Path house. So while she was in town, she, too, made a trip over there with Ruth and John Kennedy after making arrangements by phone with Jim Knapp to show them around the property.

As they walked the grounds, Debbie noticed the empty bird feeder and the untended garden.

It's all so overgrown. It never would have looked like this if Carol was here, Debbie thought.

Before Carol had even had her morning coffee, she used to water her garden, which was surrounded by a stucco wall, and feed the horses, which she used to keep in the barn. The back area also had a trampoline, an outdoor shower, a hot tub, a fire pit, an old tree house and a maze made of stones that Carol had designed to "walk the labyrinth."

Jim took them into the guesthouse and showed them the artwork Carol had stored there, telling them to take their pick. Ruth was under the impression that this was not the good stuff in her portfolio, but the discards.

"I feel free to give you any of this that you want," he told them.

Debbie, Ruth and John each chose several pieces. Debbie hung hers in her office and home, where she also displayed the dried wildflowers she'd picked from the pasture behind Carol's house that day.

"Jim just seemed like a sweetheart and talked about her with great sadness and great care for her, and like the rest of us, [he] was convinced that Steve did this," Debbie recalled. "[He] felt like he knew a lot about the ins and outs of that marriage and I think he expressed some fear . . . some desire to get out of there pretty quickly. He as much as indicated there was no telling what Steve was capable of."

While they were standing outside the guesthouse, they saw some of Steve's family pull up. Debbie felt as if they were being spied on.

"It felt like they were giving us space, but keeping an eye on what was going on," Debbie said.

"We were afraid to walk out with [the artwork] in case someone was watching," Ruth said, so Jim offered to mail the pieces to them.

* * *

Debbie exchanged e-mails with David Soule for a couple of weeks after the murder.

"He just said, 'I'm devastated. I thought she was the one I was going to spend the rest of my life with,'" she recalled recently.

The feeling was apparently mutual, because Carol had said the same thing. "I'm so incredibly happy," she told Debbie. "He's working on this sailboat, and when it's finished, we're going to go on this Caribbean cruise and it's going to mark the start of the rest of my life."

David was about the same age as Carol. He had dark hair and a graying beard, and "looked like a really kind soul, [with a] great face," Debbie said. "He had to lick his wounds and remove himself from" the situation in order to heal.

In his e-mails to Debbie, he described the altar to Carol that he'd built on his kitchen table, with some pieces of her artwork and a lit candle. Debbie did the same thing, burning a candle for two weeks next to some of the jewelry and silk bags Carol had made for her.

"She just filled my life and so many other lives with her touch and her efforts," she said.

Debbie wasn't kidding when she told Steve that she thought Carol was going to come to her in a dream and tell her what had happened. Debbie did dream about Carol a number of times, and Steve showed up as well.

One of her most vivid dreams came after talking with Detective Brown in the weeks after Carol's death. She was riding in a car with Steve and another person, who was driving, and they had to stop in a place that felt dangerous.

Steve walked up to people and "was handing out crisp big bills. He was paying people off that killed Carol."

Debbie met a female psychic, who had been involved with solving crimes, and told her that a friend had been killed.

"I'm just getting this sense that somebody was paid to kill her," the psychic told Debbie, suggesting that she tell the detectives to check Steve's bank records for a possible payment.

Debbie's husband didn't think she should bother the police with her dreams or the psychic's remarks, but Debbie wanted justice to be served, and to help however she could so the killer didn't get away with this.

"It's not all about justice," Debbie said. It was also about wanting Ruth, the girls and "Carol's spirit to be okay."

Devastated by Carol's death, Jim Knapp went on an e-mail blitz with his friends—and Carol's—spreading his suspicions that Steve was to blame. In one e-mail he mentioned something about Steve grabbing Carol by the hair.

Katherine, who spoke to him several times a day after Carol's death, didn't like that Jim was copying Katie and Charlotte on the e-mails, and told him so. Sally Butler told him the same thing.

"He was blasting their father. I mean really, really blasting their father, and this was two days after their mom's death," Katherine recalled.

When she e-mailed him back to say, *Listen, take them off, these are children,* Jim wrote back, sarcastically recounting how Carol had always spoken *so* highly of her, and he was *so* sorry he'd offended her. This time he copied dozens of other people, apparently trying to embarrass her.

He subsequently apologized and Katherine wrote it off to his being distraught with grief.

Sally talked to the girls about Jim's claims, but they said the only violence they'd ever seen was the one time Carol threw a box at Steve during an argument. Sally told investigators she thought Jim's e-mails to her seemed a bit obsessive, calling himself Carol's "loves," and saying Sally didn't know him the way he did.

CHAPTER 13

Several weeks after the murder, Steve showed up unannounced at the Van Gogh's Ear gallery with a moving van full of Carol's artwork. He said he was preparing the Bridle Path house for sale, so he had to clear out all of her belongings, including every piece of art she'd ever done.

John Lutes, one of Van Gogh's co-owners, got a frantic call from his daughter, who was working alone at the gallery that day. He drove straight over to oversee the unloading and was overwhelmed by the massive collection of items Steve had brought. Steve had not only delivered Carol's artwork, he'd brought anything even related to her art: "All her incomplete work, sketch pads, every single bit of everything she'd ever done, and he just dumped it," John recalled later.

For John and the other co-owners, this seemed like a suspicious and telling move. "Two weeks and we all thought he'd done it," he recalled in 2014. "There were just stacks and stacks of things in portfolios . . . hundreds and hundreds of pieces of art."

John felt nervous and uncomfortable at the prospect of dealing with so many pieces, not wanting to turn away

Carol's creations and works in progress, but not really knowing what to do with them, either. It was her life's work, essentially. And the gallery was now faced with the task of inventorying the cache for sale.

"This was a really weird thing, but I didn't want to refuse a home for her art, because you wouldn't have wanted him, if we refused it, to go take it to the dump," John said. "She had shown her art with us for years, and she had been a personal friend for years, and so we wanted to curate her art in the proper way and in a way to benefit her daughters."

Part of John's discomfort stemmed from Steve's demeanor, which was so businesslike and matter-of-fact about the whole transaction, a marked contrast to the spirit and power of Carol's work.

"You felt like he was expunging her or extricating her or washing his hands of everything that was personally her," John recalled. "He didn't show any emotional attachment to the work at all. And the work itself was very emotional . . . any feeling she had, feelings, bright spots in dark areas. It was about her passions, her fears . . . where the joys came from. Love."

They ultimately drafted an agreement stating that all proceeds would go to Katie as the estate's executor, and she would share them with Charlotte. Steve didn't seem interested in the money for himself.

At that point Joanne Frerking, Carol's friend and another gallery co-owner, began the daunting task of inventorying and pricing the pieces. She put them into several categories—signed, salable, and neither, as well as those the girls might want. Then she invited Katie and Charlotte to take the ones they wanted, which weren't many.

"I never had any idea there was so much," Joanne said. "She was so prolific."

CHAPTER 14

When Detective Brown interviewed Katie again on August 7, this time her lawyer, Chris Kottke, was present. They discussed the upcoming garage sale Jake had mentioned, and the one or more golf clubs that Carol may have had at the house.

"I believe my dad had said that he had given her either her golf clubs or one of his because he didn't need them anymore," she said. "I thought that he had given her one, but I personally didn't know that."

"You never saw it or anything?"

"No."

Brown explained that they could not find any such club at the house. They were trying to figure out what had become of it and what brand it was. But Katie didn't know.

Katie expressed concerns about Jim Knapp being such an odd duck, that he'd been allowed back into the house before the detectives had finished collecting evidence, and that he was spreading strange stories about her mom and dad that she'd never even heard before.

"It made me sad, because at one point, I really did feel he was a nice, normal guy that was just my mom's friend out at the property," she said. "The word around town had always been that he had a crush on my mom. That's totally fine if people are, you know, normal about it."

But, she went on, Jim had been leaving bizarre messages on her phone, "where he sounds, like, drunk. . . . He sent one e-mail that was, like, 'You know I'm sure your dad is screening your e-mails, that's why I can't get through,' and I'm, like, 'My dad's not screening my e-mails.' And we heard that he was talking to the neighbors and making the neighbors say things, like, 'Everyone knows that Steve beat Carol when she was pregnant.' We didn't even live [at] that house when my mom was pregnant."

In a small town gossip travels fast, so it was sometimes difficult to discern the source and veracity of these stories. They carried more weight when they came directly from Carol's own mouth.

As Detective Brown interviewed Carol's friends in the weeks after the murder, he heard several accounts that she'd been scared of Steve and feared for her personal safety.

Don Wood, who had known both Carol and Steve, reported that she'd called and e-mailed him that "she was in fear for her life," although she never described a specific incident where Steve did her any physical harm. Don added that he and Carol didn't have the kind of relationship where she would confide that sort of thing to him, although she did request that if anything happened to her, Don should look into it. He told Brown that "Steven had hacked into Carol's e-mails and read some of the correspondence." When Brown confronted Steve about this claim, Steve said Carol had "duped" Don into believing that she needed to fear her estranged husband.

Andrea Flanagan, a former student who had done some house- and pet-sitting for Carol, and had taken care of the girls over the years, told Brown that Carol had complained recently that Steve had broken into her house one night.

She freaked out on him and told him that it was totally inappropriate since he had been out of the house for such a long time, Brown wrote. *Steven had apparently bought Carol some Thai food when he came over. He just broke in and actually startled her. Carol said that she was very angered by it and it had really scared her. . . . Flanagan could not recall how specifically he broke in, but thought it had been through a window.*

Several weeks after Andrea's first interview with Brown, she followed up with another recollection that echoed Don Wood's, about Carol's claim that Steve had hacked into her e-mail account and read her messages.

Carol had been very upset that he was doing this, Brown wrote. *Shortly after this was happening, Carol's computer crashed.* Andrea said Carol thought Steve was getting through the windows she'd left open and the doors she'd left unlocked.

Such stories only bolstered investigators' suspicions that Steve was their killer.

In turn, Steve's fears of arrest grew as investigators seemed to be focusing on him as their primary suspect. Not surprisingly, this created a "very, very tense environment" at the condo, as Charlotte later testified.

Charlotte was not only deeply grieving her mother's murder, but she also felt a constant trepidation about the ongoing investigation into her father. "It felt awful," she said, noting that their home environment "was sad and stressed and anxious, pretty much constantly."

After detectives seized Steve's cell phone on July 3, he gave Charlotte his credit card to buy some "pay-as-you-go" phones at Walmart—the kind where users can pay for calls by the month or a certain number of minutes rather than entering a long-term contract. The GoPhones also can't be traced or monitored by law enforcement.

Spurred by his fears, Steve developed a plan to flee to a destination far, far away. But because the detectives had also seized his passport, he had to apply for a new one. He wasted no time, submitting the request on July 11.

Investigators later learned that he had lied on the application. In the space asking for details of the loss or theft of his previous passport, Steve wrote: *Don't know for certain. It is simply missing from my file at home and we cannot find it.* The U.S. State Department issued him a new passport on July 16.

On July 25, which would have been Carol's fifty-fourth birthday, Steve asked Charlotte to buy him a handheld GPS global device from REI while she and Jake were in Phoenix to pick up her cousin at the airport. The cousin was flying in for Carol's private memorial service, but ended up missing Charlotte and taking a shuttle to Prescott because of a miscommunication.

As Charlotte and Jake were returning home from Phoenix that night at eight-fifteen, they got into the rollover accident she mentioned at the service the next day. They were driving in Carol's Acura MDX on northbound Interstate 17 when they suddenly came up on a bucket that had fallen into the road. A truck, hauling something and traveling behind another car, swerved into their lane to avoid the bucket and almost sideswiped the Acura. Charlotte swerved into the dirt median to avoid the car, causing the Acura to skid and spin around, cross two lanes, crash into the opposite shoulder and roll over. The car was totaled. Jake ended up with a torn ligament in his shoulder; Charlotte suffered a minor concussion and some scrapes. Steve later managed to collect $22,000 from Carol's insurance company for the totaled Acura, even though it was deemed her property during the divorce and was part of her estate.

As part of his escape plan, Steve also bought a motorcycle on August 2, and loaded several locked metal suitcases, designed to fit the bike, with all kinds of provisions. Those locked cases, which he stored at Katie's apartment in Scottsdale, contained a DVD of Mexico street maps, $15,000 in cash, and a large waterproof "dry bag," containing beef jerky, energy bars, a loaded handgun and two loaded magazines. He gave one of the GoPhones to Katie, who was working full-time on the Obama campaign for college credit at the time.

"To be quite honest, I think I put that phone in a sock drawer and tried not to think about it," Katie testified later.

Meanwhile, Charlotte and Jake discussed her ongoing concerns that Steve was going to leave town and disappear. Steve had even given her a code word—"raspberry"—to warn him that the police had come to the condo, looking for him.

Charlotte also expressed her fears in her journal. In one entry, dated August 16, she wrote, *My dad's considering running. If he gets caught I'll never get to hug him again.* She wrote that she didn't want to live with Katie in Los Angeles and finish her high-school education there, because she couldn't leave Jake.

As investigators searched through Steve's computers and Internet browser history, they found some suspicious and incriminating activities.

On February 7, 2008, Steve had installed a computer program known as the Anonymizer, which, when engaged, hides Internet searches so they can't be traced, and masks a user's IP address by sending it through an encrypted secure tunnel between the user's computer and a proxy server. The program can also make the user anonymous. Anyone trying to track the user by his IP address will be directed back to the proxy.

Other functions allow the user to try to remove any traces of his computer activities from the operating system by deleting temporary files, tracking of websites he has visited, along with cookies, cached files and browser history.

Steve reinstalled the program on March 30. Independently, Steve also had his computer's browser history set at zero days, meaning that it wasn't supposed to keep any record of his browsing activity.

Steve may not have known, however, that the program doesn't permanently delete these files, it only clears a space that can be overwritten if needed. Or that the program doesn't stop the user's computer from keeping an Internet search history. Or that when the program "deletes" the history, it isn't a "secure" deletion, because that information isn't removed from the hard drive.

So, despite all of Steve's security measures, Paul Lindvay, a detective with the Arizona Department of Public Safety's Computer Forensic Unit, was still able to find a partial record of Steve's Internet browsing history.

Assisted by Detective Brown, Lindvay ran a series of keywords through a copy of Steve's hard drive—*suicide, homicide, insurance, hitman, invisible, fugitive, disappear* and *books.Google.com*—where he found a number of Steve's Google searches, contained in his daily browsing logs.

In between playing around on Facebook on June 1,

three days after the divorce was finalized, five of Steve's searches and the websites he visited caught investigators' attention.

Around noon that day, he searched for *payment of life insurance benefits in the case of homicide,* then did a handful of similar searches between seven and seven-thirty that night: *tips from a hitman on how to kill someone, how to stage a suicide, how to kill and make it look like suicide* and *how to make a homicide appear suicide*.

Lindvay also found a folder on Steve's computer titled, "Book Research," which was created on December 23, 2007, at 6:28 P.M., and contained eighteen files. The last time a file in that folder was written or changed before the murder was May 10, 2008. Only one file was changed in the days after the murder, on July 5. Many of them were accessed on June 1, 2008, the same date as the Google searches, but no changes were made, which could simply indicate the computer did a virus search.

In that folder was a diagram that showed a homicide in a back room with some furniture tipped over, which, as prosecutors would later point out, was "strikingly similar to the office that Carol Kennedy was found in."

Later, at trial, an Anonymizer executive testified that Steve's account—using the username "jamiebob44" and linked to his Gmail account—was accessed on June 30, July 1 and July 2, 2008, and was not used again until August 17.

Lindvay testified that one of the links took Steve to a page for a book titled *Practical Homicide Investigation,* from which he viewed a page depicting a staged crime scene, then made it a cached file.

Steve's computer also showed searches for motorcycle gear and equipment on June 1, and that he accessed a site called Writing-World.com, at 7:21 P.M., right after searching for the hit man tips and staging a suicide, and right before his search for making a homicide appear like a suicide.

Although the defense later described Writing-World.com as a site for mystery-novel writers, the site would be more accurately described as one for amateur writers and authors of any genre who are interested in getting started. The site features various links for career tips aimed at aspiring freelance writers, ads for hiring editors and consultants, as well as articles on grammar and how to write and self-publish books.

The defense also noted that Steve also had a book on his shelf that was titled, *No Plot? No Problem. A Low-Stress, High-Velocity Guide to Writing a Novel in 30 Days.*

When Lindvay acknowledged that some of Steve's computer searches went to adult websites with pornographic material, the defense tried to suggest that Steve had his browser-history setting on zero because he was viewing porn while his sixteen-year-old daughter was also living in the house.

But the bottom line was that investigators never found any actual writings by Steve—no short stories, no chapters or any partial drafts of any mystery novel.

A series of Steve's computer searches and actions concerning carbon monoxide gas and suicide raised another red flag, especially when compounded with the other incriminating searches, which prosecutors later deemed "probative of premeditation."

In March 2008, he searched for *use of carbon monoxide in suicide* and a business plant safety plan. Carbon monoxide is known as "the silent killer," because people have been found dead in their homes from undetected leaks in gas ranges and heating systems that have emitted this odorless, colorless and poisonous gas.

Steve's phone records also showed that on March 3 and 14 he called the chemical company Matheson Tri-Gas, which sells gas in bulk and delivers liquid gas to customers by truck. That same month he obtained a federal employer identification number (EIN), a prerequisite to purchase carbon monoxide.

In his "Book Research" folder, Steve stored paperwork related to these searches, including Web pages and his EIN confirmation. He also kept spec sheets from another gas distributor called Praxair, listing its Phoenix area locations, its various cylinder sizes and information for a gas safety plan. Additionally, he kept spec sheets and forms for carbon monoxide and dichlorobenzene, halocarbon 14 and C318, different gas cylinder sizes and portable compressed gas canisters.

On May 7, he filed a partially completed Matheson delivery form in the folder, listing himself as the customer, Dr. Steven C. DeMocker, doing business as DBD Research & Consulting at his Alpine Meadows address. If this was not part of an aborted scheme to murder Carol, it is unclear what other use this carbon monoxide research may have had to Steve. He did not pursue this series of tasks any further after he was told that he had to submit a detailed gas storage plan for inspection before the gas could be delivered to his home.

Meanwhile, Steve continued to engage in other behavior that caught the authorities' attention, namely that he had received a delivery of four books with titles of a concerning nature at his UBS office that summer.

Under industry standards, financial advisors like Steve

aren't supposed to open their own mail. In this case a coworker did it for him, and knowing that his ex-wife had just died, the coworker found the titles odd, if not suspicious.

Following up on the purchase, investigators found that the books had been bought from a secured wireless connection titled "Cheryl123," an address assigned to a woman between July 10 and August 20, the day of the purchase. This woman, who lived in Phoenix, and part-time in a home on Country Club Drive in Prescott, was a friend of Renee Girard, Steve's girlfriend.

It turned out that Steve, with Renee's help, had rented this house from her friend Cheryl Hatzopoulos as a place for his family to stay when they came to visit or as a "stay-cation" home.

The titles were: *How to Be Invisible: The Essential Guide to Protecting Your Personal Privacy, Your Assets, and Your Life; Cover Your Tracks Without Changing Your Identity: How to Disappear Until You WANT to be Found; The International Fugitive: Secrets of Clandestine Travel Overseas* and *Advanced Fugitive: Running, Hiding, Surviving and Thriving Forever.*

Concerning indeed.

On August 20, the same day that these books were purchased, Steve also submitted his first death benefits claim to Hartford Insurance Company, trying to collect on Carol's two life insurance policies for which he'd been paying for years. He provided a blank check to Hartford so the money—a total payout of $770,492 for the combined policies—could be transferred to his personal account at Bank of America.

But every time he tried, Hartford denied his claims, citing the fact that he was a murder suspect in his ex-wife's death. Hartford denied five such claims—on August 27, October 1, November 21 and December 16, 2008, and January 15, 2009.

In the first denial letter on August 27, from claims analyst Debbie Dettman, she told him that Hartford couldn't release the proceeds until he was cleared of involvement in Carol's death.

Steve e-mailed a response on September 3, copying his attorney, John Sears, asking how to disclaim the death benefits and to allow his daughters to collect on them, referring the matter to Sears and his daughters' attorney.

I am trying to determine if there is a way to disclaim the proceeds to our daughters, or failing that, to determine the most tax-efficient way of gifting the money to them for their sole benefit, he wrote.

As investigators continued to build their case against Steve, they put together a timeline of his activities on the day of the murder based on forensic evidence they had collected, including his e-mails, text messages, phone records and the times his remote control was used to open the gate to his condo complex:

Steve started his day at 6:32 A.M. by texting Renee, whom he usually met for coffee in the morning.

At 6:47 a.m., he logged on to his UBS computer. A satellite office of the Phoenix location, the Prescott site had only a few employees, including Steve, John Farmer and a secretary.

At 7:11 A.M., Steve called Renee, then called Carol at home at 7:41 A.M., and got her voice mail.

At 7:59 A.M., Steve sent his first text to Carol about picking up Katie's car.

Steve and Renee texted about meeting for coffee until 9:27 A.M., when someone, most likely Steve, used his gate code to enter his complex.

Around 10 A.M., Steve picked up Renee and took her to Wild Iris, a café they frequented together. As usual, he picked her up in his BMW, only this time, his bike was in the backseat, with the front wheel taken off to fit.

Steve volunteered that he was planning to go for a ride after work. But in all the time they'd been together, she'd never seen him put the bike in the car, nor had he ever mentioned going for a bike ride. Given that he lived so close to his office, and headed home to change into workout clothes after work anyway, why didn't he wait to put his bike into the car after work? Because, investigators figured, Steve was setting his alibi in motion.

After Steve dropped off Renee at ten forty-five that morning, the detectives couldn't determine what he did for the next few hours. However, forensics showed that he began texting Carol again at 1:42 P.M. about Katie's car and exchanging checks.

Steve received a text from Charlotte at three twenty-eight that afternoon—the last time he used the cell phone before turning it off—saying she was on her way to bring him some cookies.

At 3:34 P.M., Steve sent an e-mail to Jennifer Rydzewski, who was filling in for his assistant in the Phoenix office, asking if she would mind closing his and Carol's joint bank account: *And then setting it on fire and burying it? Thanks!*

Jennifer didn't read the message until she came into work the next morning, at which time she was informed of Carol's death. She printed out the e-mail and immediately turned it over to her manager. The account had a zero balance.

In early September, detectives sprayed the Bluestar blood-revealing agent on Steve's clothing, his bicycle, its tires and rims, along with various other accessories they'd seized. They also obtained a search warrant allowing them to get back into his BMW and spray it as well. But after doing so, they found no traces of blood anywhere in the car. (The reddish brown substance in Katie's car turned out to be chocolate.)

Brown checked to see if they could determine through the BMW's navigational device in Steve's car where he'd been that night, but was told that the system didn't store GPS points.

Although they were gearing up to arrest Steve, investigators still had not found the murder weapon or any DNA linking him to the crime scene. They knew that Steve was a wily, smart and cunning man, so they kept investigating him and his background, hoping for that "aha" moment.

nities . . . and agriculture, outdoor leadership,
preparation that includes multicultural education,
istic and critical response to the issues of our

verall educational philosophy is designed to pro-
xperiential learning in natural and human commu-
Burkhardt said.

ple come here because they believe in the power of
d of education," he said. The students "want to try
a difference making a living" and "change the
a positive way."

ng Steve's freshman year there, he met a sopho-
med Sturgis Robinson, who had grown up in an
suburb of Springfield, Massachusetts. Although
oung men had come from similar socioeconomic
unds, the long-haired Sturgis took an immediate
Steve, a tall, good-looking athlete who walked
eir granola campus with a country-club attitude.
e of Steve, who appeared wealthy with his coiffed
, white tennis outfit and tennis racquet, not only
from the hippie crowd, but it also offended young
iberal sensibilities.
soon realized, however, that if he wanted to
iends with an attractive fellow student named
udonym), he had to make nice with Steve. This
came after he stopped by Josie's house, peered
e glass pane in the front door and saw Steve's
om bouncing in the living room. Shocked that
educed his good friend, Sturgis was not happy.
he asked Josie about the coupling, she told him
own business.

CHAPTER 15

Born in Rochester, New York, on January 7, 1954, Steven Carroll DeMocker was the first of Dr. John and Janice DeMocker's nine children, the oldest of an educated and accomplished bunch, scattered all over the nation.

Michael, Steve's youngest sibling, works as a photographer at the *Times-Picayune* in New Orleans, where he was on the Pulitzer-winning team that covered Hurricane Katrina, and was a Pulitzer finalist in 2009. Mary is a harpist and harp teacher in Corvallis, Oregon. Sharon, a physician who specializes in integrated medicine and studied under the renowned Dr. Andrew Weil, lives in Hendersonville, North Carolina. Susan, who helped out the defense team early on as a legal assistant, lives in New York. Jim, an accountant who assisted with financial matters during the case, lives in Virginia. Information on the other siblings was not available.

Growing up in the Rochester suburbs in upstate New York, the DeMocker children had quite the hardworking role models. Steve's father earned his medical degree from the University of Rochester in the 1950s, the same graduate school that Steve and Carol attended years later.

John DeMocker interned in general surgery at the University of Illinois Research Hospital, returning to Rochester in the early 1960s for a radiology residency at Strong Memorial Hospital. In 1964, he started his own practice in Rochester, home to major corporations such as Xerox, Bausch & Lomb and Kodak, then began working as a consultant in 1971.

After Dr. DeMocker closed his radiology office in 1998, his wife hoped they could do some traveling, yet he continued to work thirty to sixty hours a week, "covering" other offices and consulting for years to come. When he finally decided to retire, he had to start up again to help pay for Steve's legal bills. Jan testified at trial that he never really stopped working.

Raising nine children wasn't enough for Steve's mother, either. She earned a master's in nursing in the early 1960s, taught obstetrical nursing for several years, then went back to graduate school in 1984 to earn a doctorate in education with a focus on counseling. In 1990, she obtained a master's in divinity and became a minister, presiding as pastor of the Hemlock United Methodist Church. She also worked part-time as a chaplain in a nursing home until she retired.

Steve attended the Harley School, a private boarding school in Rochester, as a day student. After graduating in 1972, Steve persuaded a girlfriend and some other friends to join him at Prescott College, a small alternative liberal arts school in Arizona, on the other side of the country. Majoring in wilderness leadership, he started classes there in 1973.

* * *

Prescott College opened in 19[...] Dr. Charles Franklin Parker, as its [...] a minister at the local First Congre[...] lofty aspirations to make it the "Ha[...] vision was to launch "a pioneering [...] ment in higher education," aimed at [...] could "solve the world's growing en[...] problems," according to the college [...]

But during Steve's time there, the [...] and abruptly closed in 1974. Witho[...] stubborn faculty and students regre[...] institution from an area a few miles [...] now houses the Embry-Riddle Aer[...] and into the run-down Hassayampa [...] classes.

Calling themselves the Prescott [...] Education (PCAE), the faculty an[...] Steve, apparently—stubbornly con[...] out a campus. When Steve said he "[...] elor's degree in outdoor education i[...] this very alternative college.

"It's the college that refused [...] hardt, who was provost and vic[...] affairs there in 2014.

Ultimately, a private nonprofi[...] to run the institution, which incl[...] of faculty, staff, students and due[...] the college never had to shut do[...]

Today, the college offers m[...] similar to those of the late 198[...] a sociology professor, and late[...] istration. As the college web[...] has evolved into subjects t[...] *awareness, social justice an[...]*

commu[...] *teacher[...]* *and ar[...]* *world.[...]*

The [...] vide "e[...] nities,"[...]

"Pec[...] this kin[...] to mak[...] world i[...]

Dur[...] more n[...] affluen[...] the two [...] backgro[...] dislike t[...] across tl[...] The imag[...] short hai[...] stood ou[...] Sturgis's [...]

Sturgi[...] remain f[...] Josie (pse[...] realizatio[...] through tl[...] naked bot[...] Steve had [...] And when [...] to mind hi[...]

CHAPTER 15

Born in Rochester, New York, on January 7, 1954, Steven Carroll DeMocker was the first of Dr. John and Janice DeMocker's nine children, the oldest of an educated and accomplished bunch, scattered all over the nation.

Michael, Steve's youngest sibling, works as a photographer at the *Times-Picayune* in New Orleans, where he was on the Pulitzer-winning team that covered Hurricane Katrina, and was a Pulitzer finalist in 2009. Mary is a harpist and harp teacher in Corvallis, Oregon. Sharon, a physician who specializes in integrated medicine and studied under the renowned Dr. Andrew Weil, lives in Hendersonville, North Carolina. Susan, who helped out the defense team early on as a legal assistant, lives in New York. Jim, an accountant who assisted with financial matters during the case, lives in Virginia. Information on the other siblings was not available.

Growing up in the Rochester suburbs in upstate New York, the DeMocker children had quite the hardworking role models. Steve's father earned his medical degree from the University of Rochester in the 1950s, the same graduate school that Steve and Carol attended years later.

John DeMocker interned in general surgery at the University of Illinois Research Hospital, returning to Rochester in the early 1960s for a radiology residency at Strong Memorial Hospital. In 1964, he started his own practice in Rochester, home to major corporations such as Xerox, Bausch & Lomb and Kodak, then began working as a consultant in 1971.

After Dr. DeMocker closed his radiology office in 1998, his wife hoped they could do some traveling, yet he continued to work thirty to sixty hours a week, "covering" other offices and consulting for years to come. When he finally decided to retire, he had to start up again to help pay for Steve's legal bills. Jan testified at trial that he never really stopped working.

Raising nine children wasn't enough for Steve's mother, either. She earned a master's in nursing in the early 1960s, taught obstetrical nursing for several years, then went back to graduate school in 1984 to earn a doctorate in education with a focus on counseling. In 1990, she obtained a master's in divinity and became a minister, presiding as pastor of the Hemlock United Methodist Church. She also worked part-time as a chaplain in a nursing home until she retired.

Steve attended the Harley School, a private boarding school in Rochester, as a day student. After graduating in 1972, Steve persuaded a girlfriend and some other friends to join him at Prescott College, a small alternative liberal arts school in Arizona, on the other side of the country. Majoring in wilderness leadership, he started classes there in 1973.

* * *

Prescott College opened in 1966, with its founder, Dr. Charles Franklin Parker, as its first president. Parker, a minister at the local First Congregational Church, had lofty aspirations to make it the "Harvard of the West." His vision was to launch "a pioneering, even radical experiment in higher education," aimed at producing leaders who could "solve the world's growing environmental and social problems," according to the college website.

But during Steve's time there, the college went bankrupt and abruptly closed in 1974. Without funding, a group of stubborn faculty and students regrouped and moved the institution from an area a few miles north of town, which now houses the Embry-Riddle Aeronautical University, and into the run-down Hassayampa Hotel, where they held classes.

Calling themselves the Prescott Center for Alternative Education (PCAE), the faculty and students—including Steve, apparently—stubbornly continued to operate without a campus. When Steve said he "graduated" with a bachelor's degree in outdoor education in May 1977, it was from this very alternative college.

"It's the college that refused to die," said Paul Burkhardt, who was provost and vice president of academic affairs there in 2014.

Ultimately, a private nonprofit corporation was formed to run the institution, which includes a voting membership of faculty, staff, students and dues-paying alumni, to ensure the college never had to shut down again.

Today, the college offers many areas of study that are similar to those of the late 1980s, when Steve returned as a sociology professor, and later when he joined the administration. As the college website states, the curriculum has evolved into subjects that include: *environmental awareness, social justice and peace studies, sustainable*

*communities . . . and agriculture, outdoor leadership,
teacher preparation that includes multicultural education,
and artistic and critical response to the issues of our
world.*

The overall educational philosophy is designed to provide "experiential learning in natural and human communities," Burkhardt said.

"People come here because they believe in the power of
this kind of education," he said. The students "want to try
to make a difference making a living" and "change the
world in a positive way."

During Steve's freshman year there, he met a sophomore named Sturgis Robinson, who had grown up in an
affluent suburb of Springfield, Massachusetts. Although
the two young men had come from similar socioeconomic
backgrounds, the long-haired Sturgis took an immediate
dislike to Steve, a tall, good-looking athlete who walked
across their granola campus with a country-club attitude.
The image of Steve, who appeared wealthy with his coiffed
short hair, white tennis outfit and tennis racquet, not only
stood out from the hippie crowd, but it also offended young
Sturgis's liberal sensibilities.

Sturgis soon realized, however, that if he wanted to
remain friends with an attractive fellow student named
Josie (pseudonym), he had to make nice with Steve. This
realization came after he stopped by Josie's house, peered
through the glass pane in the front door and saw Steve's
naked bottom bouncing in the living room. Shocked that
Steve had seduced his good friend, Sturgis was not happy.
And when he asked Josie about the coupling, she told him
to mind his own business.

Steve and Josie dated for several years, but in the context of that "free love" era, that didn't mean they were seeing each other exclusively. "[Josie] was probably more exclusive than Steve," Sturgis said. "Steve has never, ever been exclusive, even for a minute."

"We were young. It was the period where the fact that women could take the pill met the social revolutions of the late sixties and early seventies, so there was a lot of sex going on, and it was a big part of our college lives," Sturgis recalled.

Once Sturgis got to know Steve, he found he rather liked the charismatic young man, after all. The two became fast friends, forming a relationship that would last the next twenty-five years. In addition to enjoying extreme white-water rafting and other outdoor activities, they had one particular interest in common.

"One of the things Steve and I really shared was an appreciation for women—being with women and chasing women," Sturgis said.

Years later, Sturgis went on to become the college's interim president, from January 1999 through December 2000. One of his first acts was to reacquire the legal rights to the original college's name from the successor PCAE institution, which had by then moved the campus to its contemporary location at 220 Grove Street.

During college Steve spent a summer in Lincoln, Vermont, where one of his girlfriends' families lived. Putting his outdoor training to use, he offered to help the girl's younger brother, Alec, work on his beginner's mountain-climbing skills.

Steve's mother, Jan DeMocker, later told the story of

what happened on their outing: Steve and Alec had just parked near a cliff about five miles from Alec's house, and were heading down the path leading to a rock wall they planned to climb, when they heard the scream of an ambulance siren approaching.

The bus pulled up, two EMTs jumped out and came up behind them, carrying their medical supplies and equipment. Steve offered his assistance, recognizing that the female EMT was overweight, the man was middle-aged, both were wearing street shoes and neither had any climbing equipment.

On the rock face about four hundred feet above them, they could see the young stranded woman, who had called out for help. She'd badly injured her ankle in a fall from above and was fearfully perched on a narrow ledge, clutching onto a few saplings nearby.

Quickly assessing the woman's dangerous situation, Steve sent Alec home for some more rope and equipment, then he climbed up to the ledge to make sure the woman didn't fall in the meantime. After Alec returned, the muscular young man climbed up to join Steve and the woman. Using the additional gear to fashion a harness, Steve and Alec belayed the woman safely down the cliff to the base, where she was taken to the hospital by ambulance for treatment.

"Would she have survived had Steve not been there?" Jan asked rhetorically years later. "Hopefully, someone with the needed skills would have been found in time, but with her precarious anchor to the side of the cliff, a long wait could have led to a much less desirable outcome."

After college Steve and Josie moved back east together to work at a ski resort in Stowe, Vermont, where Steve worked as a ski patrolman and Josie as a photographer for the resort. Sturgis, Josie, and Steve also worked as Outward Bound instructors. Carol was a rock climber as well, but the risky sport was not as big for her as it was for Steve.

CHAPTER 16

Virginia Carol Kennedy was born on July 25, 1954, the daughter of a secretary and a postal worker. Raised in Nashville, Tennessee, where her family still lives today, Carol and her brother, John, who is two years older, were very close as kids.

After leaving the army as a staff sergeant, Carol's father, Alvin "A.G." Kennedy Jr., continued to serve in the reserves for twenty more years while working for the U.S. Postal Service, where he started as a mail carrier and retired as an auditor.

While Carol was growing up, she and A.G. doted on each other. "I think she loved me, but I think she loved her dad more," said Ruth Kennedy, Carol's eighty-nine-year-old mother, in 2014. "I truly do. Because I was probably the disciplinarian."

Ruth worked the first half of her career for the Tennessee Department of Education, the state Department of Insurance and Banking and its Legislative Council Committee. She later moved to the private sector to work for the American Association for State and Local History.

An avid fan of classical symphonic music and a pianist

since she was nine years old, Ruth made sure to have music playing in the house from the time the children were born.

A headstrong little girl, Carol knew what she wanted. Not liking her given name, Virginia, she began going by her middle name at the start of elementary school.

The Kennedy family spent a lot of time together, taking extended vacations on Florida's gulf coast. They also regularly attended the Church of Christ together. Spiritual from an early age, Carol was eager to be baptized at nine, sooner than Ruth would have liked.

"I thought she was too young, but I wouldn't have stopped her," she recalled, noting that Carol had a wonderful Sunday school teacher. "She was a great influence on Carol."

A high academic achiever, young Carol was ambitious, respected and well liked by her peers. She worked on the school paper, and in the eighth grade, she was elected to a board of teen representatives from all the high schools in Nashville. And with her lean build and contagious warm smile, Carol modeled for a couple of years in high school, working with a local agency and traveling for some jobs.

At fifteen she was selected as the city's representative in the Miss Ingenue contest, based on "beauty, personality, poise and presence." And in 1971, when a white crepe jumpsuit with a "laced-and-fringed crop top" sold for $44, Carol was featured in the November issue of the national *Ingenue* magazine.

"She was pretty popular in school with both her friends and her teachers," Ruth said.

Carol was also featured in a newspaper ad by the Cain-Sloan department store, billed as "the greatest store of the Central South," which invited the public to the Miss Ingenue Fashion Show in Green Hills, an upscale area of Nashville. The big ad featured an illustration of a tall, leggy model with her long hair pulled into a side ponytail, wearing a white scoop-neck sleeveless jumpsuit that laced up the front, was lined around the torso with fringe, and flowed down into flared bell-bottom pants. Inset was a black-and-white head shot of Carol, with her brown hair styled the same way as the illustration, her usual curly ringlets straightened for a more sleek and chic look.

Another photo shoot, for which Carol posed with the four top runner-ups in the competition, was full of horizontal stripes, grid patterns and generally loud fashion. Three of the losing contestants were blond. Carol, who went by "Caryl" as her modeling name, was the darkest brunette; her intelligence was clearly reflected in her facial expression.

Headed to Acapulco on a free trip to the Miss Ingenue finals, she turned sixteen and lost the contest to one of the other twenty contestants. But her family's bigger concern was that she got sidetracked on the trip home. Although she had a chaperone, she somehow missed her return connection in Dallas and ended up in New York City. "We were scared to death, but it didn't seem to faze her," Ruth said. "I think at that age you think you're invincible."

Her interest in modeling didn't last long before she'd moved on to other things. "It kind of lost its luster. She found out it wasn't all it was cracked up to be," Ruth said, noting that Carol didn't much like standing at attention under hot lights for long stretches at a time, which was less glamorous than she'd anticipated. "It got to be more of a chore than fun."

As a teenager Carol got an allowance, but she was frugal with her money, so she always seemed to have cash available for the things she really wanted, such as the cute

$13 green patterned Nehru jacket she saw while shopping with her mother one day.

When Ruth told her daughter, "It's not in my budget," Carol promptly pulled out her wallet and bought the jacket for herself.

Although she and her brother were not as close during high school, they still loved each other. One of Ruth's favorite photos features the two siblings posing together at John's graduation in 1970. But for many years after that, they drifted apart and didn't have much contact.

As John put it later, they became estranged for nearly twenty years because Carol didn't approve of his lifestyle. Between 1969 and 1975, he was a heroin addict, he later testified, a "rogue" and a "worthless type of SOB for a lot of years."

Shortly after graduating from McGavock High School in 1972, Carol went straight to Peabody College, which is now part of Vanderbilt University. In just three years she finished her education degree at what is now known as one of the nation's top schools in that field.

Living at home during college, she wasn't just in a hurry to get started on her working life, she was also in a rush to get married as well, perhaps as a way to get out of her parents' house.

Carol hadn't been in college long before she got engaged to a young man named Tom, who came from a good family and had dropped out of college to work in pharmaceutical sales. Tom was originally from upstate New York, and his family moved to the Nashville area when his father was transferred.

Ruth tried everything she could to dissuade her daughter from getting married so young. "You've just started at

Vanderbilt, and the whole world is opening up," Ruth told her. "Why would you want to get married?"

Ruth had nothing in particular against Tom. He and his family seemed very nice, and well-off, too.

"They were way above us in the social strata," Ruth recalled. "He treated her well. They got along fine."

After waitressing in high school, Carol found a bartending job at a high-end restaurant. She befriended the hostess, Debbie Wren Hill, who was a year younger than Carol. Coincidentally, Debbie was engaged to one of Tom's high-school friends, a rock-and-roll guitarist.

The four of them hung out together, and Carol and Tom attended their wedding in October 1975. Carol and Tom, who moved away and broke up shortly thereafter, were married for only eighteen months.

"It was an amicable separating, it wasn't anything bad between them," Ruth said. If there was a negative reason, she added, Carol "never told me because maybe I would have said, 'I told you so.'"

Carol spent a year at the Heartwood School in Washington, Massachusetts, where she learned carpentry, gardening and other homebuilding crafts, as well as how to use herbs.

She also taught school in Richmond, Virginia, before she moved back to Nashville in 1981, intending to teach special education at her alma mater, McGavock High.

During their time apart, Debbie's four-year marriage imploded as well. The two now-divorced women found each other again through a mutual friend while Debbie was looking for a roommate. Answering her phone one day, Debbie was happy to hear her friend's voice.

"You're not going to believe who this is," Carol said.

"I'm back in town, I have a dog named Rosie and we're looking for a place to live."

Debbie's roommate search ended at that moment, after which Carol and her beautiful Irish setter moved right in.

Within the year Carol, who had also become a certified yoga instructor, took a trip to New York and came back in a state of euphoria.

"I have just met the most amazing man," she said.

Carol and Mr. Amazing, Steve DeMocker, had quite a bit in common: "A love of the outdoors, an appreciation of the beauty and spirituality of mountain and river, a keen sense of the connectedness we have with one another," as Steve's mother, Jan, put it.

They were also both highly intelligent. Steve was a doctoral candidate at the University of Rochester's Warner School of Education. His focus was critical social theory, a rather complicated and esoteric interdisciplinary study of sociology and other social sciences, such as psychology, philosophy, history and anthropology, and how the key concepts of these areas affect us as a culture. According to Nick Crossley's book *Key Concepts in Critical Social Theory,* such concepts—which became quite relevant in the context of Steve's behavior in later years—include alienation, symbolic power/violence, power and knowledge, crisis, capital, body power and freedom.

After taking off with Steve to Mexico for a week, Carol came back even more in love. Debbie would always remember the moment when Carol shared her feelings as she folded her clothes and put them back into her dresser.

"Debbie, I know I have found my soul mate. I know it

in my stomach," she said. "There is just a knowingness and I feel it and I know it. He is my person that I'm supposed to go through my life with."

When Steve came to Nashville to visit, Debbie found herself crazy about him, too, partly because of the way he treated her dear friend. While she and Carol were at work, he stayed at the house making homemade coffee liqueur. When Carol came home, he acted "personable, friendly, engaged and loving toward her. Steve was everything every woman could want in a man," Debbie recalled. "He was gorgeous. He was smart. He was working on a Ph.D. He was in Outward Bound, incredibly physically fit. Anyone would have fallen for him."

It was only a matter of months of long-distance dating before Carol moved to New York to live with Steve and join him in graduate school at the University of Rochester.

Ruth, who didn't approve of Carol's unwed living situation, was relieved when her daughter soon announced that she was engaged. Because Ruth hadn't met her daughter's fiancé, she sent him a letter, saying, essentially, "Thank you for doing this right." Steve didn't write back.

Carol's parents flew to Rochester a couple of days before the wedding to meet Steve and his family and to have dinner with his parents, whom Ruth described as "lovely people." That said, Ruth and A.G. felt a little overwhelmed by the whole affair.

"The big family and the fact that the father was a doctor, and, of course, we were just working people," Ruth recalled. "A.G. and I were a bit intimidated, although A.G. never would have admitted it."

Now that Carol was older, Ruth felt much better about

this marriage than she had about Carol's first one. "At that time I had no misgivings about it," she recalled recently.

The couple was married on October 10, 1982, at Steve's parents' house in Webster, New York. They had a big potluck reception near the shore of Lake Ontario afterward.

This being her second wedding, Carol wore a dark skirt with a corduroy vest over a pink blouse with puffy sleeves and a pink rose boutonniere. Her hair was down, with the front strands pulled back. Steve wore dark dress pants and an earth-toned blazer. Carol also kept her maiden name.

"It was just perfect for them," said Debbie, who couldn't attend but later wished she had, because for some years afterward, Debbie mostly saw Carol when she came home to visit her parents in Nashville.

Most of Steve's rather large immediate family came to the ceremony, along with Carol's parents, aunt and grandmother. The service, conducted by a minister, was informal and low-key, but meaningful and intimate.

"They wrote their own vows, promising to support and nurture one another as they each sought the path that would allow them to create a meaningful life," Jan DeMocker recalled. "They wanted to live their lives in ways that would make a difference to others."

Sturgis Robinson came up from Washington, D.C., and met Steve's family for the first time. The DeMocker family, with Steve's numerous siblings, seemed "crushingly normal, with one exception," he recalled.

As Steve introduced his best friend to his parents, Jan and John DeMocker barely looked at Sturgis, who felt that they treated him like he was part of the staff.

"I really expected Steve's parents to be warm," he said,

explaining that his own parents were always gracious when meeting his friends. "I was really struck by how cold his parents were, particularly his mother."

He had a much more positive impression of Carol, whom he was eager to meet after hearing such glowing reports from Steve.

"He was completely in love with her," Sturgis said. Steve had described her as "really powerful and focused, and she was a carpenter, really strong and really spiritual. But then he always described the women he was with in terms like that."

Sturgis hit it off with Steve's new wife, sneaking off to the woods with her and a bottle of wine to chat during the reception.

"I was fascinated to meet Carol, and she was fascinated to meet me," he recalled.

As they were getting to know one another, Sturgis felt compelled to ask whether she was aware of Steve's serial womanizing, which he'd watched since before the start of their own friendship.

"Do you know what you're getting yourself in for?" he asked.

But Carol just laughed. "Oh, don't worry," she said. "I can take care of him."

She was right—for a time. Looking back later, Sturgis deemed Steve's courtship of Carol and their early years of their marriage as probably the purest of times for Steve.

While Steve worked on his doctorate in education, known as an Ed.D., from 1982 to 1986, Carol earned her master's in education in 1983, focusing on counseling and human development.

During that time the couple lived in a guesthouse on

Steve's parents' property and helped take care of Steve's younger siblings. Wanting to do something for her in-laws, Carol built a garden on the front circle of their house. In her mother-in-law's eyes, Carol became part of the extended DeMocker family, even going on vacation with them.

After Steve finished grad school, Sturgis helped him get his first job at Patagonia, the manufacturer of outdoor clothing and equipment, which is headquartered in Ventura, California.

Climber Yvon Chouinard, Patagonia's founder and CEO, wanted to put together a program for employees to participate in activities that required the use of the company's products. The CEO said, half jokingly, that they needed to hire a "director of fun" to run the program.

Sturgis, the company's public relations director, suggested that Steve apply for the job, which, with his outdoor experience, he landed in April 1985. His official title was personnel coordinator, a job he kept until July 1986.

"The company wanted their employees to know how the equipment they made was actually used in the field, so it was one of Steve's tasks to run outdoor programs for Patagonia personnel," Jan DeMocker said.

Meanwhile, Carol took a counseling position at a local hospital. She also volunteered at a shelter for battered women and at a crisis center hotline, working with survivors of sexual assault.

While Steve was at Patagonia, he took a group of employees on a kayaking trip in white-water rapids with a coleader who was a "world-class boater," Jan DeMocker said.

During a run down a pretty difficult stretch, Steve watched as a young woman was sucked into a class-four vortex of swirling water, losing her boat and paddle, as her body churned over and over in the current.

Feeling responsible for her, Steve immediately went into action to save her. Steering his kayak directly into the vortex, he flipped it upside down so he could spin around in sync with her. Reaching out for her, he grabbed her limp body and got her up and across the bow of his boat, which was still upside down. Then he righted his kayak, maneuvered her into it, steered them out of the whirlpool and headed down the river to a safer area, where the rest of the group was anxiously waiting.

"Steve saw her eyes flick open at last—another instance when Steve's presence made a significant difference in the life of another," Jan recalled.

Instead of living in Ventura, near the coast, Carol and Steve rented a house in the hills, about thirty minutes east, in the bucolic but sophisticated town of Ojai, where the air is filled with the scent of lavender, sage and orange blossoms and a legendary "pink moment" as the sun sets.

Similar to Prescott, Ojai is surrounded by mountain ranges, ranch land and hiking trails. And being so close to Hollywood, it also has become a haven for New Age and spiritual people, artists and actors, such as Mary Steenburgen, her husband Ted Danson, Reese Witherspoon and Robert Pattinson.

Debbie Wren Hill visited the couple in this peaceful burb, where Steve and Carol's home was surrounded with pecan and fragrant orange trees. She and Carol relaxed in the backyard and took in the scenery as they listened to Steely Dan and ate homemade orange-pecan muffins.

After Carol came home from work, she and Debbie jogged up to an area that had been ravaged by fire, where they could still see embers burning. As they breathed in the even stronger scent of flowering orange groves there, Carol explained that these trees had kept the fire from spreading any farther, perhaps because they were so green or wet with irrigation.

"That was still a happy time for them," Debbie said. "They were largely a happy couple. They had a really good connection. They were just really devoted to each other. I was envious. I felt she had really lucked out."

Eight months after Steve arrived at Patagonia, Sturgis Robinson left to enter the foreign service. Steve told him later that he'd had an affair with at least one Patagonia coworker. And that, Sturgis said, not only went against the company's internal culture, but also the personal philosophy of the owner's powerful wife, who had helped found and run the company.

"That was not considered cool at Patagonia to cheat on your wife with other Patagonia employees," Sturgis said.

It was unclear to him whether Carol knew about this particular affair. "I think she was in denial," Sturgis said in 2014. "I think it was very likely that she did not know about some of [his affairs]."

Sturgis said that this affair likely contributed to Steve's parting ways with the company. It also may explain why he didn't include the position on his LinkedIn page, which was still up in 2014.

After leaving California in the summer of 1986, Steve and Carol moved to the tiny town of Lincoln, Vermont, where Steve had stayed that one summer during college.

During the 1980s, Lincoln had a population of about 870 people.

With her credentials Carol landed a job as a teacher and counselor at the Ticonderoga branch of the North Country Community College in New York in the fall of 1986. She had to commute to work, often through the snow, more than an hour each way.

Carol told the *Post-Star* in Glens Falls, New York, which wrote about her hiring, that she and Steve were lured back to the East Coast by the beauty of the Adirondacks.

Whatever the reason, the couple had already bought ten acres in Lincoln in November 1984, and with the help of a loan from Carol's parents, they started building a house. Carol told the newspaper that Steve planned to look for a job as an educator as soon as he was done building the wooden home, which was a two-story A-frame, with an upper-level balcony looking down on the living room below.

"It was a really neat house," Ruth recalled.

In addition to counseling Ticonderoga students on how to handle the fear of failure, Carol taught three psychology courses: human development, group dynamics and a general survey course. She told the *Post-Star* that community colleges were geared toward making higher education accessible to working adults with families, who had not been able to attend or finish college earlier.

Using the analogy of athletes who use their muscles to attain goals, Carol said, "The mind, too, must be exercised. Sometimes we have to push ourselves past what is comfortable to reach the prize we seek."

The news article, which underscored Carol's past experience and interest in preventing domestic violence, stated that Carol wanted to organize a women's backcountry wilderness trip to help them build self-confidence.

Carol and Steve had already been organizing such weekend outings of rock climbing and cross-country skiing for the damaged women she'd been working with in Ventura. Jan DeMocker said this was Carol's special strength, to "teach survival skills with the deeper lessons of nature and spirit."

When a person faces a new, perhaps scary situation, and is given the skills to succeed, it's empowering, and this is what she and Steve offered to women who had, too often, been powerless, Jan wrote in 2014.

Carol also told the newspaper that she'd set her sights on a goal of her own: to write a book about domestic violence.

From July 1987 until Katie was born in May 1988, Carol worked as a psychological counselor at Middlebury College, a small private liberal arts college in Middlebury, Vermont, which is home to the Bread Loaf Writers' Conference, the nation's oldest literary writing conference. But the draw for Carol was that the college was only half an hour from Lincoln, which cut her commute in half.

Carol gave birth to Katie at their home in Lincoln on May 19, using a midwife. And when Katie was only a few months old, Carol and Steve picked up and moved across the country to Prescott, repaying the loan from Carol's parents when they sold the house in 1988.

The next thing Sturgis Robinson knew, his buddy Steve had landed back at their alma mater, Prescott College, teaching classes as a sociology professor.

CHAPTER 17

When Katie was still a baby, Debbie Wren Hill visited them in Prescott and snapped some family photos: Steve holding little Katie up in the air; Carol breast-feeding and giving the baby mini massages.

In between visits, Debbie and Carol talked on the phone and wrote each other long letters to stay in touch. Life was still good for the couple in those days. But those happy times were not to last.

As Katie grew older, but before Charlotte was born, Carol started telling Debbie that Steve was being unfaithful. And then it got worse.

Debbie isn't positive about the timing, but recalls that it was a few nights before Carol gave birth to Charlotte that Carol called her, bed-bound, sobbing and beside herself.

Carol said she'd learned that Steve was having an affair with the midwife who was about to deliver her baby, a disturbing fact that Steve had just revealed to her.

Carol really had no good answer for why Steve would commit such an insensitive act, but it was clear to Debbie that Carol had decided to stay in the marriage nonetheless. She loved him, and he loved her.

Over the years, as this pattern continued, "he kept apologizing," Debbie recalled. "The apologies were romantic—champagne, roses and great sex—and oh, my gosh, how can you turn that away? And then it would happen again. It was just a cycle."

It wasn't that Carol was weak. Just the opposite. She felt Steve was the man she was supposed to be with. He was just sick, and she was going to stick by him in sickness and in health. She believed it was her "life's work" to help him get better. She wanted to be the one there with him after he had conquered this problem and came out on the other side.

"She was a really strong, amazing, confident woman that men would have lined up on the street to have," Debbie said. "She could have had anyone. She just adored Steve and felt this incredible connection to stay with him and see him through to wellness."

As a professor at Prescott College, Steve taught a course he named, aptly and ironically, "Mass Media: The Serpent in the Garden," in which he discussed sexual imagery in advertising. He also taught a course about the politics of food, during which he took his students to a slaughterhouse to witness how animals were treated during the meat-making process. Steve and Carol were both vegetarians and healthy eaters.

"If you weren't vegetarian before that class, you probably were afterward," one student recalled.

Carol joined the faculty in 1989, and also served as coordinator of the college's Human Development Program. Both she and Steve were popular among the students.

Continuing his extracurricular outdoor activities, Steve took students on kayaking and white-water rafting trips to such destinations as the Grand Canyon, where students still visit today, as they combine rafting with water-quality monitoring.

During this period, he hung out and played poker with a group of male friends. One of them was Gareth Richards, who later launched an online athletic equipment business known as Outdoor Prolink, which sold Steve a couple pairs of trail running shoes that would become important evidence in this case.

Within a couple of years, in June 1990, Steve was promoted to dean of the Resident Degree Program, the heavyweight of the college's two dean positions.

"He is a very charismatic, attractive man, so people fell under his sway and elected him dean," Sturgis recalled, explaining that electing the dean was one of the college's unique characteristics, "a holdover from the idealistic Hassayampa [Hotel] days."

At the time Steve contended that he was the nation's youngest university dean, quite an accomplishment and an honor for such a bright and ambitious young man.

During the years they worked at the college, it was still quite a bit smaller than it is today, and was operating out of a single building on Grove Street. Enrollment jumped at the end of that decade, but was still far below its present attendance, which is slightly less than one thousand students.

Back then, graduating classes could be as small as twenty-five students. Many students were older than the norm, varying in age from recent high-school graduates to "mature" middle-aged students, who were often drawn to the "distance learning" programs.

Students tended to discover the college in offbeat ways, such as recruiting ads in the back of *Outside* magazine. The college also accepted students who might have flunked out of a traditional university. When one such student called to inquire about the ad, a college representative invited her to apply.

"Come!" the rep said.

Prescott College, this student said, "was extremely alternative, especially at the time," but it was also "very cutting-edge." Now that more of the general population is sensitive to being green, "everything that they did has become much more mainstream."

Katherine Morris, who went by her maiden name of Dean at the time, was a typical Prescott College student. After graduating from a Rochester area high school near where Steve grew up, she spent a year in Europe, then a year making her way across Central America.

Still not ready to start college, she was working at the Monteverde Cloud Forest Reserve in Costa Rica, and teaching in the neighboring community of Cerro Plano, when a dozen Prescott College students came through for a tour as part of their class.

One of her close friends and coworkers subsequently left to attend the college, and after applying and being accepted a few months later, Katherine did the same.

How she learned about the college, she said, says a lot about the school and its teaching approach. "They're out there viewing things," she said. "The universe is truly their classroom."

When Katherine first arrived at the college in 1994, she

lived in a VW bus and went rock climbing every day, which was not an entirely unusual routine for a Prescott student back then. Her peers were a like-minded eclectic bunch who grew into a tight community with shared interests in activities such as leading ecotours through South America, going on white-water rafting trips, working out "in the field" and eating vegetarian meals. Some thought nothing of swimming naked together in the stream.

"We were a hippie college," said Marilyn Walters (pseudonym), a former student who attended the college around the same time. "We were all such peace lovers. No one had a gun. We were just hippies. We weren't sixties radicals, but we were the next set of them."

There were other contingents of students as well, such as the radical athletes who were more concerned about "shredding" rocks on climbing excursions and "bagging" mountain peaks.

Student orientation consisted of a monthlong backpacking trip with eight to ten students in the wilderness. Instructors developed relationships with their students, had them for multiple classes and gave them written reports on their progress. Grades were not awarded unless they were specifically requested. These were youths who wanted to carve their own way in the world after rejecting or withdrawing from big universities.

"We were all in a very small circle and saw each other daily," Marilyn said.

Before the time of cell phones, students had open mailboxes on campus, where they left notes, poems or trinkets for each other. Passions ran high and students had sex with each other. Some swapped partners as part of the culture, while others had serious relationships.

Because it was such a small campus, drama could develop and escalate quickly. Such was a controversy in the early 1990s when Steve wanted to fire a poetry teacher and librarian, Fern Dayve, who has since died. He thought—and Carol supported his position—that it was inappropriate for Fern to have poetry nights, during which she read erotica to students and drank wine with them.

"There was a protest to try to get Steve not to fire Fern," Marilyn said, noting that some students rebelled because Fern had a following. "They were trying to kick her out of our community, and you can't really do that when the community is so small."

This controversy was considered rather ironic because it was no secret that Steve had slept with two students, who had worked as nannies for him and Carol, and one of those affairs had reportedly lasted for several months. There was also talk that he'd been involved with a couple of coworkers, and word had gotten around that Steve had slept with the midwife.

"The midwife was the first one that we, as students, had heard about," Marilyn said.

Sturgis took his best friend's side in this affair, because he harbored the perception—fueled by Steve's complaints and stories about his wife—that Carol was nagging him and acting "like an incredible harpy."

But more than that, Sturgis, who was away in 1991 while working as a white-water river guide in the Grand Canyon, actually abetted Steve by allowing him to use Sturgis's vacant house for trysts with the midwife. Sturgis was gone between April and the end of October, came back for a month, then went off to Costa Rica for the winter. He couldn't be sure exactly when the affair started, but he, too, thought it was while Carol was still pregnant with Charlotte.

"The fact that he was having this affair with the midwife

had no impact on me at all," he said, noting that this feeling has since changed dramatically.

At the time, Steve told Sturgis that this woman was "so powerful and strong and so spiritual," this outweighed the fact that she wasn't as attractive as some of his other lovers. The midwife was considered a "paragon" in Prescott, Sturgis said, and likely remains so even today.

The midwife, who was interviewed years later by Detective John McDormett, said she met Carol first and then Steve in April 1991. She told investigators, however, that her affair with Steve didn't start until June 1992, around the time that she was having her own marital troubles and had separated from her husband. (Charlotte was born in October 1991.)

The woman said Steve asked her to marry him "on a number of occasions" in the early 1990s, but she always said no because she knew Carol would always be in his life. He didn't ask her again after he'd moved into the financial industry, she said, because their relationship had changed by then as he came to care more about money and appearances. He told her that she no longer fit the standard for the type of woman he wanted to be seen with in public, but that Carol did, which "amused" her.

As McDormett wrote in his report, the midwife told him that like *Steve, a lot of people want to stay within their class and she appreciated his honesty.* Steve still tried to get her into bed occasionally, she said, but she declined and he didn't push it.

Whatever the timing of this particular affair, Sturgis said it was apparently what "cracked Carol" in terms of seeing Steve's womanizing for the problem it really was.

* * *

Steve held the dean's job for five years and five months. But the popularity he'd so enjoyed as a faculty member began to decline as word of his womanizing spread and festered.

"He would talk dirty all the time. So if he was working with a secretary, a female, sexualized banter would just be part of the day," Sturgis recalled, noting that Steve did this with two staff members, and also had a brief affair with one of them. Sturgis was not aware of Steve sleeping with any professors.

"He became a very polarizing figure on campus," Sturgis said, explaining that several complaints were filed against Steve for sexual harassment and abuse of power amid criticism that he tried to manipulate members of the faculty and administration.

"My impression is that Steve did a lot of bad-mouthing of people behind their back, starting rumors [and using] very underhanded approaches to getting what he wanted to get done," Sturgis said.

Steve, of course, didn't see it this way. In his own defense, he summed up these various controversies as "he was being pestered by bitchy, crazy people."

The practice of faculty members sleeping with students was known to happen at Prescott College until 2000, when Dan Garvey became president and took steps to curtail this behavior, Sturgis said, so "there was also a lot of forgiveness on the Prescott campus at that time."

Most likely as a result of Steve's transgressions, Carol was instrumental in putting a policy into place to prohibit faculty and staff from having intimate relationships with students. For some people on campus, this seemed ironic, because she went on to have what one female student complained to the administration was inappropriate contact with a male student by showing up at his house unannounced one evening.

This student, Richard Stevenson (pseudonym), who was questioned years later during the murder investigation, was told that his name had come to their attention during an interview with Steve's girlfriend, presumably Renee Girard.

Richard, who went on to become a sociology professor himself at a small college, and is writing a book about meditation, acknowledged that he and Carol had a "powerful, powerful relationship" and a "deep connection" while he was a student.

"Carol was a profound, profound influence on my life. As a teacher and a student, we had a deep connection, but it wasn't sexual," he said in 2014.

He and other students often hung out with their professors, he said, just as he and Carol did. And like many of her students, Richard looked up to her as an amazing and charismatic teacher, who also happened to be gorgeous and intelligent. He knew she had kids and was married to Steve, who was still a dean at the time, but they never discussed Carol's marital problems.

"Of course I was smitten with her. She was smart. She was an amazing yogi. She transformed my life," he said. "She introduced me to a world that had a depth I didn't know. In other words, it was far beyond the world of superficial meditation and yoga."

If Carol had ever made sexual overtures toward him, he said, he would have accepted them gladly and reciprocated, but she never crossed that line.

"She was a catalyst and I think that's what she was for

a lot of people. She put me on a trajectory. . . . I met her at the right place, at the right time, and she had the right skill set of a really good teacher who knew what the student needed and directed them. It's really amazing and it's rare."

Hearing about her murder was tragic, he said, and talking about it was difficult for him. "To me, it was just like she was incredible. It's just so sad, dredging it up. . . . It's heartbreaking that she was killed."

Carol really enjoyed the adoration she received from students like Richard Stevenson, but to Sturgis, Carol almost enjoyed it too much, as if she fed off it. (That is not all that unusual for a teacher, this author included.)

"When she was a teacher, her students tended to completely love her," Sturgis said. However, from his perspective she was not viewed with such admiration by her peers.

Among her peer group, he said, "Carol was a little harder to work with. She was kind of rigid. She was a little bit of a fanatic. She was very judgmental." He said she acted like "a small-town girl in a lot of ways." When Steve was dean, "she really threw her weight around as the wife of the dean."

Katherine Morris didn't see it that way. Rather, she said, it was more that Carol's peers were jealous of her beauty and intellect. "Not that they truly didn't like her, but that they wanted to be more like her," she said. And even if she was not the perfect wife, "who could fault her if she did become a little bit 'do this or do that' or controlling after she found out about all of her husband's infidelities?"

Sturgis admitted that his perceptions were filtered through Steve, who made it sound as if Carol was always nagging him to do something or other. But Sturgis did notice that she and Steve shared one key characteristic:

they exhibited "really strange boundaries" with other
people.

"They were constantly talking about sex—sex between
themselves, sex with others," he said, recalling one night
they made a dramatic entrance at a party at Gareth Richards's
house in the early 1990s.

"Oh, I'm so sorry we're late. We were screwing in the
parking lot," Carol said when they walked in.

Carol did this in private as well, confiding in her friends
what a great sex partner she had in Steve, her lover and
soul mate for life. It was clearly part of the glue that held
them together, and one of the tactics he employed to keep
her in their volatile relationship.

CHAPTER 18

In April 1992, six months after Charlotte was born, Carol and Steve decided to move their growing family to a 1.4-acre parcel on the 7400 block of Bridle Path in Williamson Valley, which they bought for $78,000. The plan was to live there in a temporary home while they built their dream house, which Carol and Steve were going to design with an architect's help.

Both of them knew carpentry well, and Steve often did woodworking in his workshop, especially when he was upset or frustrated. Steve had already built their Vermont home, he "made a bed and he made a sofa. He could do anything. He was really, really smart," Ruth recalled.

While they were designing the main house, Steve and some friends from the college quickly built interim lodging—out of hay bales to be eco-friendly and energy-efficient—for the family. During the building phase Charlotte gleefully played with the straw bales that covered the property.

By 1997, the family had transitioned into their new four-bedroom, four-bathroom house, complete with vaulted ceilings. Carol had even designed a little loft area in the house. Charlotte used to climb up and play with her stuffed animals there, using the same wooden ladder that was found near Carol's body.

The straw bale structure became Carol's art studio and Steve's workout area, with lots of shelves for storage, then later was turned into a guesthouse. They also built a double-car garage, a horse barn and a corral on the secluded parcel, which was surrounded by fruit and nut trees and by trails used by people and horses on the ranch land behind it. Far from the urban life, the house provided privacy and quiet, with a magnificent view of Granite Mountain.

Katherine Morris had heard of Carol and her great reputation as a teacher before they'd even met, and she was determined, even as a sophomore, to take one of Carol's upper-division courses. These popular classes were tough to get into, but Katherine managed. She started with Carol's "Yoga Psychology" class in 1994, then went on to take her "Dream Work" course in 1995.

In the process Katherine impressed Carol. After the midwife and nanny affairs, which Carol didn't discuss with her until years later, she wanted someone she could trust to babysit her girls.

"I couldn't believe that Carol Kennedy was calling me to watch her children. I was so honored that I was nervous," Katherine recalled, laughing. "I truly, truly was. She spoke about [the babysitting] at my graduation when she gave me away. It was funny."

As Katherine was getting to know Carol and Steve, and she first heard people gossiping about his affairs, Katherine thought, "These people are crazy. There's no way."

Initially she couldn't see Steve as a cheater. "I just didn't believe that he was that type of person," she said. He never came on to her, although she did get the sense that he would have been willing if she'd given him the nod.

"Do I think I could have gotten with him if I'd wanted to? Absolutely. But had he [come on to me], I would have told Carol," she said.

For Katherine, Carol and Steve were the ideal parents. When she started taking care of the girls, the family was still living in the guesthouse. Katie was about six years old and quite headstrong.

Katherine liked leaving the house cleaner than she found it so Carol and Steve wouldn't come home to a mess. But this practice annoyed little Katie. "My mom pays you to play with me, not to clean up after me," Katie would say, stomping her foot.

Katherine tried to explain. If she didn't clean up, she told Katie, "your mom will think I'm a horrible sitter."

Mealtimes were interesting as well. When she asked Katie what she wanted to eat, the child often gave her conflicting responses.

"I'm a vegetarian," Katie said.

"Do you want a peanut butter and jelly sandwich?"

"No, I want a hot dog."

But Katherine would oblige. "Okay, I'll make you a hot dog."

Carol sometimes brought the girls to campus with her. "They were just precious kids," Katherine recalled. "Charlotte was so soft-spoken, quiet and angelic . . . gentle. She was the total essence of peace and peacefulness. She would just look up at you, with her white blond hair, and go, 'I'm so glad you're here.'"

Charlotte liked to pick flowers, make bouquets for her mom and dad and put the blossoms in vases. She even made a crown of flowers for Katherine to wear during her graduation ceremony.

"I thought she was sent from heaven," Katherine said.

Katie had some of the same nature-loving traits and compassion for animals that Charlotte did. "Katie was extremely vibrant," Katherine said. "Extremely stubborn, passionate from an early age about whatever she was interested in, which at that time was primarily dolphins and horses. She would go after what she wanted, she was determined and she would get it. Katie was loving, way more of an adventurer and very independent."

"They both had a phenomenal imagination," she added. "They were both extremely creative in whatever they were doing."

While the girls were growing up, Carol and Steve thought it was important to expose them to the outdoors. The whole family often went hiking and camping, wearing backpacks and climbing mountains.

By all appearances they looked like the perfect American family: fit, healthy and attractive. As Debbie Wren Hill put it, they were "physically amazing specimens. Truthfully, if Steve could have been different in that way, I think they could have been a family that people would be envying to this day."

CHAPTER 19

After working at Prescott College for seven years, Steve decided to make a radical career change on October 1, 1995, when he moved into the world of finance by taking a job with much higher-earning potential at A.G. Edwards.

He and his best friend, Sturgis Robinson, made the jump together, entering a stockbroker training program at the urging of and sponsorship by one of Steve's poker buddies.

Steve's withdrawal from academia prompted a sit-down between mother and son, during which Jan asked Steve why he'd decided to stop helping people. He told her that he was still trying to help them—by investing their money so well that they could retire five or ten years earlier than they could otherwise. He also wanted to help nonprofits, such as those helping kids or the homeless.

"If I could increase the income they get from their investments by even two or three percent, that's more kids they're going to be helping. That means a lot to me," he told her.

* * *

During the first six months at the new brokerage house, Sturgis developed a relationship with a senior broker who was retiring, and who promised to give him his "book of business," worth about $40 million in assets. The broker, who also sent off a letter introducing Sturgis to his clients, was going to retire on a Friday, and Sturgis was going to start calling the wealthiest clients on Monday.

But as Sturgis began making those calls, he got a sinking feeling in his stomach that just kept getting worse. It took him about twenty calls before he could truly believe it, but Steve had already called every single one of them over the weekend, and had persuaded them to give him their business instead.

"I was blown away," Sturgis recalled.

When Sturgis came into the office, he confronted the man he'd thought had been his best friend for the past twenty-five years.

"You called them over the weekend? What the [hell]?" he asked.

But Steve looked right through him and put his head down as if Sturgis wasn't even there. "No, it didn't happen like that," he said.

This sparked a paradigm shift for Sturgis, who, after all these years, had shrugged off all the horrific remarks people had made about his friend.

"All the terrible things I'd been hearing about Steve for years were true," he said. At that moment Sturgis finally came to the painful realization that *he* was "the idiot. I'm the deluded person."

"I realized that he had some progressive narcissistic sociopathic mental disorder—and the more power he could get, the more this sort of disease took him over," he recalled in 2014.

Back in college, he said, Steve had seemed like such a

great guy. But as soon as he got access to power, he started to veer downward. And as he acquired more access to money and wealth, this "really set him off the tracks."

"It was clear that during the years that he was the dean that he was alienating more and more people," Sturgis said. "I was blind to it—I always took his side—but in retrospect people would associate me with him and look crossways at me because I was friends with him. . . . So there was no question that in his last year or two at Prescott College, he was in hot water."

Their traumatic and hurtful "breakup," only six months into their new careers as stockbrokers, "completely altered my understanding of who he was as a person and what our relationship meant," he said.

Sturgis said the fellow college alumnus who had sponsored them both in the brokerage program also became estranged with Steve around the same time because of his business practices.

As of 2014, records from the Financial Industry Regulatory Authority (FINRA) showed that Steve had four customer complaints against him, all of which essentially claimed misrepresentation of securities. Two complaints were settled; the other two were dismissed or denied.

The most serious one was filed in September 2010, two years after Steve no longer worked as a broker, alleging damages of $947,000. Settled for $297,500 in August 2011, the complaint summary states in part: *Claimants allege that UBS and their broker did not adequately advise them that the Lehman Brothers structured notes in which they invested would lose a substantial part of their value in the event of a Lehman bankruptcy filing, and allege that the Lehman Brothers structured notes were unsuitable for them and were misrepresented to them. Claimants also allege that other structured products that they purchased from other issuers also were misrepresented by UBS and their broker at UBS.* The firm, they said, also did not "adequately supervise the broker."

UBS responded that Steve wasn't asked to and didn't contribute to the settlement, which came out of repurchasing the client's securities at "par value" and "was not based on the merits of the client's specific concerns or any finding of fault or wrongdoing" by Steve.

The other complaint, filed in March 2008, claimed damages of more than $5,000. Settled in December 2008, it either didn't seek damages or they were determined to be less than $5,000. The summary states in part: *Client states that the auction rate securities were represented as cash alternatives with 7-day liquidity, and the triple AAA.* Steve blamed that outcome on "unprecedented market events" that caused the "breakdown of liquidity in the market for auction rate securities."

About 12 percent of the nation's 75,846 registered brokers have had such complaints filed against them with FINRA. Steve's former boss at UBS, Jim Van Steenhuyse, who recruited him from A.G. Edwards, said that only 5 to 10 percent of financial advisors typically last in this tough industry.

Katherine didn't see the changes in Steve come as fast or as extreme as Sturgis did, probably because Steve had always treated her well. In her view Steve seemed to try to stay true to himself for the first couple of years after moving into the finance world. He was still the same outdoorsy family man who went golfing, boating, hiking and biking with friends and family, and who attended kids' events with the girls. He also still enjoyed reading and following the news.

"He was an intellect," Katherine said. "Steve was very bright. He was worldly. He talked about worldly current events, always listened to NPR, classical music."

But over time, she said, his interests began to turn toward more material things, and his friendships with former colleagues at the college faded away. "They didn't find they had much in common with him anymore, so I think a lot of those friendships just dissipated," she said.

Money took center stage in Steve's life, she said. As a result he made friends mostly through his job, and not so much with men anymore. "Mainly a lot of women," she said.

The more money he made, the more he would spend on nice things, expensive trips, luxury items and athletic equipment. In the process people around him saw him becoming more arrogant and selfish.

He still held on to some of his old self, Katherine said, but at some point "his whole person changed. . . . He still loved the outdoors, but in a different way. Instead of being in a tent, he was at the Four Seasons. . . . Instead of duct-taping a hole in a jacket, he would go out and buy a new one."

And although she personally didn't view this change as dramatically as some, "I would hear of him being that way. That was the perception—and that was Carol's perception," she said. But "he was always wonderful with me. I still believe that he is truly *that* person and he just lost it."

Sturgis saw the change in Steve from a different perspective. He recalled the young Steve talking a "great game about spirituality, about attaining spiritual development, about being a good person, but I think the true Steve came out when he got access to wealth, and he became very focused not only on wealth itself, but all the trappings of wealth, the nice suit, the nice condo and the multiple girlfriends."

When Katherine took Carol's "Dream Work" class, it was the most powerful and intense course she'd ever taken, right around the time that Steve made the move to A.G. Edwards.

The class lasted about eight hours a day, starting in the late morning—late enough that no one needed an alarm to wake up. This was on purpose, because Carol wanted her students to wake up naturally, then write down whatever they could remember from their dreams, even if it was in the middle of the night.

They were to write them out in the first person and in present tense, as if they were happening in the moment. Then she had them go through the narrative and circle recurring symbols or images that seemed to carry energy. Only the dreamer could interpret his dreams, she said, and determine what in his waking life he needed to work through by interpreting what issues were playing across his subconscious mind. One of the goals was to become lucid in dreams so as to actively control them.

The students would share their dreams with each other and talk them through. Carol even had them sleep together for a night, head to head, with the hope of entering each other's dreams.

"She always believed in some sort of ritual to honor that dream and the gift that dream is giving you," Katherine said.

Carol also shared her own dreams. She told them about one in which she was wearing an elegant gown, fit for a presidential inauguration ball, topped off with a lavish jeweled necklace. The outfit was gorgeous, she told the class, "but so not me, I'm in this, so uncomfortable, walking around, like, 'What am I doing? Why am I in this?'"

As she processed the dream with her students, she attributed it to her discomfort "with Steve's career change, and how different what he's doing is for me and how out of my element I am with that." The dream told her that she "must really be very uncomfortable" with the vastly different direction her life with him was taking and showed "how she wanted it to slow down."

"It's all a different world for me, and it's not a comfortable one," Carol said.

Like Steve, Carol finally left Prescott College as well, but for different reasons. It's unclear exactly when or why she left, details that college officials said they were unable to disclose because of privacy laws.

Katherine got a much closer view of Steve's personality shift after she graduated from Prescott College in 1997 and moved down to a condo in Phoenix that she occasionally shared with him while she attended graduate school at Arizona State University. Her sister lived in the condo for a time as well.

Steve and Carol stayed at the condo together sometimes, and when he was in town for work, he stayed there without Carol, bringing over his assistant Barb O'Non instead, under the guise that they were working together. He and Barb would relax by the pool before a meeting, or before they drove back to Prescott together after work.

One day Barb put on Carol's bathing suit and paraded around in it, which really rubbed Katherine the wrong way, especially when Barb said, "I feel just like Carol."

In 1999 or 2000, Barb came to a Christmas party hosted by Steve and Carol, during which Katherine watched Barb act "all goo-goo gaga" toward Steve in front of his wife and their guests. The behavior was so noticeable that Katherine even remarked on it afterward.

"If that woman doesn't have [a thing] for Steve, I don't know who does," she said.

Around that same time Steve came down to stay at the condo before a meeting, showing up after work around five o'clock.

"I can't believe it," he told Katherine and her sister. "I've left my wallet up in Prescott. Thank goodness for Barb. What an amazing assistant she is. She's going to drive down and meet me halfway."

Before he left, Katherine's sister needed to move Steve's car to go somewhere, because it was blocking hers in. Grabbing his keys, she got into his car, where she was surprised to see his wallet sitting on the console.

Steve left for the night and snuck back into the condo at 6 A.M. When she and Katherine compared notes, she mentioned seeing the wallet in his car the evening before. Katherine was just as surprised as her sister had been.

"Really?" she asked. Katherine didn't want to believe that Steve—even though he could be a jerk and controlling at times—had concocted such a tall tale.

"Maybe it's not really his wallet?" she offered.

But they had to face that he'd made up the whole wallet story as a way to hide the fact that he was staying the night with Barb.

There were days when Steve disappeared around dinnertime and couldn't be reached, so Carol just went ahead and took the girls out for pizza. On those occasions he offered some excuse when he showed up later, saying that his phone died or he was in a meeting, but he didn't take responsibility for his absence.

"He would always blame it on [Carol]," Katherine recalled. "It was her fault."

Carol's response was not to yell or scream, although Katherine did see her neck getting noticeably tight as she calmly disputed whatever excuse he'd given. "Steve, that is not what happened," she would say.

"Carol was so tolerant," Katherine recalled. "She wanted to believe the best in people. And that's why she stuck with Steve for so long. She fought for her marriage. Hard."

Katherine never really liked Barb, especially the strange way Barb seemed to be trying to win her over. But Katherine never tattled on Steve to Carol, because she couldn't be sure what was going on between him and Barb, and she didn't want to cause trouble unnecessarily. Instead, she waited until Carol brought it up.

One day Carol got so upset by something Steve had done that she finally told Katherine that Steve was having an affair with Barb. When Katherine apologized for not having said anything sooner about her suspicions, Carol told her not to worry. She never rebuked Katherine for not reporting what she'd witnessed.

"It's so okay," Carol told her. "It's fine."

But after that initial disclosure, Carol and Katherine talked about Barb quite often.

Curiously, Sturgis said that Steve kept a lid on his emotions as well. He either hid his feelings or did not show an overt response to them, apparently keeping them bottled up inside.

"He was a very controlled person," Sturgis said. "I never saw him angry. I would see him compress his lips and tighten his face and wrinkle his forehead. I never saw him shout or be angry that I can recall. At the very most he would get stern and contemptuous, say something cutting, but even that was fairly restrained."

Sturgis never saw Steve get violent, either. "I never saw him hit anybody," he said. "It would have been inconceivable for him to get into a fistfight with anybody. He was more subtle than that."

CHAPTER 20

Carol and Steve both doted on their daughters, being the best parents and educators they knew how to be. This came easy with Charlotte, but Katie was more of a challenge early on.

"Charlotte soaked up the information like a little sponge," Ruth Kennedy said. "She could outspell Katie. She was a precocious little thing."

Katie, Ruth said, is "really a smart person. She really is. They both are. But they're totally different personalities."

When Katie was still in elementary school, she was having a difficult time staying engaged. In other words she was bored.

"At home Carol struggled with Katie because she was very stubborn and could be very oppositional with Carol and with Steve, but not at school," Katherine said. "She is extremely intelligent. Her IQ is off the charts."

Carol encouraged the girls to be creative by sending them to schools that used the Waldorf method of teaching, a philosophy that encourages children to use their imagination. She even set up a Waldorf-type school for them and some other kids in the guesthouse for a time, painting the interior with pastel colors.

Like her mother before her, Carol loved to have music in the house, turning on the stereo as soon as she walked in—usually something classical or a soft lilting CD by Enya, the New Age Irish singer-songwriter who was one of Carol's favorites.

By the time Katie got to junior high school, Carol tried to engage her by homeschooling her. But after a couple of years, Carol felt that wasn't best for Katie—for Carol to be her mother *and* teacher. Instead, they found an alternative that excited Katie: the Orme School, a private boarding prep school that she could attend as a day student.

Carol drove her forty-five minutes to an hour each way to Orme, which was down a long dirt road in the middle of ranch land. To pass the time on the long drive, she often called her friend Debbie to chat.

"I spend half of my life in the car," Carol told her.

Katie loved Orme and excelled there. She played three seasons of sports and became a prefect in the dorm, where, by her junior and senior years, she was spending two or three nights a week. She went on to become class salutatorian and gave a speech at the graduation ceremony in 2006, making her parents proud.

From there she went away to Occidental College, with a goal of going to law school.

Charlotte attended a school closer to home, entered the Waldorf-inspired Mountain Oak School once it opened in 1999, then graduated from Prescott High School.

During these years Carol's mood often alternated between extremes, depending on whether her relationship with Steve was in a good or bad place. At one point, when Carol called to tell Debbie the latest, she sounded so down that Debbie was worried for her friend's emotional health.

"I feel like you are my best friend and I keep calling you when these things happen," Carol said.

"Do you have anyone there you can confide in?" Debbie asked.

"No," Carol said, "I'm never quite sure whether they've slept with my husband."

Debbie didn't think she could've stayed with a man like Steve. "Do you still respect yourself?" she asked Carol. "Because I'm worried you're losing respect for yourself. I've never loved a man the way you love Steve, and I hope I never do. I just don't get why you're still there. I just don't."

Because Carol was so strong and so intuitive, Debbie and other close friends actually went to Carol for counsel, support and advice. But they could see how very difficult it was for her to heed *their* advice, to even think about letting go when Steve kept coming back to her with such emotional force. Despite all of his affairs, he just wouldn't let her go.

"I don't think he ever quit loving Carol. I think he just wanted everything that he wanted at the same time," Debbie said. "And that's what we all really held against him. He was bringing this woman to her knees."

Lots of couples have problems with infidelity, she said, that's not what was unusual or extraordinary about this relationship. It was the way that Steve kept toying with Carol's psyche.

"He just never could say, 'We're done, I'm done.' He kept apologizing," Debbie recalled. "He would tell Carol who the woman had been, [and] they would go back to treatment. It's like an alcoholic. . . . He really was addicted."

One time Carol counted up the affairs that she knew of, that she had proof of and that Steve had confessed to. It came to fourteen.

Still, Steve stuck by Carol. Debbie called her friend one Valentine's Day to complain that her then-partner and soon-to-be husband had let her down. She'd asked him to get her a particular book as a gift, but he didn't come through.

"If we didn't live together, I'd leave his ass," Debbie told Carol.

Carol sympathized, then told Debbie how Steve would have handled the situation. "Steve would never have done that," Carol said. "He'd have gotten me that book. And there would have been roses, there would have been champagne . . . . But here's the deal, he might have been in bed with his secretary."

"It was like pick your poison," Debbie recalled. "I was, like, 'I guess I'd rather have a boyfriend who didn't get me the book.' Steve always came through in a wonderful way for Carol. But not *just* for Carol."

Some say that people who become therapists do so because they're trying to figure out their own issues, and along the way they become fascinated with the psychology of others as well.

"Carol had always been engaged in her own therapeutic process in one shape or form," Katherine Morris recalled, noting that Carol saw a therapist in Prescott.

At Carol's urging, she and Steve went together for

marital counseling. She also tried to persuade him to get therapy for love and sex addiction at an upscale rehab center known as The Meadows in Wickenburg, about forty-five minutes from Prescott.

The Meadows website describes the term "sexual addiction" as a condition in which a person has an "unusual fascination with or fixation on sex." This can involve incessant fantasizing about sex, making it difficult to maintain healthy relationships, as well as indulging in reckless and risky behaviors that may result in serious consequences. All the while these individuals justify their actions to themselves, blame others, and deny that they have a problem.

Carol discussed Steve's pattern of behavior with Katherine and Debbie, given that they were all therapists.

"We knew there was some sort of sex and love addiction going on there that needed to be treated," Katherine said.

To Debbie, Steve seemed somewhat aware that his behavior was wrong. He seemed genuinely remorseful when he came clean about his latest affair; he would say it had ended, and promise to stop cheating. Carol told Debbie that Steve admitted he needed help. The challenge was getting him to go to treatment, let alone comply with the changes he needed to make.

Originally, Carol proposed that Steve go for a thirty-day inpatient program, but Steve bucked that idea. "I can't with my work," he said. "There's no way I can do that."

Short of that, Carol tried to get him to go for some kind of treatment, *period*. She wanted him to get well. But even if he dabbled, such as attending a couple of group sessions, he never made any significant effort to deal with the problem.

"He always had a way of finagling himself out of it,"

Katherine recalled. "If he did do anything, he didn't really *do* it. He did it for an extremely fleeting and sporadic time."

Steve had a dark side that began to emerge, and having sex with other women was not the only troubling behavior he tried to hide from Carol.

Around 2002, Katherine and her future husband came to Bridle Path for a visit. Katherine had just finished working out on the treadmill in the guesthouse, where she and her boyfriend were talking to Steve about its shelving and structure.

Steve mentioned that a neighborhood cat used to come in and get into their stuff. He would try to shoo it away because it also tormented and scratched up their cat, but it kept coming back.

One day, Steve said, he decided to lure the cat in by leaving the back door open and trap it inside. His plan worked. After closing in the cat, he grabbed an object—a shovel, kayak paddle or baseball bat (Katherine couldn't remember)—and went after it. As he chased the cat around the guesthouse, the animal tried to escape by climbing and clawing at the walls, but Steve was determined not to let him get away.

Laughing as he told them the story, Steve said, "I just got my [kayak paddle or other object] and beat it to death. And from then on, Katherine, that cat was just gone."

Katherine could not believe what she was hearing. She knew Carol would never approve of this animal control method.

"Surely, Carol does not know about this," she said.

Steve acknowledged that no, Carol didn't.

When Katherine told this story to investigators after Carol was murdered, they told her that they had tried, but they couldn't find any neighbor who had lost a cat.

Wondering if she had misremembered the story, Katherine called her then-ex-husband and asked him about it. He not only confirmed her recollection of the conversation, he remembered even more details about it than she did.

"No," he told her, "that totally happened."

CHAPTER 21

Earlier in the marriage Carol executed her last will and testament on June 23, 1998, leaving assets of her estate to a trust and listing Katie and Charlotte as the two beneficiaries. Her wish, stated in supporting documents, was for the trustee to *be guided by my desire to provide for the education of my children and to encourage them to obtain a college degree, and to provide adequately for [their] health.*

The will provided for the trust to be administered as a single trust until Katie reached the age of twenty-five, at which time the first shares would be distributed equally, one to Katie and the other to continue in trust until Charlotte reached twenty-five, or until the trust was otherwise spent for the purposes she'd specified.

Around this same time, Carol and Steve took out a couple of Hartford life insurance policies on her, naming Steve as the primary beneficiary. The first, issued July 24, 1998, was for $250,000, and listed the Virginia Carol Kennedy Trust as the secondary beneficiary. This policy's annual premium was scheduled to increase from $237 to

$2,812 in July 2008, but due to the timing of Carol's murder, Steve never had to make the higher payment.

The second policy, issued January 2, 2001, was for $500,000 and named Steve as the owner and sole beneficiary. As a financial advisor and licensed insurance broker, Steve took both of those policies with him when he moved from A.G. Edwards to UBS. But he didn't get the paperwork in order, switching the official broker of record to UBS, until February 2008.

In 2003, Carol called Debbie to tell her that Steve wanted to move out and have his own space—a condo on the golf course.

"We're still married," Carol said. "We're still in an exclusive relationship."

Steve had told his wife that he needed his own place so he could get some sleep. He'd been working as a broker for some time now, going to bed around eight-thirty at night and getting up around four in the morning, before the stock market opened on the East Coast. The girls and the barking dogs kept waking him up, though.

"Carol, really?" Debbie asked, stunned by this flimsy excuse. "Are you serious?"

"Yes," Carol said, "and I think it's going to be fine."

Carol told Katherine the same thing, noting that Steve would now have a place to exercise his obsessive-compulsive urges to straighten and keep things orderly.

"He can have all his cans of soup lined up, and all the drawers organized," Carol said, adding that she had no problem with him moving out. "There's nothing wrong with that. It just doesn't work for me. I'm not going to spend my life organizing cupboards."

Katherine had noticed this tendency as well. Steve's car

was always spotless and clean. "There was never any dirt in it," she said.

He even acted like a perfectionist when he and Katherine played golf together. "He didn't get angry, but he was always critiquing himself," she said. "What an awful way to lead your life. And I think he did that a lot."

That said, he didn't pick at Carol until after the divorce battle started. "He praised her, put her up on a pedestal, because she was that phenomenal and because it made him look good," Katherine said. Because that, she added, is what narcissists like Steve do.

Before he moved out, Steve always talked about building himself a "man hut" in the side yard at the Bridle Path house, someplace he could call his own to meditate, smoke a fine cigar with a good glass of wine or do whatever else he pleased. Today some might call it a "man cave."

"He never built it, and then Carol would kind of laugh about it, say that the condo could be his man hut, his thousands-of-dollars man hut," Katherine recalled.

It took Carol only a couple of weeks before she realized that Steve was still having an affair with Barb, and that the "need" for the condo was more likely a desire to have alone time with his mistress.

That point, it seems, was the beginning of the end of the marriage—when Carol began to realize that she was too codependent and had to get some help for herself to really let go of Steve. But, unfortunately, her psychological torture was far from over.

Steve did move out, but he didn't file for divorce for three years, and even then he withdrew the petition six weeks later. Carol had to be the one to make it stick when she filed in 2007.

When Katherine got remarried in 2004, Steve and Carol were separated, but still doing things together. They both came to the wedding in California, for example. He came on his own, and Carol with the girls. Katherine was surprised and yet overjoyed to see Steve, because Carol had said he had a lot going on and might not be able to make it. But there he was.

CHAPTER 22

Steve's affair with Barb O'Non was his longest lasting romantic relationship outside his marriage.

Barb started working as his clerical assistant at A.G. Edwards in July 1998, shortly after she and her husband moved to Prescott. She answered phones and basic client questions while she studied for her Series 7 security and insurance licenses. She said their personal relationship began a couple of years later.

After earning her licenses in the spring of 2000, she was allowed to perform the duties of a stockbroker and financial advisor, and Steve gave her a 10 percent split of his commissions. At A.G. Edwards, Steve was in charge of $75.2 million in assets. In 2004, his last year there, he earned $816,000 in commissions, a chunk of which he gave to Barb, and a smaller sum of $5,000 to another member of his team.

Steve and Barb's personal and professional relationships continued to be intertwined after he took a job at UBS as a senior vice president of investment in September 2004. Barb and another team member went with him to UBS, where Barb's title became investment associate.

Although she went into an investment training program, Barb was still working as his assistant.

Because she and Steve were trying to make their respective marriages work, she said, their relationship was "on-again, off-again, but it was always friendly."

"It was as it always had been," Barb recalled. "We worked very well together."

By 2007, Steve's gross earnings at UBS had jumped to more than $1 million, of which he gave $350,723 to Barb, a 30 percent share of his "book of clients" value.

Soon after Barb got divorced in 2004, Steve asked her to marry him. They were sitting in his car at the time, and she responded to his proposal by flattening herself against the window with shock.

"Look how you reacted to that," he joked, trying to make light of it.

"You're still married," she said, trying to joke back and sidestep the question.

After Steve's own divorce battle began in March 2007, he often complained about how it was proceeding, that Carol should get a job and that he was frustrated with her "unwillingness to do that."

Upset at how much he was going to have to pay Carol, he groused that his settlement offers had been "generous," that she was being unfair by rejecting them and that it was difficult to support "all of the households." Although he never told Barb directly that he was having a tough time, he did indicate at one point that he was a million dollars in debt.

Barb knew he was borrowing money from his parents, because she handled the transactions. It was around this

time that he got angry with her a couple of times at the
office and she began feeling afraid of his temper.

The relationship between Steve and Barb started coming
apart in late 2006 and early 2007, when she announced that
she wanted to dissolve their partnership and take her fair
share of Steve's business, which she believed she'd helped
him create.

"We tried to work out our differences," she said, acknowledging that they continued to have sex and work
together. "We were in dispute over money, primarily."

As she tried to break away and go it alone as a broker,
they were trying to divide up the client list in a way they
both thought was equitable. But Steve wouldn't agree to
her terms: Barb wanted a boost, to a 50 percent share.

"I felt that the [30 percent] split wasn't fair," she said.
"I felt as though I was doing more work than I was being
paid for."

So in October 2007, UBS management moved her to an
office in the town of Surprise to ease tensions. Their partnership was set to dissolve in July 2008, but UBS didn't
officially end the arrangement until the fall, because Carol
was found dead just as management was about to approve
the deal.

After months of negotiations Barb finally buckled,
agreeing to walk away with her same 30 percent share of
the investment assets they'd managed together. They also
split up their client list.

"We managed the assets together," she said. "So if we
had stayed in the partnership, it wouldn't have been that I
handled half of the clients and he handled half. We handled
them together."

Barb described the two incidents when Steve lost his

temper in 2007, saying she'd never seen this happen before. The first was triggered by an argument over "which clients were going where."

She was standing in the doorway of his office when she said something that prompted him to jump out of his chair with such force that it went flying backward into the credenza. He came around his desk and got into her face aggressively until his nose was only a few inches from hers. He didn't raise his arm to hit her, but his demeanor communicated that he might do her physical harm.

"He was angry," she testified during a pretrial hearing in 2010. "I don't even remember the words that were spoken, but he was angry with me."

The second incident, which occurred several weeks later, also came during an argument over clients as she was sitting across the desk from him. This time he pounded his fists on his desk, flew out of his chair and left the office. They'd been angry with each other before, but they'd never argued like that, she said.

"For the most part we got along pretty well," she said.

She admitted, however, that she didn't report the incidents to police or seek a restraining order. She simply confided in a close friend and asked to be transferred to another office. She said the move didn't stem from these incidents alone. Steve apologized, and they subsequently slept together again. They continued to negotiate their financial split through the first half of 2008, at the same time Steve was negotiating his marital division with Carol.

Barb wasn't enough for Steve, either, it seemed. As time went on, he appeared to be unsatisfied with just one woman on the side.

After being told that Steve had used escort and "adult

dating" services—i.e., hookups for sex—investigators looked into his online dating habits and found that, sure enough, he was using Great Expectations Dating Service, as well as AdultFriendFinder.com. Carol had known about some of these services, because they'd shown up on his credit card bills, and she'd told Katherine about them.

Steve joined Great Expectations, which bills itself as "an upscale dating and matchmaking service," on October 12, 2004, choosing a global membership that encompassed Los Angeles and New York City, because he traveled.

During his four-year on-and-off membership, he repeatedly switched the status from "separated" to "divorced" and back again, often listing himself as both on different parts of his profile. He selected 116 members from across the nation and downloaded numerous photos. One member complained to management in January 2007 that she was upset to learn that Steve was not actually divorced.

In May 2008, when he was already involved with several women, he paid $620 in membership fees. On July 6, four days after Carol's murder, he e-mailed the service again, asking to be placed on inactive status due to a death in the family. On October 17, he requested that his account be reactivated.

Jim DeMocker contacted the service on November 7 to cancel Steve's membership, stating that Steve was incapacitated.

In December 2006, as his relationship with Barb was disintegrating, he met Leslie Thomas (pseudonym) on AdultFriendFinder.com, a service that advertises itself in sexually explicit terms as the world's largest site to find "worldwide sex dates, adult matches, . . . [and] hookups."

Launched in 1996, the site claims it has helped "millions

of horny members" meet one another through "online chat, chatrooms, sex cams, member blogs, groups and emails." It describes its mobile app as "A Party in Your Pocket."

During a phone interview with Deputy Doug Brown in March 2009, Leslie said she and Steve mostly conducted a long-distance relationship by phone and saw each other only occasionally in Phoenix or in Southern California, where she lived.

However, she said, they saw each other twice in June 2008, just before Carol was murdered, once for dinner in Phoenix when she had a layover there, and once a few weeks later in Chicago when she was in town on business. Leslie said it was rare for them to see each other twice in three months, let alone twice in one month. They also had traveled together to St. Maarten.

In between visits, she said, they usually spoke by phone for about an hour at a time. But after Carol was murdered, their conversations typically lasted only five minutes, except for the two-hour discussion they had about his urge to leave town to escape arrest. Steve mentioned going to Bora Bora, where they'd previously discussed traveling for their next vacation.

[Leslie Thomas] explained to Steve that there is a truth to our lives and that is to tell the truth as you see it, Brown wrote in his report. *She asked him if the best way to tell his truth is to live away (Bora Bora) as an innocent man and leave behind his life, or is it to stay and face what happens and to tell the truth in a court of law.*

In his AdultFriendFinder profile, Steve described himself as divorced, and shortly after he met Leslie in person, he acknowledged that he was actually separated, but going through a divorce. Nonetheless, Leslie believed that they were in a monogamous relationship during the two years they were involved.

They met in person for the first time in January 2007. Told she was a fellow aspiring author, Leslie and Steve discussed the novel that he said he'd started working on. Noting that she'd already written three novels, she sent him information on National Novel Writing Month—known as NaNoWriMo—during which aspiring authors are encouraged to write a fifty-thousand-word draft of a novel in the month of November.

Steve told her about a couple of hero characters he was developing. In 2007, the character was similar to James Bond or Jason Bourne. By 2008, *[he was] a hitman who had not planned on being a hitman but by accident found out that he was good at doing it,* Brown wrote.

[Leslie Thomas] explained that the assassin would kill people in a very sophisticated/intelligent manner throughout his spy work. The hitman, however, is "kind of bumbling and kind of lame, but he discovers that he is good at killing people and having it look like an accident," Brown wrote.

But Leslie said that Steve never sent her any of his writings, not even an outline.

Asked if she knew of anyone who might have known about Steve's writings and then committed the murder in a way to frame him, she said Steve had never mentioned having a contentious relationship or that anyone was out to get him.

To her, Steve was kind and gentle, so she was in shock for a couple of days after learning that he'd also been seeing Barb and Renee during their relationship. She was so upset, in fact, that she called both of them to talk. And once Steve was arrested, Leslie never spoke to him again.

As if the two online dating services weren't enough, Steve started dating Renee Girard in November 2007, while he was still seeing Leslie and carrying on with Barb and who knows who else.

Renee, a massage therapist, first met Steve and Carol when their daughters were little. Renee, who was then thirty years old, about five years younger than Steve, worked at their doctor's office.

Steve was still the dean at Prescott College back then, and Prescott was such a small town that she'd already heard through the grapevine about Steve and his affairs.

"There was a general tarnish on his character in my eyes, and seemingly in the community . . . related to womanizing and having relationships outside of his marriage," Renee said later.

Because she moved in the same circles with college faculty and staff, she'd also heard of Steve's power struggles there. "There were certainly people who were not fond of him because of that," she said.

In the fall of 2007, when Renee was forty-eight, she and Steve ran into each other at Coffee Roasters, where they struck up a conversation. Learning that she was a massage therapist, Steve scheduled an appointment, saying that his regular masseuse was leaving her practice. At the time Renee got the sense that he was already divorced.

A couple of massages later, Steve asked her out. She accepted, not knowing that he was seeing other women. Everything she'd heard about him was rumor, and although she'd believed it, he now "sounded like someone who was moving on, moving through."

Steve helped ease her concerns by offering to tell her which rumors were true and "which people he'd actually had affairs with. Then he insisted that other things were urban myth, and weren't true, and this is just what happens in a small town. So I frankly was liking the person that I was meeting. . . . I mean we had only had a few dates at that point so it wasn't like I was marrying him. I didn't know if . . . a tiger can change its stripes or not, and I didn't know how striped he was."

When Carol learned Steve was dating Renee she told her friends that she really disliked Barb, but she had no problem with Renee. In fact, she told her daughters that Renee was "a good person."

CHAPTER 23

Throughout her ever-evolving relationship with Steve, Carol dug deep to find a place of healing and a way to move on, perhaps to handle all the struggles he threw at her, or to discover why she was putting herself through them. Nurturing the artist in herself, she created handmade cards, adorned with yarn and tassels, and wrote messages in beautiful calligraphy to family and friends. She also discovered Touch Drawing.

While Carol was still teaching at Prescott College, she found a couple of women whom she asked to come to town to give guest lectures or presentations, and with whom she formed lasting connections. One was Deborah Koff-Chapin, the founder of Touch Drawing, who conducted weeklong sessions on Whidbey Island, Washington.

Between 1997 and 2007, Carol traveled to the island for five of these retreats, which proved therapeutic and inspirational for her, as she and other spiritual women bonded through drawing, dancing and exchanging dreams to heal, get in touch with their inner selves, and achieve "wholeness." The bonds were so strong that she was able to call on these women in times of need.

"Touch Drawing is a practice of creative, psychological and spiritual integration," Deborah explained.

Carol found one of her most satisfying forms of creative expression in monoprinting. This medium involves making individual prints through the application of inks with brushes or rollers, known as brayers, on a flat hard surface like glass or Plexiglas, and running the plate through a press. After putting the ink design down, the artist lays a piece of paper over the surface, then runs it through a press to push the ink into the paper. More ink can be added to the design after the first run if desired. Multiple passes can be done on the same piece of paper, or a fresh piece can be placed over the ink that's already been used once, to make a lighter "ghost" print.

"They're so whimsical, you never know what you're going to get," said monotype artist Joanne Frerking, who was a yoga teacher when she met Carol. Carol invited Joanne, who taught yoga in a therapeutic manner, to guest teach her class, "Yoga Psychology," in which she focused on the spiritual side of the social science.

Carol had been working on her art for many years, but she'd always been "afraid of hanging out her shingle, declaring herself an artist," Debbie Wren Hill recalled. So Carol started out small and worked her way up to have her first gallery opening.

As she approached her fiftieth birthday, which represented a significant milestone to her, she'd created enough pieces to hold a special birthday show at an art frame shop in Prescott, The Frame & I Gallery.

The start of the show was announced in the *Daily Courier* on September 24, 2004. The article stated: *Becoming a professional artist will be her last career and the best*

50th birthday present she could ask for. The show, which ran through October 15, displayed fifty of her best pieces.

"Instead of having a regular birthday, I wanted to do something more symbolic," Carol told the *Courier.*

As Debbie had described, Carol told the newspaper that she didn't allow herself to become a professional artist until she'd stopped teaching. Carol said she'd always felt she was an artist, but somehow couldn't give herself "permission" to be one. Explaining her approach in somewhat abstract terms, she said that when she was creating art, she felt vulnerable as she struggled to let herself acknowledge her feelings and stay in the moment. As such, her artwork represented images of healing, reflecting a parallel of sorts to the work she performed in other parts of her life.

The gallery opening, which featured live music and refreshments, was well attended. And although she and Steve were separated, Carol was thrilled that Steve not only came, but he bought a number of her pieces "because he loved it so much."

"That's what I remember her telling me. It meant so much to her that he came," Debbie recalled. "He wanted to support her work, didn't want it to get away."

By that time, Joanne Frerking was working in the same medium, also adding collage to her monotypes. When she saw Carol's show, she was so taken that she approached Carol about selling her art at Van Gogh's Ear.

Prescott may be a small town, but quite a few local artists live there. And yet, only in recent years has it become a decent market for art. Carol's work stood out among the more typical southwestern cowboys-and-Indians fare.

"Her artwork wasn't the norm for the area," said John

Lutes, a blown-glass artist of thirty years and one of Van Gogh Ear's four co-owners. "It's very different for Prescott to see someone with such a sophisticated contemporary form."

Starting in fall 2004, Carol began showing and selling her art at the gallery, where she worked as a lab assistant and also in sales as an art consultant, about fifteen hours a week for the next two years. She earned an hourly wage plus commission.

She dressed conservatively in flowing silk skirts, pants or dresses, with short heels or flats. Also, because the store sold jewelry, the sales people were encouraged to wear the wares, which Carol did in a tasteful way.

"She had a classy presentation of herself. She was very beautiful," John said. "I think she was very, very pretty, myself, but not in a flashy sort of way."

Carol's sales performance ranked reasonably well in the store. "It requires a lot of knowledge and finesse to sell art, and she was very good at it," he said.

He added that she wasn't an exceptional saleswoman, however, because she had so much distraction in her life with Steve and the family problems he created for her by calling and stopping by the store while she was trying to work.

"Steve would come in all the time, sauntering in, bringing coffee. This was when they were separated. You would just feel it. He'd walk in and you could just feel the bad vibes," Joanne recalled. "He was sucking up to her. . . . He had this way of ingratiating himself, just being the nice guy, and you just wanted to throw up. But she fell for it."

While Steve acted magnanimously toward the women, John said, Steve never paid much attention to him, acting as if he were of "finer stock" than John. "He was just that sort of haughty kind of person, you know, arrogant."

John tried not to listen to the discussions between Carol and her estranged husband, but he couldn't ignore the raised voices. Steve was more quietly firm and stern than loud, John recalled—and Carol seemed angry and vehement as well. Steve was still seeing Barb, but he would tell Carol it was over and then Carol would see them together. But more often than not, the conversations were about financial matters.

"I would never say Carol was a weak individual. I would see her as strong also," John said, noting that she used to stand her ground with Steve, "with good reason."

At this point Carol still had hope for her marriage. "She wanted it to work out. She always felt he was her soul mate and he'd learn," Joanne said. "He had to learn to be on his own. In a sense he had to work his way back to her. He had to earn her trust back, which, of course, he never did, because he never stopped seeing other women. That was horrible. It was like a knife in her chest. . . . And then there were the girls. They'd see each other because of the girls. . . . In the beginning she allowed it. They just didn't really separate."

Art—whether it was selling other artists' work or creating her own—seemed to make Carol happy, and so did her daughters.

"If her daughters were in town or visiting or came into the gallery, she always seemed very happy to be their mother and to work things out with them," John said.

To John, Carol seemed like a lovely but troubled soul who was in a constant struggle to be happy, striving to help others and make herself a better person. But as her interactions with Steve became a festering sore in the workplace, the gallery owners finally had to talk with her about the tensions he was creating.

"It went on for months and months. It was a cumulative

thing," John said. At the time, he said, "We all really liked Carol. We wished things were working out better, but it seemed like her personal life was becoming too much of a distraction for her to be able to work. It wasn't like we felt anything negative about her as a person or even as an employee—it was just tumultuous."

These issues led to her being let go from the gallery in 2007, which was ironic, given that Steve complained she wasn't working hard enough or earning enough money.

After she died, Carol's friends could see the spiritual healing she'd attempted to do through her artwork, pouring herself into producing a sizable collection with many, many pieces.

In August 2009, Van Gogh's Ear held a posthumous opening for her very best work, which hundreds of people attended. Ruth Kennedy and Debbie Wren Hill even flew in from Tennessee for it.

"I think we sold like thirteen thousand dollars that night," John Lutes said. "That's a lot for us in Prescott."

The framed art alone spanned one whole wall, starting from the front window back to the sales desk.

"Art is sort of worthless until someone buys it," John said. "The most valuable piece of art in our gallery is the one that's sold."

In late 2013, when Katherine Morris was in town, she and Joanne Frerking took two of Carol's unsigned prints and laid them side by side. As they compared their images in grays, burgundy, dark oranges and browns, they interpreted what Carol was trying to express with those forms. And one or both of them exclaimed, "Oh, my God!"

For Joanne these two pieces represented "the story of what Carol hoped would happen" between her and Steve.

It looked as if Carol had used an old X-ray as a stencil, cutting out two shapes: one appeared more male, and the other more female, but also otherworldly, with an angel-like shape—a round head and wings—that seemed very abstract to Joanne.

Carol had used the stencil to print the shapes once, then turned them over and used them again to make ghost prints, one following the other. In the first print, a heavy line connected the two. Their interpretations varied: Joanne saw the line as an arrow, while Katherine saw it as a phallic connection, or a link between their cores—a thread that extended from the angel's heart toward the male figure's center and his genitals. The male figure looked athletic to Katherine, and was leaning in a seductive stance against a shape that looked like a surfboard or warrior's shield.

In the second print Carol created two versions of each figure, one dominant and one ghost. The ghost male figure was right side up, while its darker dominant twin was flipped and heading down, as if subdued or dead. The ghost angel was right side up, and its dominant twin floated above, wings extended.

"In the first one—she was, like, stabbing at him, the part of him that was so awful to her, the sexual part, the addictions and women," Joanne said. "In the next one he was vanquished and she was floating up—her spirit—she was free. It was angel-like."

Judging by the second print, Katherine felt that Carol "was ready to leave that earthly body. She was so evolved. She was ready and she just went," ascending to heaven even stronger than she was on earth.

"That's like the good and evil, the good prevailing up to the heavens, and the dark part of your stuff you don't ever work through, it just pulls you down and you don't get to experience the other realm," she said.

Another more literal interpretation could be that Carol was portraying Steve killing her or her spirit, then sending her up to heaven.

The gallery was still selling Carol's art in 2014, with a tribute to her memory on the wall.

"We're down now to sort of the end of the stuff," Joanne said. "We may have a hundred, maybe seventy-five pieces. . . . But we truly sold . . . at least one thousand or fifteen hundred pieces. I knew it would be thrown away otherwise and I couldn't bear that."

CHAPTER 24

While Carol and Steve were living apart, but still not truly separated, Carol's friends encouraged her to stop seeing him altogether so she could move ahead on her own.

"You have so much to lose, don't do this," they told her.

And yet, she allowed herself to continue along the same downward trend, accepting Steve's apologies and promises—like the time he came over with a couple dozen roses and the deed to the Bridle Path house.

"I'm not going to [screw] up again, but if I do, here's the deed to the house," he told her. "I'm serious this time."

However, that, too, proved to be just another ruse to keep Carol tied to him.

One night before Thanksgiving Day in 2005 or 2006, Carol called Debbie Wren Hill, sobbing. Steve was with some woman, she said, and she felt sad. She missed having her family around her.

"It is so hard," she said.

Debbie was concerned about the level of despair she heard in Carol's voice. She sounded suicidal. "I am really worried about your safety," Debbie said. "I'm wondering if I need to call somebody."

Carol assured her that wasn't necessary under the circumstances. "I would never make that my kids' legacy," she said. "But without them . . . I would probably do it."

Hearing that, Debbie wanted to castrate Steve. "I wanted revenge on this man. I was just so sickened," she recalled. "But I knew that Carol was going to see her way through to the solution."

Debbie was right. In the last couple years leading up to her divorce, Carol did do the emotional work she needed to break free of Steve. But the years of conflict had taken a toll on her.

She lost quite a bit of weight, and although it's unclear when, Carol was diagnosed with Graves' disease, an autoimmune condition exacerbated by stress that can lead to an overactive thyroid gland. In women Carol's age, symptoms can include weakness and fatigue, rapid or irregular heartbeat, memory loss and chest pain. If it goes untreated, the condition can lead to depression.

"She was not only emotionally distressed, she was physically falling apart from the stress of this relationship," Debbie said.

With this stress came a change in the mood and tone of her artwork, which became much darker. "She used to use vibrant colors, and she was doing really interesting introspective work. It just became muddier," Joanne Frerking said.

As did her mood. "She just became very depressed. She didn't look good. She lost even more weight and she was thin. She was trying then to get past him and he would never leave her alone."

And that, Debbie said, is what she still holds against

Steve to this day. "The fact that he would not let her go. It was just a travesty the way he messed with her mind."

When Carol finally realized that she had to permanently let go of Steve to save herself, she filed for divorce in March 2007. And this time it stuck.

It was baby steps from there.

As Carol began to move away from Steve emotionally, her friends encouraged her to start dating and try meeting men online. Steve had certainly been doing enough of that.

So she did. According to Steve's defense team, Carol engaged in "risky behavior" by being on seven dating websites, but Katherine Morris said she knew of only one that Carol had really used: Match.com.

"I don't believe she was an active member on seven," Katherine said.

As investigators tried to identify the male DNA under Carol's fingernails, they went through her e-mails to find men she'd met online, and obtained DNA swabs from ten of them nationwide. In interviews with some of these men, they said that they, too, were using multiple dating sites so they often couldn't be sure if, when or how they'd met Carol. It appears that Carol was enrolled with dharma-match.com, Match.com, thesoulmatenetwork.com and spiritualsingles.com, often using the moniker "Carolita."

In August 2011, the defense named one of these online friends—John Stoler, of Missouri—as a possible third-party culpability candidate for Carol's murder, along with David Soule and Barb O'Non.

Among the many men pulled into the investigative web of this case, John Stoler was asked to provide a DNA swab based on what one defense attorney called Carol's "terse kiss-off" by e-mail on May 14, 2008. Stoler, however, hired an attorney and stonewalled investigators by refusing several requests for a DNA sample. Detectives never got a search warrant to force the DNA issue.

Instead, they tried to determine where he was at the time of the murder through his bank and phone records. Those records showed that someone used his ATM or credit cards between July 1 and 3 in California, at a restaurant in Toluca Lake, a Holiday Inn in North Hollywood and a McDonald's in Blythe, then someone used those cards on July 4 in Scottsdale, Arizona. The records also showed that this man called Carol's house at eight-sixteen on July 2, the morning she was murdered, from a number with the Phoenix area prefix of 602.

Another of Carol's online friends, Edward McCollough, told investigators that he and Carol dated from October 2007 to February 2008, but they were never sexual. During that time they took two ten-day trips to Hawaii and New York on his dime. But when she hinted that it would be a good idea for her to move into his home, he told her he wasn't ready for a serious relationship.

They stayed in touch because he thought she was such a great person, and they were still e-mailing until the day she was killed. Carol never spoke to him about her tenant, Jim Knapp, in anything but positive terms, which was not the case with Steve.

Edward told authorities that Carol had "disclosed more than one episode" in which Steve "'went off' in a way where Carol was afraid for her physical safety," including one time a year earlier when she'd insisted on meeting Steve in a public place because of such concerns, Sergeant Tom Boelts wrote in his report.

CHAPTER 25

Once the divorce battle was fully under way, Carol kept closer track of Steve's spending and expressed her frustrations by e-mail. She conveyed her particular disapproval on October 10, 2007, their wedding anniversary.

Steve had e-mailed her to complain about the debt he was accruing by covering her bills, the girls' expenses and his own. Despite his monthly take-home pay of $9,000 to $12,000, he wrote, he was still going into debt by $5,000 to $9,000 a month. These figures seemed to vary widely over time, depending on when and to whom he was speaking.

In a financial affidavit he filed during the divorce, he claimed this amount was even higher—Steve contended that he was spending $17,000 more than he earned every month, and had amassed a total personal debt of $1.4 million.

Listing his expenses, he said he had to pay income taxes, interest on their jointly acquired credit card debt, the principal and interest on a loan he'd borrowed against his 401(k), Katie's student loan and tuition payments, and the girls' health insurance, car payments and other basic living costs. And after that, he still had to pay Carol's mortgages, utilities, her car, health and life insurance policies, and $700 a month in "temporary 'support.'"

Carol came back with details backing up her argument that his discretionary spending was more the problem. Since they'd come to an interim financial agreement in April 2007, she wrote, Steve had traveled to St. Maarten (she assumed he went with Barb O'Non, but it may well have been with Leslie Thomas). He'd also taken a pleasure trip to Zurich and Italy, to which he'd added an expensive three-day stay in New York City, treating the girls to Broadway shows and dinners. And then he paid for a "pricey family reunion" at the Albedor, a seventeen-thousand-square-foot historic vacation rental home with fourteen bedrooms in the Adirondacks.

Furthermore, she wrote, he leased a new BMW for Katie, who was a sophomore, treated his dad and brothers to a week of fun at the Hassayampa Golf Club and took the girls on numerous shopping trips in Phoenix. Steve was also buying himself all kinds of expensive athletic equipment, clothing and accessories. And he'd withdrawn so much cash in October that he'd pushed up the minimum payment on one credit card from $570 to $900 a month, only a month after driving up the interest rate from 9.29 percent to 24.24 percent.

All of this sounds like the wonderful, richly blessed, privileged lifestyle that would naturally accrue to a man who makes the income you have made for the past seven or eight years, she wrote. *You should be entitled to do all of these things—because you have earned it and you can.*

Nonetheless, she wrote, all of this "financial irresponsibility" would not exempt him from a reasonable settlement for spousal maintenance.

* * *

Due to a confluence of factors, the worst financial crisis since the Great Depression began to hit the United States in mid-2007, resulting in huge stock market losses that led to the Great Recession, all of which significantly decreased Steve's income.

And yet, in the last two months of 2007, when Steve was borrowing $20,000 a month from his father to "pay bills," he was still frequenting the same upscale hotels and resorts he loved and still spending $2,444 at a time to play golf.

One of Steve's favorite self-indulgences was to stay at the exclusive Phoenician resort in Phoenix, where he spent more than $1,250 in the first two weeks of December 1, 2007. He also enjoyed the Westin chain of resorts, where he spent an additional $787 later that month. In January 2008, he spent $4,465 more at a Westin resort and spa, and hundreds more on dinners at Olive & Ivy in Scottsdale.

"He did that as a routine," said Mike Sechez, the prosecution investigator. "His wife was never there." Steve also didn't keep his fancy hotel stays to just Arizona. He was flying around the country "just to have sex with women."

"He was one sick customer. He was trying to win the girls away, to get Carol, that way," Joanne Frerking said. "Then it got ugly. They were going through arbitration, to try to save money . . . but did he stop spending? No."

All this time Carol was having problems making ends meet. She worked several jobs, but she was still struggling even with the "temporary support" Steve sent her before the divorce was finalized. She started the counseling gig at Pia's Place in late February 2008, and she worked Fridays in the print lab at Yavapai College.

"She knew she was in a very bad financial situation and he wasn't giving," Joanne said. "It was just getting so ugly and so awful, it was taking her down too, and Charlotte was sort of turning against her."

On November 19, 2007, Carol texted Steve that she was **overwhelmed by the $500,000 of debt** she was supposed to pay off, and also by knowing that she couldn't make a living with her current work situation. *And you don't think it's reasonable to help me for even as many years as you were having affairs and lying to me about it,* she wrote. She added that she needed to stop arguing with him about this, because it was harming both of them.

But those arguments only escalated. On February 25, 2008, Steve complained that he was out of money, and he blamed her. *The sand has run out, Carol,* he said in an email. *Wake up. . . . At this point we're here because of you. You alone.*

Noting that he'd borrowed $40,000 from his father in November and December, he said he was awaiting a tax refund check in April, but *until then, all I have is whatever I can borrow.* And yet, even when he was allegedly so cash strapped, he still spent at least two nights that month at the Phoenician, at $493 and $506 a night.

In March and May 2008, Steve borrowed an additional $20,000 from his father, continuing to complain that Carol was coming out of the deal better than he was. *I will not be pushed any further, Carol,* he wrote on June 14, 2008, still fighting even after the divorce agreement had been finalized. *You have extracted all you will extract from me.*

He claimed that his financial state was far worse than hers, because she got "to start clean," living off a settlement based on his best income year ever in 2007, while he tried to "dig out of a staggering hole" and pay $400,000 to send their daughters to college.

Steve's trading performance at UBS reached more than $1 million that year, ranking at the highest or second-highest level among his fellow brokers, who earned, on average, $700,000 or $800,000 in commissions that year.

But Steve's gripes rang empty in the face of his continued hypocritical overspending. Although his income dropped significantly in the months of 2008 before Carol's murder, Steve still spent $13,740 on stays at resort hotels, and $3,200 more in the subsequent four months. Between November 2007 and September 2008, he spent $9,440 on golf alone, as he fell deeper and deeper into debt.

CHAPTER 26

The last time Carol saw her mother was Thanksgiving in 2007, when Ruth flew up to Prescott and stayed in the guesthouse. They drove out to Sedona for the day, where they had lunch and visited a little chapel together.

Carol took photos all day—handing over her camera at one point to someone they met on a trail to capture mother and daughter. She later sent Ruth an entire photo album of their adventure, which Ruth still cherishes today.

"[We] had a wonderful day together," she said.

They had five for Thanksgiving dinner that year at Bridle Path, including Charlotte, Katie and her boyfriend.

During the visit Carol told her mother that Steve had been in the house when she wasn't there, even though he didn't have a key.

"I'll show you how he comes in," she told Ruth as she led her to the back room that had been Charlotte's bedroom, which Carol was just starting to use as her office. At the time the room was bare, with nothing but a bookcase, computer and chair.

Carol pointed to the window, where she said Steve had been climbing in. "He's never taken anything," she said.

"You can put a stick in that window and he wouldn't be able to open it," Ruth suggested.

But to the best of Ruth's knowledge, her daughter never took her advice. "I don't think she thought that he was ever capable of doing something like that," she said in 2014, referring to Carol's murder.

Based on her conversations with Carol in her last months, Ruth could see that her daughter was terribly anxious about her finances.

"She was not making enough money to keep that house up, even though she was working full-time," she said.

Carol tried to get rehired at Prescott College, Ruth said, but she was told she couldn't rejoin the faculty without a Ph.D.

"Her whole focus in her life was, in those later years, to keep that house so Katie and Charlotte would have a place to come home to, because she'd had a place to come home to, and that was one of her guiding principles," Ruth said. "She designed the house. She just wanted it for them. And that was such a sorrow to her, I know, that she couldn't do it."

When Carol called her mother each night, she often cried. It was upsetting for Ruth to hear her daughter so unhappy and yet be too far away to be able to do anything more to comfort her.

Carol met up with her friend Katherine Morris for a spiritual retreat at La Casa de Maria in Santa Barbara, California, in late January 2008.

Just back from a break in the activities, Carol told Katherine about some bad news she'd just gotten from a friend she'd known for years.

"I just got an awful, awful call from Jim Knapp that he's got this cancer," she said. "My heart is just so hurt for him."

After further discussion Carol said, "He's going to move into the guesthouse. I need the money."

Every morning of the retreat, Katherine drove into town to get a cup of strong coffee. One morning she saw Carol out walking so she stopped to see if she could pick up a cup for her, too. Carol asked for so many special ingredients in her double latte that Katherine had to write them down.

When Katherine delivered the latte, Carol thanked her effusively and tried to pay her for it, but Katherine said that wasn't necessary. Carol seemed so grateful, but it really wasn't that big a deal to Katherine.

Later that morning, February 2, when they were going around the circle and sharing with the others at the retreat, Katherine came to understand Carol's reaction.

Breaking down in tears, Carol said, "That's why, Katherine, when you bought me a latte this morning, I was overjoyed, overwhelmed, because I don't even have enough money to buy myself a coffee. Until Steve puts my money in the account, I don't even know how I'm going to get gas to drive back to Prescott." Carol explained that the money was due the day before, but Steve was late making the deposit.

Katherine had no idea. She was floored. Infuriated, in fact. This outburst was a "big eye-opener." She'd had no idea that Carol was so financially dependent on Steve.

Carol said she was going to have a garage sale and sell a golf club or set of clubs he'd given her, and had stacked the clubs with some other sale items in the back bedroom. Sometime later Katherine recalled Carol telling her that

Steve had taken them back and Carol was upset that she couldn't sell them.

As they talked about how hard her life was and how difficult the divorce had been for her, Carol said, "And sometimes, Kat, I don't even feel safe in my own home."

Looking back, Katherine inferred from that comment that Carol was referring to Steve, but she didn't press her. Today she wishes she had.

Carol went further in discussing these fears with her friend Sally Butler, who later recounted to investigators a similar conversation in which Carol said Steve had been sending her some very erratic e-mails—professing his love in one and saying horrible things to her in the next. To keep from feeling like she was going crazy, Carol read some of the e-mails to Sally.

Around this same time Carol found a close friend and confidant in Jim Knapp, who moved into the guesthouse around February. Carol liked having a man there, and although she needed help with her finances, it's unclear whether Jim ever paid her any rent, because he had financial troubles of his own.

"Carol, being the wonderful helper type, brought him in," Debbie said. "She needed a friend, needed someone to commiserate with her. . . . They would have a glass of wine in the evenings and help each other through hard times. And if he had feelings for her, it didn't get in the way of a friendship."

Jim and Carol had known each other since their kids were young; Charlotte and Jay, Jim's older boy, had attended the same school. More recently, Jim had done some house-sitting for Carol.

After a dozen years of marriage, Jim and his wife, Ann

Saxerud, had divorced in January 2007, and were going through child custody battles in mediation. As Carol went through her own struggles, she and Jim had plenty of mutual woes to discuss.

In August 2007, he'd been exploring the purchase of a Maui Wowi Hawaiian Coffees & Smoothies franchise in Prescott. He and the owner had settled on a price of $260,000, and Jim said he was talking to his accountant and prospective investors to move forward. In discussions with corporate representatives, Jim mentioned Carol as a manager who would run the store and restaurant operations and also help expand the business.

The owner had to close the store in November 2007, because his employees quit after hearing it was already sold, but Jim said he was still enthusiastic about buying it. Shortly thereafter, however, Jim e-mailed the owner, informing him that he had skin cancer, saying that he was about to have surgery to "excise the tumor" and to "graft it to patch it." He also mentioned that Carol's divorce settlement was coming in three weeks, as if she was going to be financially involved in the franchise deal.

But at the end of February 2008, right around the time that he moved into the guesthouse, Jim backed out of the sale.

I am still VERY INTERESTED, but I'm not healthy enough to do it, he wrote to the franchise reps. *Maybe in a year or two after I bounce back.*

Carol Walden, the area franchise developer, later concluded that Jim was more talk than money. "He was pretty bold in his assertions but he wasn't able to back them up," she later testified.

Asked if Jim ever told her that Carol Kennedy was his financial backer, Carol Walden replied, "No, he did not."

By the time Carol was killed, Jim had just lost his job as a fund-raiser for Project Insight, Inc., a nonprofit that provided services for people with special needs. He also had racked up nearly $50,000 in medical bills from the Mayo Clinic, where Carol often drove him for appointments.

When Jim Knapp moved in with Carol, it was right around the time he broke up with Suzanna Wilson (pseudonym), a physical therapist from Montana he'd met on eHarmony, the online dating site, in September 2007.

Jim and Suzanna met face-to-face for the first time that October, when she used her frequent-flyer miles to fly into Phoenix. He'd told her he had problems with his bowel, but his eHarmony photo and profile made him look and sound healthier than he really was. The very pale and out-of-shape man she met that weekend was not who or what she'd been expecting. Nonetheless, she spent three days with him in Prescott, where she met his sons and ex-wife at a football game. He seemed quite manic at times and she enjoyed his sense of humor.

"He was funny, bright, witty," she later testified.

They saw each other again in November on her home turf in Montana, where she paid for him to fly in for a three-day weekend because he said he didn't have any money. This time he seemed lethargic and really out of it, but he surprised her with something else.

On the last day of the trip, as they were taking a walk to Glacier National Park, he announced his intentions. "I really, really want to marry you," he said.

Suzanna was taken aback. "This is a bit premature," she replied. "I need more time to get to know you."

For their next rendezvous, they planned to meet in

Kona, on the Big Island of Hawaii, a trip for which they both bought their own plane tickets.

Jim acted more mentally "with it" on this trip, and although Suzanna was exhausted after the flight, he insisted on taking her on a scavenger hunt. He led her along a path of white stones, laid out on a black lava sand beach, then excitedly took her to collect her prize: a handmade ring with a yellow topaz-colored stone.

The next day, when she met his brother, Jim introduced her as his fiancée. She'd been having gallbladder attacks before flying to Hawaii, and she ended up in the ER that night, vomiting.

After she recovered, they went to the beach, where she went swimming. And even though he seemed lethargic and out of it again that day, he still managed to be romantic. He drew a love note for her in the sand: *Jimmy James loves [Suzanna]*.

Jim told Suzanna he was taking medication for pain related to ulcers and his lower bowels, as well as for anxiety, depression and to help him sleep. She thought that he was overly self-medicating, and that it was strange the way he kept disappearing for hours during the day, but she never said anything to him about it. She decided to wait until she got home, then end the relationship.

Once she was back in Montana, she called his brother, Bobby, to talk about Jim's drug use. Bobby told her that Jim had been in rehab in the past.

The day after she had her gallbladder surgery, Jim called to report that a doctor had told him that a mole on his cheek was cancerous and he was dying.

"Because he told me that he was a PA, a physician's assistant, I believed him," she testified later. "And he said he knew that this was really dangerous."

When Jim found out that Suzanna had talked with his brother about his drug issues, he was very angry and accused her of going behind his back. When she told him she was breaking up with him, he got even more angry, accusing her of abandoning him when he needed her the most.

Then the angry e-mails started. *You're not getting off that easy,* he wrote in one of his last e-mails to her.

He didn't elaborate, which frightened her. "I didn't know what that meant," she testified. "It just left me hanging. I felt scared. I didn't know if he was going to come up and shoot me. I didn't know if he was going to stalk me. I had no idea what was happening."

Still, she wasn't so scared that she felt she needed to report the remark to police. She stopped responding to his e-mails, but he continued to write her and her family, asking for money to help with medical bills because he was dying of cancer.

CHAPTER 27

In late May 2008, Carol called out to her closest friends for help. Right before her divorce trial she sent out a group message, asking them to please think of her on the Wednesday and Thursday of that week, when she expected to be in court. Steve had forced them to go to trial by not accepting her last two counterproposals.

Most of you know that I have lived in a kind of self-inflicted, unconscious relationship-hell for the past many years, she wrote, noting that she'd filed for divorce after finally waking from this "trance state of self-torture."

Steve is fighting me over the simplest of issues, and he is truly one of the smartest and most persuasive people I know, so I am more than a bit nervous about my ability to stay unwaveringly grounded in my own truth and integrity and not devolve into fear & anxiety.

Underscoring that asking for help was something she'd only recently learned how to do, she requested that they think of her while they did what they loved most, then to write her passionate and enthusiastic descriptions about it. Her e-mail closed with the repeated exclamation of "thank you!" in multicolored fonts, followed by a string of capital *O*'s and *X*'s.

After the brief trial was over, Carol sent out an update, thanking them for the inspiring and overwhelming "outpouring of love" and joyous energy she'd received—more, in fact, than she'd felt in her entire life, which filled her with gratitude. Even her clients at Pia's surprised her with a plethora of gifts, from poems to drawings, flowers and hugs. All of this, she wrote, helped her through the settlement talks, feeling "held and guided."

I got a clear vision of how it had taken me not only 25 years to position myself for this moment in time, it had taken lifetimes! she wrote.

As she felt waves of fear and anxiety coming, she told them, she felt herself opening up to accept rather than resist the feelings as she asked for help to see what she hadn't been able to see before—what her part and responsibility had been in her own emotional pain. It had been a process, she said, but she felt as if she'd reached a new place.

This week, she wrote, was her time to win. She went on to describe her feelings of triumph—feelings that some close to Carol suggested could have been her downfall in the end: Carol had finally found the strength to say no to Steve. She would not continue this struggle, she said, and she would not prolong this relentless, torturous relationship anymore. And that, they say, may have been too much for Steve to bear.

On May 28, Carol described in a subsequent e-mail how she walked into court, strong, to face her old fears and old wounds, her "self-lies about unworthiness." She found a way to make it up to her inner child for all the years she'd "abandoned and betrayed" her. Carol had learned how to love that inner child, to love herself and to stand up to her fears.

Haggling to the end, Steve made a concession he hadn't been willing to make before, and, in turn, he got Carol to agree to pay him child support. Within a couple of hours, they were able to reach a settlement without going to trial and calling witnesses.

As part of the agreement, Carol would have to pay off her credit card balance, which was $32,000 in June 2008, as well as the full $12,500 balance on one of Steve's cards, and $20,000 on another, the last of which she paid in June. She also assumed the liability for the Bridle Path mortgages as well as a home equity line that Steve had taken out in his "sole and separate name," which she subsequently wrote to him that he'd "succeeded in sticking [her] with, rendering Bridle Path an unsalable albatross."

Steve had refinanced the Bridle Path house in June 2003 for $408,000 and took out a second mortgage for $70,000 in January 2004. At some point he also took out a second mortgage on his condo for $59,000.

During a long series of e-mails, Steve wrote her back on June 15, 2008—Father's Day—that while he thought she was being "incredibly grasping and unreasonable" and "self-absorbed," he viewed her actions from a position of compassion. He believed she was actually trying not to let go of him, that she was acting out of "some deeper fear of being finished with each other." Despite his many years of acting to the contrary, he contended, he was just *as uninterested in hanging onto our old attachment as I remain open to the possibility of something new.*

Either way, he was done arguing. *Please let this marriage be over,* he pleaded. He closed by saying that he'd tried calling her twice on Father's Day, during which he thought of her "with gratitude."

As part of the settlement, Carol was to receive Steve's 401(k) payout, which turned out to be $197,367 before taxes and penalties for early withdrawal, and netted her $149,334 after they split the excess over $180,000. But Carol didn't see how she was going to make it after having to pay income tax on that sum on top of covering the credit card balances.

After their day in court, Carol drove out to Watson Lake. There, she told friends, she gazed at the water, the sky, the birds and the clouds, and she wept—"with deep sadness, huge grief, profound relief and uncontrollable joy." She'd finally managed to step up and love herself. As she said in an e-mail, *It was huge!*

Carol called Katherine from the lake, crying. "I love myself too much to lose myself to Steve," she said.

It seemed, at last, that the prolonged dissolution was finally resolved. Or so she thought.

A few weeks later, on June 18, Carol dropped off a bundle of clothes to sell at a friend's resale clothing boutique, Whatever Was. Teary and depressed, she explained that she was worried about her finances and the credit card debt hanging over her, not to mention that her youngest daughter had chosen to live with Steve over her.

Whatever her friend Linda Harrison couldn't sell at the shop, Carol said, she would try to sell at her upcoming yard sale. The two women knew each other through the store, and also from Unity Church in Prescott.

Linda often saw Steve having coffee at least once a day at the Wild Iris, a coffee shop next door to her boutique.

* * *

Carol told friends she was surprised to learn that Steve had been able to take out the second mortgage on Bridle Path without her knowledge. The house was still in her name even though he'd been making the payments. It was basically underwater, she said, and she was going to have to move out because she couldn't afford to make the payments. Carol was unable to qualify to take over the mortgages and credit line because of her poor credit rating.

As Carol wrote her divorce accountant on June 30, 2008: *It's upside down, because of the second [mortgage] in Steve's name that got given to me as an encumbrance on the property, so I can't sell it in this market.*

As Carol put it to Joanne Frerking, "I am going to have to just have a yard sale and walk away, and go do something somewhere. I don't know what."

A couple of days before the murder, Joanne ran into Carol at Costco and was concerned by her appearance.

"She was just distraught and upset, and she didn't look good," she recalled. "She looked sort of disheveled. She looked skinny. She looked worn. She didn't have the bright light Carol used to have."

Just as Carol would tell Katherine, she told Joanne that she'd just seen Steve and he was trying to get back together with her.

"Steve was over last night," she said. "He just doesn't get it."

One of Carol's neighbors later told Joanne that within a day or two of the murder, she was walking her dogs when she heard someone crying. It was Carol, out for a run. Carol stopped and they chatted.

"He said he wants us to get married again," Carol said. "He just doesn't get it."

Married in 1982, Carol Kennedy and Steve DeMocker were very much in love and considered each other "soul mates."
(Photo by Debbie Wren Hill)

Soon after the family send-off at the airport for Katie, Carol told her mother that Steve had texted her, asking to meet for coffee.

"Carol, don't go," Ruth pleaded. "Don't be a fool. He's going to try to sweet-talk you."

Carol didn't bring up the coffee date again, so Ruth was surprised to learn years later that her daughter had actually met up with Steve. "What an insane—after the divorce went through? Oh, gosh. He never gave up on his charm, did he?"

Carol hiking in Ojai, California, around 1985, before she and Steve had children.
(Photo by Debbie Wren Hill)

CHAPTER 28

On July 2, the day Carol was murdered, Barb O'Non spoke with Steve by phone. Their conversation, she recounted later, was "warm and friendly."

She remembered this well, because that day was also her son's seventeenth birthday. After having her nails done, she and her son celebrated his special day at Buffalo Wild Wings restaurant in Phoenix before heading home to Anthem.

She texted Steve at 8:46 P.M., as soon as she got home, but she could tell that he didn't open the message. Like Renee, she immediately thought he was "probably with another woman again somewhere," because it wasn't like him not to respond to her text right away.

In her experience Steve was never without his cell phone. It was always on and he took it everywhere. "I don't recall a time ever in the years that I was with him, the many years, that the phone was ever left unattended or away from him. I remember once watching him take it into a shower," she later testified.

Steve called her at 12:14 A.M. on July 3, but she didn't

Five-year-old Carol Kennedy and her mother, Ruth, in 1959. *(Photo by A.G. Kennedy)*

Carol and her brother, John, on his high-school graduatio in 1970. *(Photo by A.G. Kennedy)*

Prescott College, where Steve earned a bachelor's degree,
taught sociology and went on to become dean.
Carol taught "Yoga Psychology" and "Dream Work" there as well.
(Photo by author)

Steve holding their first daughter, Katie, as an infant in Prescott.
(Photo by Debbie Wren Hill)

In 1992, Steve built a small hay bale house on Bridle Path, which later became the guesthouse. *(Photo by Rich Robertson)*

Carol designed the main house on Bridle Path, into which the family of four had moved by 1997. *(Photo by Rich Robertson)*

A majestic view of Granite Mountain from Williamson Valley Road, about a mile from the house. *(Photo by Sue Willoughby)*

Carol worked in sales and also showed her own art at
Van Gogh's Ear gallery on Whiskey Row. *(Photo by author)*

Just before her death, Carol gathered some of her artwork
in preparation for a garage sale. *(Photo by Rich Robertson)*

Carol and her close friend and former student, Katherine Morris, spoke by phone just hours before Carol was murdered. *(Photo by Jason Hales)*

A private celebration of Carol's life, just for friends and family, was held in Sedona. *(Photo by Katherine Morris)*

Ruth and John Kennedy flew in from Nashville to attend the ceremony. *(Photo by Katherine Morris)*

Sheriff's detectives said they found bike tire imprints and shoe prints similar to Steve's on the ranch land side of this Glenshandra Drive trailhead.
(Photo by Sue Willoughby)

Close-up of the barbed-wire fence, gate and decomposed granite sand at the Glenshandra trailhead.
(Photo by Sue Willoughby)

Steve claimed he went riding on a different trail, here at the end of Love Lane, two miles west of the house.
(Photo by Rich Robertson)

Authorities said Steve put his bike in some bushes, stepped over this gate, which he'd built to keep out wild animals, and entered Carol's house. *(Photo by Rich Robertson)*

The front and rear tires of Steve's trail bike had different treads. He said the rear got a flat the night of the murder. *(Photo by Rich Robertson)*

The defense argued that Steve's bike tires were a very common brand and model: the WTB (Wilderness Trail Bike) VelociRaptor. *(Photo by Rich Robertson)*

Sheriff's detectives bought a golf club similar to what was believed to be the murder weapon: a Callaway Big Bertha Steelhead III #7. *(Photo by Rich Robertson)*

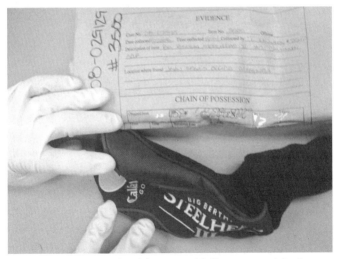

Steve gave his Big Bertha club cover to his first attorney, John Sears, to secure. Sears held onto it until Steve was arrested. *(Photo by Rich Robertson)*

Investigators could tell from the blood spatter pattern around this ladder and on some bookshelves that they'd been moved after Carol was killed.
(Photo by Rich Robertson)

Carol's former tenant, Jim Knapp, was found fatally shot in this closet six months after her murder. Authorities ruled it a suicide.
(Photo by Prescott Police Department)

The courthouse in downtown Prescott, across from Whiskey Row.
(Photo by author)

Judge Thomas B. Lindberg

Judge Thomas Lindberg collapsed from a brain tumor in June 2010,
just a week into the first trial, and had to step down.
(Photo by Les Stukenberg/The Daily Courier)

Prosecutor Joe Butner was lead counsel during the first trial. He later retired and became a judge. *(Photo by Les Stukenberg/ The Daily Courier)*

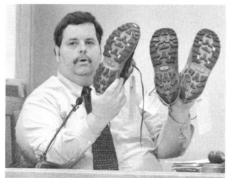

FBI forensic examiner Eric Gilkerson said the Pikes Peak was one of three models of La Sportiva athletic shoes that "could have made" the imprints found by investigators. *(Photo by Les Stukenberg/ The Daily Courier)*

Yavapai County Attorney Sheila Polk's office was effectively put on trial in the "Docugate" scandal, which delayed the second trial for about a year. *(Photo by Les Stukenberg/ The Daily Courier)*

Yavapai County Sheriff Scott Mascher testified that Steve asked if he was a suspect even before Carol's death was deemed a homicide. *(Photo by Les Stukenberg/ The Daily Courier)*

Medical Examiner Philip Keen was criticized for transporting Carol's body to Phoenix in the back of his pickup truck. *(Photo by Les Stukenberg/ The Daily Courier)*

Steve's mother, Janice "Jan" DeMocker, was granted immunity before testifying about the transfer of Carol's life insurance money to pay Steve's first defense team. *(Photo by Les Stukenberg/ The Daily Courier)*

Prosecutor Jeff Paupore used the "exemplar" golf club
and a rolled-up rug to reenact Carol's fatal beating
during his dramatic closing argument.
(Photo by Les Stukenberg/ The Daily Courier)

Steve's second defense team: Attorneys Craig Williams (from left)
and Greg Parzych, and investigator Rich Robertson.
(Photo by Les Stukenberg/The Daily Courier)

Judge Gary E. Donahue presided over the second trial and sentencing.
(Photo by Les Stukenberg/The Daily Courier)

Steve DeMocker was sentenced to life plus twenty-one years in prison.
(Photo by Les Stukenberg/ The Daily Courier)

Steve is serving his sentence at the state prison in Florence, Arizona. *(Photo by Arizona Department of Corrections)*

Carol dancing at a Touch Drawing gathering on Whidbey Island, Washington. *(Photo by Deborah Koff-Chapin)*

answer because she was asleep. She didn't hear the phone ring or realize he'd called until later.

She learned of Carol's death later that morning, in a six forty-five call on her way to work. John Farmer, a coworker from the UBS office in Prescott, told her that sheriff's detectives were there, looking to talk to Steve. John called back moments later, informing her that "Carol had been found dead in her home." Stunned, Barb pulled over to process the news.

Minutes later, Barb heard from an attorney friend who called to tease her that the police had descended on the UBS office, and had put up crime scene tape, because she and Steve had been arguing over the dissolution of their business partnership. Once she told him the true nature of the detectives' visit and asked if he thought she needed an attorney, he called back with the name of a Phoenix lawyer he'd contacted on her behalf.

"You need to call him now," he said. "He's waiting to see you."

When Steve called her that afternoon, she told him she was going to consult with an attorney.

"Why?" he asked.

"Because I could be seen as a suspect," she said.

"You couldn't have murdered Carol any more than I could have," he said. "Anyway, it was an accident. There was a ladder there and she fell. It was an accident."

That same day, Barb hired attorney Michael Terribile, who advised her not to talk to law enforcement until they stated in writing that she was not a suspect. The county attorney's office initially refused to do this; Detective Doug Brown said they were trying to interview her to rule her out as a suspect because Steve or one of his family members had indicated that she might be involved somehow in the murder. But, ultimately, Brown was able to get the prosecution to write a letter saying that Barb was not a target of the investigation, which enabled him to schedule an interview with her for July 12.

The fact that Barb hired her own attorney raised a few eyebrows, including Katie DeMocker's. In talking with Renee and Katherine, who then relayed these conversations to investigators, Katie said that if her father had wanted to kill Carol, he would have done so before finalizing the divorce, and he also would have planned it better. Because of his imminent split with Barb over the client list and accounts, Katie suggested that Barb could have killed Carol because she'd always wanted to be with Steve. If Barb made it look like Steve did the murder, then she would also get to keep his entire $110 million portfolio.

Brown subsequently investigated Barb's alibi, confirming through her cell phone records her whereabouts on the night of the murder. Both her text to Steve and his call to her pinged off the cell tower near her house in Anthem.

Barb told Brown that Steve had tried to persuade her not to go through with their financial split, saying she wouldn't be able to make it on her own. She also recalled that Steve had been furious with Carol during the divorce proceedings and had said several times that he'd wished Carol were dead. Barb said she didn't think he was joking.

Two years later, when Barb testified at the pretrial hearing, she changed her story, saying that Steve had made comments several times that "he thought that they would all be better off if [Carol] were dead. I didn't take him seriously." She couldn't remember the context, but she said, "There were instances where he was unhappy with Carol around the children, and he thought that they would be better off if the kids were just with him."

She told Brown that Steve's habit of spending more than he earned, and specifically his frequent stays at the Phoenician, had been an issue in their personal relationship as well.

She also raised another curious tidbit. About six months earlier, she said, Steve had begun injecting himself daily with HGH (human growth hormone), and was also getting testosterone shots. He made an appointment for Barb to see his naturopathic doctor so she could get HGH injections, too, but she refused.

Because of tensions relating to their split, Barb tried to cut off most of her personal contact with Steve. But on June 27, 2008, as they were finalizing their settlement and division of clients, Steve wanted to meet for dinner at the Westin Kierland Resort.

"He wasn't happy about either [our business or personal] relationship ending, and I was trying to keep things on a friendly note," she testified, adding that she really wanted to break personal and professional contact with Steve after that.

Instead, they ended up spending that Friday night together at a hotel. She blamed her lack of resolve on too much alcohol. The way Barb told the story in court later, it had an uncanny parallel to Steve's meeting with Carol and the girls at the airport that Saturday, and his subsequent coffee meeting with Carol that Sunday.

"The dinner was very friendly," Barb said. "It was the way it used to be. It was warm. . . . It was the first time in many, many days, weeks and months that we'd had friendly conversation."

The next morning when they woke up, Barb told him she was concerned to see him looking flushed, but he said he always looked like that. He told her, *[the HGH was] a miracle drug that helped with mental acuity, pains and made his workouts much better,* Brown wrote in his report.

Barb had been intent on talking to him that morning about breaking off contact for a while, but Steve was distracted, texting with Carol about going shopping with the family before heading to the airport for Katie's send-off. This, Barb said later, left her feeling "pretty disgusted" with herself.

"I felt as though I had been . . . fooled one more time," she testified in 2013, that "all of the flirtatious, charming, seductive talk over the night before was really nothing but talk."

She'd tried repeatedly to break up with him in the past, but he always managed to talk her out of it, telling her how important she was and that he was sorry.

"He would be in tears. He would tell me I was all that mattered, that it was a terrible mistake he had made. It meant nothing. He would spend the rest of his life making it up to me."

The tears always seemed to work on her. Parting with Steve was so difficult that she started seeing a therapist to help her do it.

A couple of weeks after Carol's murder, Steve asked Barb to go hiking and camping with him near Durango, Colorado, but she declined.

"I was really trying to be done with the relationship," she said later, but he was trying to save it, to "fix things between us. He wanted to talk. He wanted to go camping, and we never went camping. I thought it was odd."

"You didn't think Steve was going to take you up in the

mountains and kill you, did you?" defense attorney John
Sears asked during the 2010 pretrial hearing.

"I didn't know what the purpose was. I wasn't going to
go up into the mountains with Steve at that time."

"You weren't afraid of Steve, then, were you?"

"I was. At that time I was."

Prosecutor Joe Butner asked Barb why Steve's camping
invitation was more worrisome in light of Carol's recent
murder.

"Because I had no idea what happened, and I wasn't
going to place myself at that time in a position where—
we've already established . . . I am not an outdoors person.
I wouldn't know how to take care of myself outside, out of
doors. . . . I wasn't willing to go camping with him."

Sears argued that much of Barb's testimony at the pretrial hearing should be inadmissible at trial because it was
too prejudicial. Butner disagreed, arguing that "this is
highly probative of the kind of pressure that he was experiencing when he cracked and killed his wife."

Two weeks after the camping invitation, Barb went out
to La Jolla, California, to get away from everything going
on in Prescott. She was horrified by what had happened to
Carol and wanted some quiet alone time.

Steve continued to insist that they really needed to talk;
he just didn't want to do it in Arizona. He flew out to meet
her at the hotel, where she'd been staying for the past week,
arriving the day before she was planning to leave. They
had dinner, then went back to her room.

Given that she'd turned down his camping offer, Barb
could not explain later why she'd agreed to let him join

her in La Jolla so soon afterward. "I don't understand it myself," she said.

By now Steve was no longer able to claim that Carol's death was an accident. "It was obvious, at that point, that it was a homicide," she said. Steve told her he didn't kill Carol and was worried about being falsely accused and arrested for her murder.

It was then that he told her where he'd been the night Carol was killed, recounting a story somewhat similar to what he'd told law enforcement, but also similar to the story Jake first told investigators, which Steve denied.

Steve told Barb that he was at the fitness center, intending to finish his workout that night after the aborted bike ride. He was going to use the club phone to call Charlotte when he realized he had a spare cell battery in the car. So he went out to his BMW, loaded the battery into the phone and called his daughter, who reminded him that they were supposed to have dinner together that night.

"He said he had forgotten that," Barb said.

As Barb listened to his story, parts of it sounded fishy. She'd done regular workouts with him in the past and had never known him to let his phone go dead or to find himself without a spare battery. He rarely, if ever, had gone for a bike ride while he was living at Alpine Meadows. Plus he made such a big deal about the physical exertion it took to get the bike back to the car with a flat tire, it didn't make sense that he'd go for a workout after all that. She also doubted his forgotten-dinner explanation.

"Charlotte was very important to both of her parents, and at that time, in my opinion, there's no way that Steve would forget he had a dinner with Charlotte," she said.

Steve had been with other women during the course of their relationship, including Carol. Barb had heard or suspected that he was involved with Renee, but he always claimed that she was simply his masseuse and friend. While Barb and Steve were talking in La Jolla, she asked him about Renee again. This time he acknowledged sleeping with her and apologized, just as he had more than half-a-dozen other times after having sex with other women.

"He told me that it was a huge mistake and that he had only slept with her once, and it was all an error, and that it was over, and that [Renee] was upset." None of this turned out to be true, Barb said, but his apology was tearful, "warm and genuine."

In early October 2008, just as UBS management was finalizing the split between them, Steve proposed to Barb one last time while they were on her back porch in Anthem.

"He said that he had learned a lot about what he wanted out of life, and that the business didn't matter, that none of it mattered, that he wanted to be together, and we could go wherever I wanted and do whatever I wanted, but that we could get married," she said later. "I don't really recall how I answered him. I don't think I did."

CHAPTER 29

On October 8, 2008, a *Daily Courier* article ran a story with this headline: POLICE HOPE TO MAKE ARREST IN KENNEDY MURDER SOON.

The DeMocker family had been feeling the walls closing in on Steve because the detectives had never said they were looking at any other suspects. But after reading this article online, Steve's mother got excited, thinking that investigators had finally settled on another suspect to arrest.

They have found the right person, she thought.

Then she talked to Steve. "So they are going to arrest somebody," she said. "Have they found a suspect?"

Steve knew better. "I think they are planning to arrest me," he said.

Two weeks later, Steve surprised Carol's mother with a call. Ruth had invited Katie and Charlotte down for Thanksgiving, and they were planning to come. But Steve told

Ruth that he was concerned she might not be up to having the girls stay with her and cooking them a big meal.

Still miffed that he hadn't offered his condolences, Ruth did not take kindly to Steve's feigned "concern."

"Of course I'm up for having them here," she told him. "I love them and I want them to come."

That remark sent Steve into a monologue about his struggles with his own grief, which Ruth did not believe. The whole call seemed entirely manipulative to her. It was the only time she could remember him calling her, other than when he was leaving A.G. Edwards for UBS and he asked if he could take her and her husband's account with him.

The next morning, on October 23, Lieutenant Dave Rhodes, Sergeant Luis Huante and Detective John McDormett showed up at the UBS office on Camelback Road in Phoenix to talk to Steve.

Announcing that they had search warrants for the office and Steve's condo, Huante read Steve his Miranda rights. They patted him down, then took him into a room to question him.

Their first query was about the golf club head cover. "It was laying on a shelf in the garage, and when we went there two hours later that golf club sock was gone," Rhodes said.

"Right," Steve said.

"We'd like to know where it is," Rhodes said.

Steve contended that he didn't know the deputies were looking for it at the time. When he found it the next day, he gave it to his attorney. "I said, 'John, what do I do at this point?' and he said, 'Let me look into it,' but there is an explanation—"

"Yeah, we're very—our curiosity is very high about that."

"He came back to me and he said, 'Give it to me.'"

"Why did you give him the golf club sock?" Rhodes asked.

"Because he's my attorney, and I've been—I—I—because that seems wise."

"I don't mean that, Steve. I'm kind of confused," Rhodes said. "The detectives came back, and they were looking for it, and then it was gone, but what made that something that you—"

"Because I overheard them in my garage saying something about a golf thing," Steve said, acknowledging that he'd heard the detectives talking in "hushed tone around the corner" about it, then made him sit on the stairway while they compared photos taken earlier in the day.

Huante said the golf sock was listed on the search warrant that he'd handed Steve that day. This issue became a matter of debate and interpretation later, because the defense contended that the warrant listed only golf clubs.

Rhodes told Steve that they'd been in contact with his attorney, John Sears, who told them that he'd gotten plenty of information from Steve "that made him confident that you weren't involved in the death of your wife, but we'd asked him and asked him and asked him to . . . provide that information, and it just never happened."

Rhodes went on to say that the killer rode a mountain bike into the forest behind Carol's house, jumped the fence and went in the back door. "Mountain bike tires are kind of common, but they had the exact same kind of tires that you had on your mountain bike," he said.

"I've always wondered what it was that made you guys

so focused on me other than the fact that I'm an ex," Steve said, admitting that he also "didn't have an alibi that night."

"Well, that was a big deal," Rhodes said. "Is there any way that you could have ridden behind her house that night?"

"My bike has not been at or near that property in I don't know how many years—not with *me* on it. . . . And I have been out in that area in days or weeks previous, once in a while, but not right there behind the house. I mean, if I were going to go over there, if I were going to enter that property, why would I go over the fence there? I mean, I built that gate."

Since the day the detectives had searched his condo, Steve said, he'd learned that Jim Knapp had been making accusations that Steve had been physically abusive to Carol. But that, Steve said, "never, ever happened. Not ever."

McDormett assured Steve that Jim Knapp and his comments had nothing to do with this. "No, it comes down to, you know, the time frame is huge, and the mountain bike tracks behind her house are big. I mean, it rained that day, earlier, and there's no other tracks out there except these . . . and most reasonable people are going to say, 'Wow, that's extremely coincidental.' And so we've never had the benefit of hearing from you about it."

"I've never had any experience like this," Steve said, noting that he talked to them for hours at the station without an attorney, and had since been roundly scolded for it. "I've assumed that being innocent counted for something. . . . I loved Carol."

Steve said they'd gotten together for coffee the day after Katie's send-off, and the tone between them had only grown warmer since they'd gotten past the roughest part of the divorce. "I asked her if she'd be interested in starting to see each other again, and she said, 'I'm here. We'll take it from there.' I don't know that we would have reconciled. I don't know."

Rhodes brought the interview back to the golf sock. When the detectives came back, he said, "Why would you have taken the sock at that point?"

"I didn't take the sock."

"No, no, I mean—"

"I never touched it."

"You moved it off the shelf."

"I never moved it off the shelf. I haven't touched that thing. I told you, I have an explanation. I've given it to my attorney."

From there Rhodes honed in on the books that Steve ordered on Amazon, about "basically hiding your identity and covering your tracks and that kind of stuff."

"How to live abroad," McDormett chimed in.

"Right. Stupid fear-based stuff," Steve said. "My brother—"

"Your brother suggested it?"

"I don't want to get him in trouble," Steve said. "If you guys arrest me, I'm going to face this down in trial. I'm not going anywhere."

Rhodes said they needed to take him back to Prescott and ask him more questions. If he wanted to talk to his lawyer, that was fine, but he would be in custody until they got their questions answered.

"Am I under arrest?"

"Right now you're in investigative detention."

"We've got serious questions about that night and about your involvement in your ex-wife's murder, and if they don't get resolved, you definitely could be facing charges."

They drove Steve back to Prescott in the passenger seat

of the cruiser without handcuffs. He was placed in an interview room at the Yavapai County Jail, but after his attorney told detectives that Steve didn't want to talk to them, they booked him on felony charges of first-degree homicide and burglary.

That same day the investigators served search warrants at Steve's office and condo, his storage facility in Prescott, Katie's apartment in Scottsdale, where he stayed sometimes, and for his rental car. They were looking for the books he ordered on Amazon and the golf club head cover.

During the searches they found a book, *How to Be Invisible,* some e-mails between Steve and Barb, as well as his handwritten notes about a pro-and-con competition involving Carol and Barb. On the last page he'd written, *games, sets, match, tournament,* and listed Barb as the winner. When she learned of this competition from detectives, she described it as "frightening."

A couple of hours later, attorney John Sears turned over the golf club head cover to Detective Theresa Kennedy.

Steve had taken the head cover to Sears's office on July 5, where the attorney examined it for bloodstains or other biological evidence, then put it into his safe until he was specifically asked for it.

Some in law enforcement, including then-Sheriff Steve Waugh, believed that Sears was wrong to do this, viewing it as evidence tampering and obstructing the investigation. Waugh filed a complaint against Sears with the State Bar of Arizona, alleging that Sears acted improperly.

But the bar association, from which Sears had received

a "pre-read" at the time on whether he was required to turn it over voluntarily, did not agree.

"They told him to preserve it and if he was ever asked for it by law enforcement, he should produce it, which is exactly what he did," defense investigator Rich Robertson said. "It was in a paper bag on a shelf with a note attached. It sat there until [the detectives] asked for it and he gave it to them." That's because a defendant has a Fifth Amendment right not to volunteer evidence that could be incriminating, he said.

The bar counsel dismissed Waugh's complaint, noting that Sears "safeguarded the item from damage, deterioration or destruction until the police agency obtained a more specific search warrant." He noted that Sears did so based on advice from the bar's ethics counsel and another criminal defense attorney.

Later that day Detective McDormett, Sergeant Huante and Lieutenant Rhodes went to Steve's condo to interview Charlotte again.

Katie had just walked in the door after flying in from Los Angeles, where she was a senior at Occidental College, majoring in politics. In big-sister protective mode, she was not thrilled to see the officers through the peephole.

The officers tried to persuade Charlotte to come outside to talk to them alone, but Renee and Katie would not allow it. Renee asked if the officers could come inside to talk to Charlotte, then went to call John Sears. That's when Katie stepped in.

Huante tried to assure them that neither Charlotte nor Katie was in trouble. "My motive is I want to find out what happened to your mom," he said.

"We all do," Katie said.

"Okay, but based on that I want you guys to tell me the truth. That's all I'm asking."

"Have we given you some reason to believe we have not told you the truth?" Katie asked.

"Yes," Huante said. "You were asked a couple of questions and your answer was 'I don't feel comfortable answering that.'"

"That was not lying to you," Katie countered. She said it was a difficult night for all of them and she wanted to take care of her sister, who was upset. "Am I obligated to speak with you right now?"

"No, ma'am," Huante said.

"Okay, then I think we're going to do this another time."

"Yeah," Charlotte agreed.

"I really do appreciate everything that you're doing, and I'm not trying to be difficult here, but I don't think you understand what it is we're going through," Katie said.

Huante pressed on, trying to engage Charlotte right in front of Katie. "When can I speak with you?" he asked.

"That's not up to her," Katie snapped.

Renee refused to talk to them as well, saying that she wanted to speak to a lawyer before doing so. "None of us are lying to you," she said. "I know that you think we're trying to cover for Steve, but even if Steve did this . . . he would never compromise himself by telling any of us."

Katie apologized for being short with them, but said she still had heard no reason why the interview needed to happen immediately, especially when she'd just finished telling them by phone that she would prefer to wait until the next day. Then she asked them to leave.

Trying to soften the impression left by Huante's confrontational approach, McDormett said, "Before I leave, you guys just have to understand we're working for your mom. We're not the enemy."

Katie said she wasn't trying to prevent them from finding out what happened to her mother, but she was "a little bit insulted by you treating me like this. . . . It has nothing to do with wanting to hide anything about the investigation."

CHAPTER 30

When Detectives McDormett and Brown interviewed Renee several days later, they assured her that Jim Knapp's stories had no bearing on Steve's arrest. In fact, they said, the stories made Jim seem "like an idiot."

"You would have to think we were the biggest fools on the face of the earth and the most unprofessional Mayberry RFD Department if we were basing our investigation and taking our lead from Jim Knapp," McDormett said. "I would find that to be very insulting."

Asked about the "mysterious golf club head-cover story," Renee explained that Steve was using her car because investigators had seized his, so hers was parked in his condo garage. The windows were down, she said, and Steve told her that the wind must have blown the golf sock off the shelf and into her backseat, where he found it.

"Do you really believe that?" McDormett asked. "I mean, just seriously, do you really—"

"Well, it's . . . I think it's a stretch," she said, but "it was monsoon season. There was some wind."

McDormett reminded her that the garage door was shut

when the detectives had left a few hours earlier. When they returned, they discovered that the shelves in the garage had been straightened and the head cover was missing. They had photos to prove that a dramatic cleanup had taken place between the first and second searches.

"I'm still trying to figure out how a monsoon can straighten out three garage shelves," McDormett quipped.

Asked about Steve's books and his plan to flee, Renee said she and Steve started discussing his escape plan in the weeks after the murder, and it became a joke between them. She said she might consider leaving, too, if she'd been in the same situation, "facing something where the entire community thinks that I did it. He's got this reputation that proceeds him, not being violent or a murderer, but being, at the very least, a dog."

Although Steve seemed to seriously consider leaving town, she said, he usually reversed himself, concluding, "I just can't leave my girls. I won't leave my girls. I have to stay here and fight this."

Hearing Renee rationalize Steve's behavior, McDormett tried a more direct approach, explaining that the killer slammed Carol's skull so hard it broke into fifty pieces.

"I believe Steven DeMocker did this," he said. "This is a crime of rage and I know that you guys see one side of Steve, but rage indicates some type of personal relationship. Can you definitively say in your heart that you know he didn't do it?"

"No," Renee said, quickly adding, "I'm not saying that he did."

Asked if the girls would talk to the detectives, Renee explained that Katie and Charlotte viewed both of their parents as victims and that they saw investigators as "the enemy," especially aggressive ones like Sergeant Huante.

* * *

Steve was a master manipulator, and Renee stuck by him for many months after he went to jail, even after finding letters on his laptop that showed he'd cut and pasted the same poems and descriptions of his romantic feelings—the language altered slightly, depending on the recipient—into missives to the various women in his life.

Based on the way Steve went back and forth between them, insisting that he loved each and every one of them, it is difficult for an objective observer to ascertain whether he was sincere in any or all of these emotions. But he apparently came across persuasively enough to keep them on the line.

Renee showed the letters to her friend and Unitarian minister, Dan Spencer. "There's a part of me that's sympathetic to Steve," Reverend Spencer said in 2014. "I can see a man who was genuinely torn about who to love, and it was the weird thing, because it was also an indication of his emotional deficit. . . . He looked at things very mathematically."

Reverend Spencer said he never really knew Steve, but from talking with Renee and reading some of his e-mails, Steve sounded like a genius. When he was trying to reconcile with Carol, for example, he was poetic and convincing. He knew how to be vulnerable, he pretended to take responsibility and he talked about being soul mates. He would also tell stories about people who had helped him.

But the people who weren't sexually involved with Steve weren't as receptive to his antics. "People who knew Steve either liked him or didn't, and there wasn't a lot of gray," Reverend Spencer said. They thought he was "creepy at best and a sociopath at worst in pretty much everything he did."

Fairly early on, he said, Renee "started to put two and two together that Steve was probably a sociopath, and there were obvious deception and honesty issues, . . . but she wanted to overlook it."

CHAPTER 31

The day of Steve's first court appearance on October 24, 2008, Deputy County Counsel Bill Hughes asked that Steve be held without bail at the request of Carol's mother.

"It's the state's intention to seek the death penalty in this matter," Hughes told the judge magistrate.

Because of the way Arizona's laws concerning victims' rights work, Hughes requested that Steve not be allowed to have any contact with his two daughters or Carol's mother, unless they actively requested such contact, which would involve waiving their victims' rights under the law. The girls were considered victims because their mother had been murdered, but they were also the daughters of the man accused of killing her.

Steve's attorney, John Sears, countered that Katie and Charlotte "by no means consider themselves victims," but they would also not want a "no-contact order with their father. . . . I think they are very much in support of their father, love their father, and want to participate in this case."

So, to continue to have contact with their father, Charlotte and Katie had to waive their victims' rights. As

Detective Brown stated during his interview with Katie, the detectives, and now prosecutors, were concerned that it would compromise the case against their father if the girls were given information about the investigation.

Feeling they were being shut out, the girls later regretted that decision. With the help of an attorney, Christopher Dupont, they requested that the state comply with their constitutional rights to meet and confer with the prosecutor.

One of the first steps in being more actively involved was a request to be heard at a hearing concerning conditions for Steve's release in November 2009. Dupont sent numerous letters and made calls to prosecutor Joe Butner, seeking a meeting to confer around that time, but Butner did not respond.

It got even more surreal after that. Later, during jury selection as the trial neared, county victim advocates who watched Charlotte hug Ruth Kennedy in the courtroom took the girls aside afterward and told them the jurors couldn't see them having contact with their own grandmother.

The prosecution filed its official notice on November 20, 2008, that it intended to seek the death penalty. To help John Sears defend Steve against these more serious charges, Steve hired the firm of Osborn Maledon. His parents covered the legal bills, and attorneys Larry Hammond and Anne Chapman joined the defense team.

After several judge changes, based on requests from attorneys on both sides, Judge Thomas Lindberg was appointed to the case.

With a bail hearing set for December 23, the DeMocker family hoped that Steve would be released on bail for

Christmas. Testimony continued over two days, during which Sears said the defense aimed to prove that someone other than Steve killed Carol.

With three more hours of testimony to go by day's end on Christmas Eve, Lindberg continued the hearing until January 13, and Steve spent his first Christmas behind bars.

The hearing spilled into two more days in January 2009.

Knowing that the national media had cameras and producers from *48 Hours* and *20/20* in the courtroom, Steve was allowed to change out of his previous attire of orange jumpsuit and shackles. Instead, he sported a dark suit, with a pale yellow tie, and his graying hair in a spiffy new haircut.

Sears filed a motion asking to send the case back to the grand jury for a new determination of probable cause, arguing that the prosecution had misstated and mischaracterized evidence. But Judge Lindberg would set bond only if he was persuaded that the case lacked enough evidence to exceed the standard of probable cause that Steve had killed his ex-wife.

Prosecutor Mark Ainley laid out his theory: Steve was deeply in debt, and he wanted to save himself $576,000 in alimony over the next eight years. So he conducted incriminating computer searches on how to kill someone and get away with it.

"Somebody using Mr. DeMocker's computer was sure thinking about someone dying," Ainley said.

On July 2, he said, Steve took a bike ride over to Carol's house. Wearing a backpack containing overalls and gloves, he laid in wait in the house while she was out running, surprised her while she was on the phone, then beat her to death with a golf club. Afterward, he burned his bloody clothing in a bonfire somewhere. When authorities confiscated his passport, he claimed he lost his old one in order to obtain a new one fraudulently as part of a plan to flee.

Defense attorney John Sears countered that the computer searches were part of Steve's research for a novel, explaining that one of the searches led to a link for a joke site that said one way to kill someone, but make it look like an accident, was to give the victim a cigarette.

The shoe prints didn't match any of Steve's shoes, Sears argued, and investigators' photos were not only of poor quality, but they also lacked a scale from which to judge size. The same bike treads detectives said were made from Steve's tire could have been virtually anyone's because the brand was so popular. Detectives failed to properly investigate Steve's claim that he'd been riding his bike on another trail, which eliminated his ability to prove his alibi. And the ME had never said definitively that the murder weapon was a golf club.

But most important, Sears said, was the fact that the prosecution did not present specific exculpatory evidence to the grand jury that a complete profile had been compiled for the unknown male DNA under the fingernails of Carol's left hand, and it specifically ruled out Steve.

"The inference to be drawn from that is a powerful one and clearly exculpatory, that there was a struggle with an unknown man who is *not* the defendant in this case," he said. "If you had to pick one place in the entire crime scene where that presence of that unknown would be relevant, it's under the fingernails of the victim," Sears said.

"The police put the blinders on twenty minutes into this case and they are still there today. This was a terribly bloody event," he said, noting that investigators found no blood on Steve or anywhere at his condo.

Although Steve prepared to flee because he feared being falsely accused and arrested, Sears noted that his client Steve never actually left town.

Nonetheless, Ainley stood by his theory that Steve burned his overalls. He also offered an explanation for why the trail running shoes that detectives found in Steve's closet didn't match the shoe prints.

"It's not a real big leap that he probably got rid of the pair of shoes because it's going to be covered with blood."

Issuing two separate rulings, Judge Lindberg determined that the prosecution did not meet the required legal threshold to bind the defendant over for trial. That standard, which is higher than probable cause, must establish that "proof is evident or the presumption great" that a defendant committed capital murder.

Lindberg said the prosecution failed to tie Steve De-Mocker to the murder scene with conclusive physical evidence, and it also didn't prove that he had a financial motive to kill his ex-wife.

Though the actions and statements of the defendant have properly given rise to suspicion, more is required, Lindberg wrote, setting bail at $2.5 million.

The judge sent the case back to the grand jury for a rehearing, saying that the prosecution had presented misleading, incomplete, prejudicial and erroneous evidence—some of which was based on "unsolicited" opinion, not on fact—to the panel.

He cited the prosecution's failure to mention, for example, the exculpatory evidence of the unknown male DNA under Carol's fingernails, and that other unknown male DNA was found on her cordless phone, on several unscrewed lightbulbs in the laundry room and on a door handle. (Exculpatory evidence meaning it wasn't Steve's DNA.)

During the hearing Steve turned around from the defense table and smiled like the Cheshire cat at his family behind him in the gallery.

But that brief victory didn't last. After the prosecution presented the case to the grand jury a second time, the panel indicted Steve once again with the same two murder and burglary charges, in February 2009. Sears's attempt to get a third grand jury look was rejected.

Representatives from both sides of this case agree now that it was a mess from the start. The shortfalls in the prosecution's case that the defense identified in the beginning were still being challenged by the defense in the years to come.

The problem with Ainley's theory about Steve wearing a biohazard suit and gloves, then burning them in the ranch land behind the house, is that "there's absolutely no evidence that Steve ever purchased anything like that or of any burn pile of paper suits," defense investigator Rich Robertson said recently.

If writing a book on this case, Robertson said, his working titles would be *Even the Smallest Things Can Attack* or *Tunnel Vision.*

The first title references testimony early in the case by Detective Steve Page, who, Robertson said, had minimal computer forensics training and was being mentored by the state DPS.

As Page was testifying about Steve's Internet searches, he mentioned one for "even the smallest things can attack." Asked what that phrase meant to him, Page replied something to the effect that "Steve was being very careful to the smallest details in planning this murder."

But as Robertson pointed out later, this phrase was actually an innocent message from a decal on Steve's car, which detectives photographed on July 8, 2008, well before this hearing. Based on a family catchphrase, Steve's daughters had made the decal as a Father's Day gift before Carol died, in memory of a childhood adventure at the tide pools. When Steve told Charlotte to pick up a little hermit crab, she replied, "Dad, even the smallest things can attack."

Robertson cited this as a prime example of the prosecution's confirmatory bias toward evil intent, "because there's so much of the story that they don't know." As a result, he said, they ended up with accusatory misinterpretations like this one, when there could be a "completely benign explanation."

In this case the defense was able to counterbalance this claim by showing Page the decal photo. But other prosecution theories came up later—such as numerous possible scenarios for how the unidentified male DNA #603 ended up under Carol's fingernails—and may have influenced the jury, he said.

If you interpret evidence wrong, "you get the story wrong, and that's how people are wrongly convicted," Robertson said in 2014.

Carol's friend Katherine Morris has since offered another theory for why none of Steve's DNA was found at the house, and none of Carol's blood was found on Steve's person, clothing or car. She said she's always felt this in her gut, out of instinct, not from any particular hard evidence, but from the lack of it.

"He went and jumped in the lake and then got on his bike and went home," she said in 2014, noting that Watson Lake and Granite Basin Lake are both very near the Bridle Path house.

But she added, "I don't believe there wasn't DNA all over the crime scene. I think the sheriff's department did a horrible job, and I think he took the murder weapon up to Colorado."

That remark stemmed from Steve's call to Katherine just a few days after the murder, when he mentioned that he was in the car, driving to Colorado alone.

"They took my passport, but they didn't tell me I couldn't leave the state," he told her.

He even made note of that trip during Carol's memorial service. "I think it was his narcissism that made him do that," Katherine said.

It wasn't until Renee's interview with detectives in April 2010 that other details came out about Steve's trip to Colorado. Renee said she'd gone with him, and because they were both stressed out, they had lots of sex. They also went to some of his favorite areas, such as Durango, and his favorite restaurants, such as Ken & Sue's. It wasn't clear if this was a separate trip from the one Katherine described.

CHAPTER 32

Six months after Carol was killed, another death and a twist of fate sent the murder case against Steve into an entirely new direction, although it took some time for the shift to play out.

At eight-thirty on the night of January 7, 2009, Jim Knapp's ex-wife called one of his closest friends, concerned. Ann Saxerud hadn't seen or heard from Jim since Monday, a day and a half ago. He'd said he was going to a meeting in Phoenix before moving there to take care of some property, and would watch their boys on Tuesday if he got back in time.

But, Ann told Sean Jeralds, Jim never called, so he missed a visit with his sons, which was totally uncharacteristic of him. He also hadn't returned any of her subsequent calls or e-mails.

"Okay," Sean told her, "I'll go check."

Sean was celebrating his birthday with his family that night, but after Ann's call he immediately alerted Dave Roy, another close friend of Jim's.

"We've got to go over to Jim's," he said. "Ann hasn't heard from him. We need to go check on him."

They agreed to meet at Jim's place, a mutual friend's condo in the 3000 block of Peaks View Court, where Dave had also lived for a time.

When they arrived, the lights were off in the condo, but the front door was three-quarters ajar. Pieces of broken glass were scattered on the porch, the screen door had some small holes blown through it and the front window frame was damaged.

"Jim!" Sean called out.

No one answered.

Entering the condo cautiously, Dave and Sean turned on a light in the living room and noticed that it looked messier than usual. That's when Dave saw a small metal object on the floor among more glass shards.

"There's an empty [bullet] casing right there," he said.

"Jim!" Sean called out again.

Still, no response.

Taking a step around the love seat and turning the corner, Sean saw a second bullet casing on the floor and started backing away. The bedroom door was closed, and despite his training as an EMT and reserve firefighter, he didn't want to investigate on his own.

"Dave, we need to call 911," Sean said.

The two men headed outside. As they stood in the parking area, waiting for the police to show up, they called their good friend and coworker, Bill Thompson, to join them. The three of them stayed at the condo all night, talking to police.

* * *

At first glance the scene was confusing, even for Prescott Police Department detectives, who always investigated death scenes as homicides to ensure they didn't overlook evidence that could be important later. And this scene did seem suspicious, at least initially.

For one, they found five bullet casings, four bullet holes and several live rounds, but only one spent bullet in the condo. And it wasn't the one that killed Jim Knapp.

When the officers entered the master bedroom, they found his dead body lying halfway into the closet, barefoot and shot in the chest. A semiautomatic nine-millimeter gun lay by his left hip, with a bullet casing next to his right foot, and a live round between his legs. Still wearing a gold ring on his finger, he wore a white T-shirt and brown pajama pants. His arms were folded at the elbow, hands up by his chest.

The officers saw what looked like gunshot residue on Jim's shirt around the wound, and also on his chest underneath, but they found no suicide note. And although that was not unusual, the state of the condo didn't look like one might expect for someone who had just killed himself.

"It was a unique scene, and it was something that we looked at very carefully," Sergeant Clayton Heath said.

In the living room the base of the phone rested on the coffee table, but the receiver was on the floor. An open briefcase containing paperwork rested nearby, with more papers fanned out in front of it.

They found a bullet casing in the hallway just outside the master bedroom, and another one inside, between an unmade bed and a dresser. On top of the bed was a kitchen chair on its side, with a bullet hole through its seat. Tracing the bullet's projectile, detectives determined that Jim had shot through the chair and the common wall between the master and spare bedroom, sending the bullet into a pillow on a child's daybed.

As soon as Sergeant Heath realized that Jim was connected to the DeMocker case, he called the sheriff's office to come over.

"I knew it was going to be a big deal," Heath recalled in 2014. "It was a critical thing in my mind that they got in on the front end of that investigation so that they weren't blindsided by something that we found, because I knew that the defense was going to latch onto that, regardless of what we found."

The detectives determined that the bullet holes in the front window, blinds and screen door had come from the inside, because the holes in the metal screen protruded outward. The front door showed no marks or bullet holes, indicating that it had been open, with the screen door pulled to, when the gun went off. Tracing the trajectory, investigators determined that the shots were fired from the hallway outside the master bedroom.

Examining the area outside the condo, the detectives saw no signs that an intruder had entered the unit, and they found no bullets or casings outdoors.

"There was like a breezeway out to the side of the building, and it was full of dead leaves," Heath said. "It didn't appear that anybody had walked through those. It was all pristine."

Later, Steve's attorneys drew parallels between the "very clumsy and hurried" staging at the Bridle Path crime scene and the same type of staging at Jim Knapp's condo six months later. The two scenes, attorney Craig Williams contended, couldn't be viewed in a vacuum.

"You have to say to yourself, 'What was building up to

this? How did this happen?'" Williams stated rhetorically at trial.

Because Jim couldn't answer for himself, Steve's defense team was able to argue later that Jim's anger could have killed Carol and perhaps had gotten him killed, too. Although none of Jim's friends, including his ex-wife, believed that theory, they could not deny that he had led a troubled life toward the end.

Sean Jeralds, Dave Roy and Bill Thompson had all been swabbed for DNA by investigators in the DeMocker case as they tried to match—and rule out—subjects for the unidentified male DNA under Carol's fingernails. All three of them had been at Carol's house, helping her move some heavy items about a week and a half before her murder. Dave had also helped Jim move into the guesthouse and to carry a refrigerator over there from the garage.

Although Jim shared his struggles with his divorce, custody and health issues with Carol during their nightly chats, it's unclear how much she knew of his prescription drug use. But his ex, Ann Saxerud, reported that he'd been resisting drug testing, a requirement of their mediation agreement, for months.

That agreement, dated October 23, 2007, noted that Jim hadn't complied with this requirement. It also stated that he'd transported his and Ann's son Alex in his car in May 2007 while under the influence, but there was "no evidence of a plan for addiction treatment/recovery."

As a result, Ann later testified, Jim was allowed to visit their boys at her house, but not to take them anywhere in his car, or to keep them overnight at his house, because "he was struggling with prescription drug overuse."

On January 8, 2008, shortly before he moved into the guesthouse, Ann filed a restraining order against Jim, claiming that he was harassing her by phone and making disturbing remarks.

She cited a series of calls on January 7: *Yelling & swearing on the phone, threatening litigation related to child custody—unable to reason with him,* and a *disturbing phone call stating 'Goodbye'—unsure if this was a suicidal gesture or threat, reported to PPD, check welfare,* followed by two *prank calls to YRMC* (where she worked) *recorded on voicemail. . . . One of the calls was about me and sexual & vulgar. Another call that was difficult to interpret, saying 'Ann Saxerud, Fear!' . . . Late message left on my cell phone threatening no more cooperation & swearing with abusive language.*

Jim e-mailed Ann two days later, asking why she kept hanging up on him—*Just because I used profanity and shared anger? Why did you lie about the incident to both Jay and the police?*

He explained that when he said "good-bye," he simply meant that he wasn't going to call her again that night, not because he was going to harm her or himself. And when police showed up at his door that night, he added, they were there to check on *his* welfare, not because they were worried about hers.

In handwritten notes he listed the points he apparently planned to make at the upcoming hearing: *Strike the restraining order, seems too adversarial. . . . I NEVER threatened her w/ violence, or implied it—I have never been "physical" with her ever—my understanding (from the clerk) was there had to be minimum 2 threats or acts of violence.*

Jim Knapp was the only one to show up at the hearing

on the protective order, so he was successful in getting it dismissed.

At first, Sean Jeralds was angry at his longtime friend. He wasn't entirely surprised, but he also hadn't seen Jim's death coming. Jim had only recently asked for Sean's and Dave's help to move him to Phoenix, nearly two hours away from his kids, after the condo owner had told him to be out by mid-January. It was time.

Sean and Jim had been friends for nearly twenty years, and roommates a couple of times. They lived together for nearly a year when Jim split up with Ann, after which Jim moved to Hawaii for a while.

"He was having a bad time in Hawaii, and I thought, that's when he was hitting rock bottom," Sean recalled.

Jim had gone to visit a friend there who arranged an interview for a university fund-raising development job. "He really kind of blew it, and, unbeknownst to us, had started taking a lot of prescription drugs, which kind of sent him over the edge," relapsing after he'd been "clean and sober for decades," Dave said.

While in Hawaii, Jim tried to get into bamboo housing, but that was "a lot tougher than he anticipated," Sean said. Jim was always coming up with moneymaking ideas, such as hurricane-worthy coastal housing, known as "airplane on a stick."

Knowing that Jim missed his sons, Sean could sense how bad his friend's depression was getting. "Hey, you want to come back here?" he asked.

Jim accepted his friend's offer to move back in with him in Prescott. "I owe you my life, because I was getting ready to kill myself in Hawaii," he said. "If I couldn't come back and live here, I probably would have done that."

"Oh, Jimmy, you can't even be thinking that," Sean told him.

Jim said he was experiencing a lot of pain, but the medications he took for it caused problems in their friendship. One time Jim had Alex over, went downstairs while he was cooking and forgot to turn off the stove. Another time he wrecked the garage door by trying to drive out while it was closed. Jim paid to fix the damage, but these incidents began to add up. Finally, after Jim left the stove on again and lit a bunch of candles, Sean worried that his roommate was going to burn down the house, and told him that he had to leave.

"Jim, you can't stay here anymore," he said. "I don't trust you in any way."

Jim said he understood, moved into a third-story walk-up apartment, and things were better for a time. He seemed upbeat, happy and full of ideas.

After meeting Suzanna Wilson online, he fell head over heels in love, and took her to Hawaii for what Sean called the "whole circle-of-life thing," bringing her together with his love of the ocean. But that relationship went bad right around when Jim was diagnosed with a malignant melanoma mole on his cheek, which doctors had to surgically remove.

After Jim moved into Carol's guesthouse, he told Sean he loved living there, that it felt as though he and Carol were like an old married couple, just like he and Sean had been when they were roommates.

The morning after Carol was murdered, Jim called Dave Roy, who was in Tucson with his wife: "He was just in tears, just completely torn up over what had occurred. It was the beginning of a real downhill slide for him, and part of a relapse, that he felt it was just the last straw."

Describing Jim as very complex, interesting, compassionate and full of life, Dave said, "Carol was that way, too. The two of them were cut very much from the same cloth, just great individuals, which is really part of some of the tragedy here."

Jim went downhill in the coming weeks and months. "Everything changed," Sean said, noting that Jim took Carol's murder "very, very hard. It was the deepest sadness I'd ever seen out of Jimmy. And it stayed, that sadness . . . It was from climbing a hill and smiling to just going to the deepest, darkest spot and staying there."

Deep in that emotional darkness, Jim became convinced that Steve had killed Carol, and now Steve was going to kill him. No matter how Sean tried to talk him out of it, Jim was convinced. He even went so far as to borrow a gun for protection—the gun that ultimately killed him.

"Jim, what's the deal?" Sean asked when Jim showed him the weapon.

"Well, I've told the sheriff's office I have it, so they know," Jim replied.

Not happy with the choices Jim had made since he'd lost Carol, Sean still drove him to medical appointments, but stepped back from regular contact as his friend's caretaker, and let Bill Thompson step up.

After Jim was found dead and Sean's emotions had cleared a bit, it started to make sense that Jim might have felt he'd solved all his problems by committing suicide. The depression, the pain, the debt and the sure feeling that he was dying of cancer—it all added up. After watching his mother suffer a long and painful death from the disease, and having his father die in his arms from cancer as well, Jim had told his friends he didn't want to go that way.

Sean told police that Jim had been acting particularly strange the last time they'd seen each other, a few evenings earlier at the video store. Jim had walked in with Alex, smiled and approached his friend.

"Mr. Jeralds," Jim said, surprising him with a long, slow, tight hug and a kiss on the cheek. Sean thought the random kiss and hug were a bit inappropriate, but he shrugged off the behavior, attributing it to Jim having "a lot of pain meds on board."

Jim had also told Sean that he'd recently seen an attorney to ensure that his sons—and no one else—got his belongings in the case of his death. It was as if he were preparing for this, getting his affairs in order.

Over the recent Thanksgiving and Christmas holidays, Jim Knapp had traded e-mails with Ken Korn, a friend who had grown up with him and his brother, Bobby, in the San Fernando Valley, where their parents taught together at Valley College. Ken and Jim met when they were twelve, and went on to attend Grant High School in Los Angeles.

"We all grew up surfing together and hanging out," Ken said.

He and Jim moved down to San Diego County during the 1980s, and lived together in Carlsbad for five years. Jim worked as an orthopedic surgical tech at Scripps Clinic in San Diego, and took flying lessons at a small airport, which prompted him to apply to Embry-Riddle Aeronautical University. He then moved to Prescott, where he met his future wife, Ann Saxerud, an ER nurse.

To Ken, Jim was like a brother, which is why he asked

Jim to be his best man in 1988, a few years after Jim's own wedding to Ann.

Jim received an associate's degree in aeronautical science in 1991 from Embry-Riddle, then went on to earn a bachelor's and a master's degree in education from Northern Arizona University.

Years later he returned to Embry-Riddle as the director of development, helping to raise money for capital projects and new buildings. In that job Jim rubbed elbows with wealthy donors such as the billionaire entrepreneur who gave millions for a library that was named after him and his wife, the Christine and Steven F. Udvar-Hazy Library and Learning Center.

After leaving the university in 2004, Jim, his wife, mother-in-law and their family moved to the state of Washington, where he taught grade school. But missing Prescott, they all moved back eighteen months later.

Jim and Ken weren't as close during the last five years of Jim's life, but in his last months, he talked about his melanoma diagnosis, biopsies and medical tests, receiving unemployment and being in debt. Jim gave Ken and other friends the impression that he thought the cancer had metastasized and he was going to die.

The last time Ken saw Jim was in Carlsbad, a year or two before he died, where he came to get his "ocean fix" for a week, met up with old friends, went surfing and camped out at the state beach.

Jim had always enjoyed surfing and flying, Ken said, because they "gave him a good feeling and allowed him to channel" his urge to get high on drugs and alcohol, with which he had struggled in the past, and focus on healthier activities.

After Carol's murder Jim exchanged some last e-mails with Ken, in which he seemed out of sorts, listing his struggles in bullet points. Between Carol's death and his health and financial concerns, "he was not himself," Ken said. "He was devastated that Carol was taken away—she was like an anchor for him."

Even so, Ken said, "He was still positive, and still upbeat. He was the kind of guy who always had something new going. Very funny guy. Great sense of humor. Was always open to new [things], kind of spiritual, just open to improving his life. Loved his kids. A very dedicated father."

Jim's brother, Bobby, called Ken to tell him the sad news that Jim was dead and they both thought he "took his own life."

How would Ken explain the odd scene at Jim's condo? "He might have gone through a couple different phases before he decided to do what he did," Ken said. "I guess we'll never know for sure."

Sean Jeralds and Dave Roy came to a different conclusion: Knowing that life insurance companies often don't pay benefits in suicide cases, Jim might have purposely left the room in disarray.

Both thought that "in some twisted way, Jim had made it look like there had been a struggle" at the condo, Dave said. "That would have been a Jim thing to do, [to] make it look like there was another reason [for his death]."

They didn't know whether Jim had any life insurance, but Dave suggested that another "motivation may have been for his kids not to think that he committed suicide, and that it was something bigger than that."

Jim Knapp was pronounced dead at 9:20 P.M. on January 7, nearly an hour after Sean called 911. And by the next day, the detectives had looked at the totality of the circumstances and determined that Jim had shot himself four days before his fifty-third birthday. However, they still asked the ME to confirm their finding, which he did.

Dr. Philip Keen and his assistant, Karen Gere, rolled Jim over and determined that the bullet had gone through his body and the closet floor, through a three-quarter-inch-thick piece of plywood, and into the dirt in the sub-basement.

"I've been doing this job for twenty-six years, and that was the one time I can remember I had the medical examiner and his assistant come to the scene, examine the body and see what his determination was as well, before we removed Mr. Knapp," Sergeant Heath said.

By seven o'clock the next morning, detectives had obtained a search warrant for the condo, which allowed them to collect the bullet casings and look for a note or other evidence concerning the cause of death.

Inside a drawer in a plastic storage bin in Jim Knapp's bedroom, the detectives found a black nylon handgun holster, with an extra magazine and a note that stated Jim had borrowed the gun from a former coworker at Project Insight, Inc., whose phone number was written there.

Investigators also found quite a few vials of medication in the kitchen. After Ann Saxerud showed up, she told detectives that Jim was addicted to the prescription meds he took for chronic illnesses and depression. He'd had cancer, she said, and he'd planned to get a new growth checked. He also was unemployed and in financial trouble.

A termination letter from Project Insight stated that Jim had worked there from January 25, 2007, until June 3,

2008, but he was let go after his position was eliminated "as part of a larger administrative downsizing."

Jim's next-door neighbor told police she'd been startled awake by two loud noises at 12:30 A.M. on January 6, which caused her to jump up in bed. She listened for a short time and went back to sleep when she didn't hear anything else. The last time she'd heard Jim in his apartment was on January 5, and she hadn't seen him for a while before that.

Dr. Keen, the same pathologist who conducted Carol's autopsy, also performed Jim's on January 10. Doug Brown, who was back to being a sheriff's patrol deputy, but was still working on the DeMocker case, observed the examination.

Keen's report noted that Jim was five feet seven inches tall, weighed 189 pounds, had "mild to moderate" alcoholic liver disease, a "history of malignant melanoma," and a 1 3/8-inch scar on his left cheek, a remnant of the skin graft placed where his melanoma had been removed.

This man died of a self-inflicted contact perforating gunshot wound to the chest with shored exit wound in the back, Keen's report stated. *There is a surrounding dark muzzle imprint and powder imprint ranging up to 1.5-inches in diameter with no discernable stippling of the adjacent skin surfaces. There is black soot residue on the anterior surface of the white T-shirt overlying the wound.*

Stippling, the term for a pattern of unburned gunpowder grains, like a tattoo, is usually found when someone is a shot from a short distance away. A self-inflicted gunshot, straight to the body, does not leave such marks.

Keen said the shot went in right to left and steeply

downward, perforating the center of Jim's heart, leaving an exit wound in the back, left of the spine, which he determined was consistent with Jim holding the gun, probably in his right hand, and firing it into his chest.

Cause of death: gunshot wound, thorax, the report stated. *Manner: suicide.*

Before Jim Knapp's toxicology tests came back, Prescott police were still hedging about the cause of death, telling the *Daily Courier* that they were searching Jim's computer for threats against him and more solid evidence that he had committed suicide.

But that search didn't turn up any threats. And when the toxicology results landed on January 22, they showed that his body was full of prescription drugs—with no undigested pills in his stomach and no alcohol in his system.

Jim's blood contained six different substances, including metabolites, the chemicals still present after the body has processed a drug. If no traces of the original drug are present, this usually indicates that the person took the drug some hours or days ago, depending on its half-life, said forensic toxicologist Dwain Fuller, who testifies as an expert in homicide cases. Fuller, who had no official role in this case, looked over the toxicology and autopsy reports before commenting.

The toxicology results showed that Jim had elevated levels of zolpidem, better known as the common sleep aid Ambien, which could mean he took a higher than therapeutic dose, Fuller said. But the elevated level could also result from postmortem redistribution, because drug concentrations can rise between the time of death and when toxicology samples are taken.

Jim's blood contained less than a therapeutic level of chlordiazepoxide, otherwise known as Librium, a Schedule II controlled substance and muscle relaxant used as a sedative for anxiety and symptoms of alcohol withdrawal. Because this is an older drug, Jim might have been taking it for quite some time, Fuller said.

The tests also showed the presence of tramadol, which is a quasi-narcotic painkiller marketed as Ultram, and promethazine, which is used to control allergy symptoms, nausea and vomiting.

Three different metabolites were found—for tramadol, for the antidepressant Zoloft, and for nordiazepam, a product most likely of metabolizing the Librium.

Asked how this combination of medications might have affected Jim's state of mind at the time of the shooting, Fuller said that antidepressants don't tend to acutely affect a person's mood and the Ambien would have made him sleepy. If Jim had been taking the Librium for some time, that shouldn't have been debilitating, either.

But based on the "malignant melanoma" notation and the number of surgical scars described in the autopsy report, Fuller said Jim may have had more than one growth removed. He already had one surgical scar—and a skin graft—on his left cheek, as well as two other scars on his right arm, one on his left thigh and two along the midline of his abdomen. A Mayo Clinic "order for photograph," dated February 2008, had boxes checked for his right shoulder, "face and chin."

"Once melanoma gets going, it's not a good thing," Fuller said. "A lot of times it can metastasize to the brain and you will be dead in six months. Melanoma is a very serious condition. I can see him very fearful that he didn't have long."

It's difficult to try to speculate about a suicidal person's state of mind, Fuller said, but "having cancer, owing a lot of money and thinking you're going to die probably has as much psychological impact as anything he would have taken."

Knapp's Mayo Clinic records, which were entered into evidence in the DeMocker case, show that he did, in fact, have a number of serious health issues requiring surgery over the years, and had been prescribed narcotic painkillers for some of them: a diagnosis of diverticulosis in 1999, with symptoms still present through 2008; a partial colectomy, with subsequent infections and revision surgeries in 2000 and 2002; treatment for abdominal adhesions in 2004; a diagnosis in 2006 of Barrett's esophagus (a precancerous condition where abnormal cells grow in the esophageal lining), reconfirmed in 2008; an open xiphoid resection in late October 2008 (which left a scar near the gunshot wound); and consistent complaints of pain in various parts of his body. His history of melanoma included growths frozen and surgically removed and skin grafts. In 2008, he reported concerns about various skin flaws, as well as a tumor in the perineal area, which a biopsy in May proved to be benign.

"He'd obtained pain meds for those things, and his temptation was that his best friend, [Carol], probably as close as they could be without dating, here she was murdered, he was upset about this and really felt like that's it, 'I'm out of here, life isn't worth living,'" Ken Korn said.

The Northern Arizona Department of Public Safety crime lab conducted DNA and other tests on the nine-millimeter gun, bullets and casings found in Jim Knapp's condo. The results all came back to Jim, not to an unknown intruder.

This lab found that James Knapp's DNA was located on this firearm, Officer Ryan Hobbs of the PPD wrote in his report. *They also tested the spent casings located at this scene as well as several unspent rounds [which] . . . matched this firearm.*

After Jim Knapp's death, the Embry-Riddle alumni website posted a blurb about him, which was similar to an obituary that ran in the *Courier: Jim will always be remembered as a deep emotional person with a tireless entrepreneurial spirit and endless enthusiasm for fresh new ideas.* The notice described him as someone who could share deep philosophical insights, then immediately break into a joke. The writer also noted Jim's deep love for his two sons, his affinity for the ocean, his easygoing surfer sensibility and his "constant quest for knowledge, friends and fun."

A celebration of life for him was held January 17, 2009, at the Watson Lake Ramada. Recommended dress was aloha shirts, shorts and sandals. Organizers asked that donations be made to the Surfrider Foundation in lieu of flowers.

Interviewed by prosecution investigator Mike Sechez, Bobby Knapp said his brother had talked about committing suicide at least once during phone calls in his last months. Once Jim was diagnosed with melanoma, he told Bobby he would rather kill himself than go through the same ordeal as their mother had. Jim's struggle with prescription drug and alcohol abuse dated back to his twenties. For this and other reasons, Bobby was certain his brother had taken his own life.

Bobby told Sechez that he'd gone over to Jim's condo a week after his death to retrieve his belongings, accompanied by Sean Jeralds, Dave Roy, Ann Saxerud and her sons. Among Jim's things they found a diary, with a note asking Bobby to give it to Alex and Jay once they were old enough. On the kitchen counter they found a camera, which Jay asked if he could have as a keepsake. Dave took the camera to his car to check the photos on his laptop and make sure they were appropriate.

Three photos featured Jim wearing a Santa's hat and holding a black semiautomatic handgun, the same one that was found next to his body. One, time-stamped December 25, 2008, at 10:01 P.M., showed him pointing the gun across his chest. A second, taken a minute later, had him pointing the gun into the air. And a third, taken a minute later, showed him holding the gun in his right hand and a knife in his left. Roy deleted the images before giving the camera to Jay.

When Sechez retrieved the camera from Jay, he couldn't find the deleted photos on it, so he collected the memory card and adapter from Prescott police and sent them to the DPS Computer Forensic Unit. The unit was able to recover the deleted images, which were necessary for the prosecution to illustrate Jim's state of mind around the time he shot himself.

Jim was truly in dire financial straits. When Bobby looked through his brother's bank statements, his accounts showed that he had $5 in his saving account and $172.51 in his checking, as of November 30, 2008. After closing those accounts six months later, Bobby received a check for a whopping $241.

In January 2012, Detective Norman Peterson of the PPD met with Steve's attorney to discuss evidence found at the condo.

A month later, Peterson went there with prosecution investigator Sechez and sheriff's Deputy Doug Brown to follow up on a photo Peterson had snapped of a bullet hole through the master bedroom ceiling the day Jim's death was reported. Climbing on the roof, Peterson found a bullet hole in the shingles above the bedroom, but he was unable to find the actual bullet. Brown also crawled into the attic space to track the bullet's course, and photographed the hole in the ceiling and where it had exited through the roof. The bullet that killed Jim Knapp was never found, even after investigators ran a metal detector through the crawl space under the condo floor.

CHAPTER 33

After his arrest, Steve stayed busy behind bars, making phone calls, and writing letters to the Hartford Insurance Company, trying to collect on Carol's policies. He also took steps to ensure that his daughter Charlotte was being cared for, and that Renee stayed on his side.

On November 9, 2008, Steve wrote Renee a six-page letter, explaining his affair with Leslie Thomas, and asked for Renee's forgiveness. Renee hung in there.

Charlotte started off staying with her aunt Susan De-Mocker at the condo. However, after they butted heads, the very upset teenager called Steve to complain, and he subsequently called Renee.

"Charlotte is coming over. She needs to talk to somebody," he said. "How would you feel about her staying with you for a few days?"

"That's fine," Renee said.

Within a week Susan had packed her bags and left town. Renee later learned that Susan was upset about this chain of events, but Renee never found out exactly why. Apparently, Susan had a falling-out with Steve over parenting issues and decided to return to New York.

At this point Renee's caregiver relationship with Charlotte became a more long-term and more serious arrangement. And because Renee's house was old and had no closets, she thought it best that she move into Steve's condo with Charlotte.

As the personal representative of her mother's estate, Katie DeMocker had hired attorney Chris Kottke on July 11, 2008. And on October 14, the probate court officially made her the trustee of Carol's trust.

On January 2, 2009, Steve called his parents to tell them he'd just met with attorney John Sears and had gotten some good financial news.

"The news is definite and will happen soon," Steve told his mother.

"It was seven-five-oh?" Steve's father asked, referring to the $750,000 value of Carol's insurance policies.

"Yeah."

"Makes life a little easier," John DeMocker said.

As Steve called Renee and his brother Jim to share the news, little was said on the recorded line, but all would soon be revealed.

When he talked with Katie the next day about the cost of their car leases and worries about his credit rating, she said, "I don't know what this new pile of money is, and I don't know that I want to spend it on cars."

In conversations that day with Charlotte and his siblings Jim and Susan, Steve discussed how this new money should be enough to cover his debts. He also told Susan that Katie would need to be "managed" on this.

Steve's money situation, coupled with his escalating legal bills, had placed an escalating stress on him and his parents. On January 20, Steve told Jim that he'd met with

Sears that day and was told that the cost of his defense was now twice the initial quote of $400,000 to $500,000. In the three months after Carol's death, Steve had borrowed an additional $40,000 from his parents, bringing the total they'd loaned him in the past year to $100,000.

In a call with his mother, Steve learned that his father had not only had to go back to work to cover Steve's legal bills, but he'd also taken out a $50,000 line of credit on their home, and applied for a second line of $150,000.

Steve's lawyers ultimately agreed to cap the fees if they could get the money in a lump sum, but the question remained where those funds would come from. The legal firm of Murphy, Schmitt, Hathaway & Wilson, which specialized in estate planning, was hired to help Steve with *"securing payment and disposition of the proceeds under the two Hartford life insurance policies . . . owned by Mr. DeMocker and insuring Carol V. Kennedy, deceased,"* according to a letter the firm wrote to Hartford on February 4, 2009. Within a couple of months, Steve and his team of attorneys had worked out a solution.

In March, after his attempts to collect on the life insurance failed, Steve submitted to Hartford signed disclaimers of any interests in Carol's will and payouts from her insurance policies. This cleared the way for the $750,000 to be paid to the contingent beneficiaries—Carol's trust and estate, which were under Katie's control.

At this point Steve brought all of his persuasive powers to bear on his older daughter to convince her that this money needed to go toward his legal costs—not the girls' education, health and welfare, as their mother had intended and stated in her trust.

Katie had apparently learned about this new estate plan

just before Steve called her on March 17, but she clearly had other ideas in mind. Exercising her stubborn streak, she asserted herself as Charlotte's protector during an antagonistic discussion with Steve, who then applied countermeasures by asserting himself as Katie's father. These were apparently supplemented later by pressure from other family members, to convince her that this plan was, essentially, her familial duty.

In two back-to-back recorded calls that morning, Steve told Katie that "these are resources that, you know, for reasons you understand need to be set aside under your control for now, but . . . these are resources I have to be pretty sure you know . . . that I am going to make the decisions about how they're deployed."

After Katie replied that she was holding on to some of the insurance money to ensure that she could send Charlotte to college, Steve said, "I understand your concern, but . . . that, unfortunately, at this point has to be down the scale of priorities below bond first, defense second. . . . We may need every penny of it for defense and I need to make certain that you understand that there will be no impediment to that."

"And I need to make sure you understand that I'm trying to take care of my little sister," she countered.

"I understand that you're trying to do that, but we're going to get an acquittal here, and if we don't—"

"You don't know that. I'm really sorry to be that harsh . . . but you cannot say beyond a shadow of a doubt that this is what is going to happen. . . . I'm setting aside money that I'm not just going to hand over."

"How? What are you talking about doing?"

"Maybe you should get your lawyer to explain it to you a little better—"

"Hey, hey, hey."

"—before criticizing me in my decision."

"Sweetie, the only reason those resources will come under your control will be if I give them up," he said.

"If you can take them yourself, go for it."

"These are resources that, otherwise, wouldn't come until this is all over and we need them now for the defense. And so, this is a completely legal and appropriate way that the attorneys have constructed, but we need your cooperation, and if you're going to exert control here," he said, "I'm asking you simply to step aside and don't exert this sort of—"

"I'm not going to do that," she said.

"Oh, pumpkin, I'm counting on you," Steve said, trying to soften his approach. "My life is in the balance."

"Stop saying that."

"It's the truth."

"It's not true," she said. "I have some decisions to make now, and you can't always play the daddy card."

"Sweetie, I will make certain, first of all, ninety-nine percent probability here, that if we can get me out and . . . back to work, whether or not there's a civil suit against the county that succeeds, as long as I'm acquitted and back to work, I will take care of both of you, as I always have. And if for some reason I am not able to, my family will. But the resources we have at our disposal right now have to go to this without any interference and I need to know that from you. . . . As long as we're clear that, if we need it, it comes to my defense or my bond. I have to be out and I have to be acquitted. The two go hand in hand. I need to get out so I can raise money so that I can help with my defense."

When Steve pressed Katie on her plans to do something

different, she said they hadn't been drawn up yet. Asking how she had come to a point of not trusting him, he said, "Laughing at me is incredibly hurtful and insulting right now."

"That kind of question is completely irrelevant, how it is I've come to trust you won't handle it, because you can't handle it," Katie replied, saying she needed to take care of her "little family right now."

Tensions heightened as they argued over who was really trying to care for their family and Steve increased the pressure to comply with his wishes. "I need you to stop, to not be part of the problem here, Kate," he said. "On top of everything else we're battling here, don't you enter here and become something—"

"I am not the problem. How dare you?" Katie said, telling her father to stop trying to dictate what she needed to do. "There are some things that I'm not your daughter about anymore. When I'm the executor of this estate, I'm Mom, I'm not Katie."

Turning to a victim ploy, Steve replied that he didn't know why she was being so "harsh" with him, "as though I was somehow asking you to do something inappropriate."

Katie countered that she would talk to her lawyer, family members and some friends "to cool off from this infuriating conversation." Then she would call Renee, Charlotte and even Steve's lawyer "if that is what you would like, Father. Anything else?"

"I don't deserve any of what you just dished out to me," Steve said, playing the guilt card now. "You do whatever you have to do, sweetheart."

"I don't deserve what you said to me, either."

"You don't deserve the pain that has been inflicted on you anytime recently," he said. "None of us do, and I'm sorry. I want to get out of here so that I can do what I can to resume taking care of all of you guys, first of all emotionally, and second of all in every other way. But don't make me the enemy here."

Steve said he wasn't trying to take away anything that belonged to her. "We are a family," he said.

With that, they told each other, "I love you," and hung up.

The following month Steve's accountant brother, Jim DeMocker, created a spreadsheet totaling up all of Steve's family financial obligations, including loans from their parents, outstanding student loans for the girls, $309,000 in legal fees and more than $70,000 in credit card debt. The financial picture, as he put it in an e-mail to attorney John Sears, was "sobering."

Hopefully this will help Steve see the depth of his obligation to Mom and Dad and the need to move away from fantasies about vacations to Bora Bora, at least anytime soon, and will keep the girls' feet planted on the ground too as they ponder big checks from Hartford, he wrote.

Behind the scenes it had been decided that Katie would *resign as trustee in favor of [Renee] Girard, who was not only Steven DeMocker's girlfriend, she was also Charlotte's custodian under a parental power of attorney given to her by Steven as Charlotte's father,* Marlene Appel, an estate and trust attorney and a licensed fiduciary, later stated in a written analysis for the prosecution.

On April 13, 2009, Hartford issued two checks, one for $256,831 to the Virginia C. Kennedy Testamentary Trust, and one for $513,661 to Katie as the estate representative. Both checks arrived at her attorney's office in Prescott on April 14. Within a week or two, those checks were deposited into the respective Bank of America accounts for the trust and the estate.

The Bridle Path house sold at a foreclosure auction for $398,654 that same month, according to Zillow, a real estate website.

Looking back in retrospect, the next few months represented a frenzied period during which Steve later claimed his behavior was motivated by fear, not guilt. Prosecutors saw it the other way around.

Whatever the motivation was, prosecutors said, Steve used this time to perpetrate a chaotic fury of emotional manipulations, financial machinations and fraudulent schemes from behind bars. In doing so, he involved his girlfriend, daughters and family members to the point that four of them had to obtain immunity before testifying in court or face criminal charges. These schemes also resulted in additional charges being filed against Steve down the road and placed his defense attorneys into an unworkable position of conflict.

Within a month of the Hartford checks being issued in April, Steve had put the insurance scheme into play. Confident that he would get control over the money eventually, Steve told Renee he had it covered.

Using his sexual and intellectual wiles, Steve made sure to keep Renee on the line by having her act not only as his advocate and proxy, but also as a guardian to Charlotte when it came to the steps necessary for Carol's insurance proceeds to pay his legal costs.

Their recorded jail conversations illustrated such tactics during calls like this one on May 26, 2009:

"Hey, baby," Steve said.

"Hey," Renee said.

"Got a minute?"

"Yeah."

"God, you sound good. Let's make love."

"Yeah, so do you."

After these pleasantries Steve went right into the trouble he was having with Katie and his brother Jim following through on his plan for the money.

"Katie is not getting it done, because Jim is just—"

"Shopping for a car."

"No, it's just that Jim won't sit Katie down and say, 'Look, we really need this done here, while you're here, here, sign these things. Let's get this estate closed and let's get this, you know, other thing, this trust thing going,' and blah blah blah."

"Yeah."

"And so, John is going to see if, in addition to being my POA (power of attorney), you'll take over as, well, he'll explain it to you. . . . It is not actually any genuine discretionary responsibility. It's just a matter of, you know, doing that—well, you do have discretionary responsibility."

"Okay."

With business out of the way, it was back to sex talk. "We've made love numerous times, too, are you tired of it?"

"No."

"There you go."

"Some things are not going to wear out."

"Yeah, I'm glad about that."

"And when they do, there's Vitamin Blue," Steve said, using his own nickname for Viagra, the little blue pill.

Between the Viagra and his daily injections of testosterone and HGH, Steve seemed to have no shortage of sexual enhancers before he went to jail. Dwain Fuller, the forensic toxicologist, said the testosterone would have increased Steve's already overactive sexual drive, and it also could have caused more "aggressive and competitive behavior, including feelings of dominance and increased self-esteem."

On June 5, Steve told Renee, "I have seven hundred and ten thousand dollars to play with . . . that's the hard truth. . . . I can come up with another forty thousand dollars, so tell John [Sears] that $1.1 million is the total amount."

A week later, Steve told Renee that Sears had come up with the idea to put her in charge of the trust so she could help funnel the insurance payouts to the defense team. (But, in fact, as Renee later told prosecution investigators, Sears had told Renee that Steve was the one who suggested she take over the estate's trust, because Katie was "worn-out, tired of doing it, didn't want to be bothered." So Renee agreed, without consulting an attorney of her own.)

"You don't have to do what anybody tells you to do," Steve told Renee. "You can do anything you want with the money after you get in that position."

Katie's attorney, Chris Kottke, told investigators that Sears called him and asked if the estate money could be used to pay for Steve's defense costs, but Kottke claimed that he didn't commit one way or another. Kottke also claimed that he and Sears spoke "hypothetically" and he told Sears he was not giving him official legal advice on the matter.

The price tag for Steve's defense costs soon rose to $1.25 million. In a series of calls, Steve gave explicit directions to Renee and various family members on how to move money around to cover most of that sum from the estate and trust accounts. He said an additional $20,000 to $25,000 could come from a personal-injury lawsuit his divorce attorney, Anna Young, was handling.

Meanwhile, on July 10, during a hearing under seal with Judge Lindberg, Steve and his attorneys filed a pleading to declare that he was indigent. This was the same day that he and Renee accepted Katie's resignation as trustee and installed Renee as the successor trustee.

Prosecutors later expressed indignation about not being notified of the indigency hearing, not receiving a copy of any indigency motion and not getting to object during an open public hearing process for the indigency claim. They argued that such a hearing should have occurred as a precursor to the hiring of taxpayer-subsidized expert witnesses to support this allegedly indigent defendant's case—especially given that he had facilitated the transfer of $750,000 of his ex-wife's insurance money to pay his private defense team.

In a public filing dated late November 2012, outside attorneys for the prosecution accused Steve's attorneys of holding improper secret communications with Judge Lindberg on "dozens of occasions," both in motions and at secret meetings that were likely "multiple" in number, to discuss issues relating to the case that were not meant to be protected, including the indigency claim and names of expert witnesses with whom the defense wanted to consult. (By this time another judge had unsealed records concerning witnesses who had been discussed in those meetings.)

An indigency determination is a public process and, indeed, prosecutors have standing to appeal indigency determinations, the attorneys wrote.

As a result County Attorney Sheila Polk testified in 2013, "I would say our position has been that Mr. DeMocker wrongfully received public funds [to hire these experts], that those funds assisted in the defense."

But these allegations came long after the fact. At the time prosecutor Joe Butner simply put any motions labeled "ex parte" or appointments of defense experts and investigators into a pile on his desk "and didn't pay attention to them," Polk testified. Butner intended to wait until the defense actually chose which witnesses were going to take the stand.

Once Steve was declared indigent in July 2010, he and his attorneys helped direct the insurance money transfer to the defense team. But it was not without some more bumps along the road. In August, Steve told Renee that Katie was still "not cooperating" with the plan.

Based on a series of Steve's recorded jail calls, prosecutors, their estate expert witness and even Renee concluded that Katie ultimately transferred the money under duress, allowing the estate account to be closed with a zero balance on August 12.

Nowhere do I see any indication that either Katie or Charlotte were advised to seek independent counsel or in fact consulted with independent counsel, Marlene Appel, the prosecution's estate expert, wrote in her August 2010 opinion. *Nor do I see any indication that they were advised of any conflicts of interest any of the attorneys representing Steven DeMocker may have had. . . . It should also be pointed out that Attorney Kottke represented Katie as PR/Trustee and it would be a conflict of interest for him to also represent or advise Katie or Charlotte as beneficiaries, given the obvious adverse interests the facts disclose.*

Although Katie later denied in her testimony that she made the transfer under duress, Renee told investigators that she didn't see it that way. "There was some pressure, because had there not been pressure, she never would have released the money," she said.

The same day Katie resigned as trustee, she transferred $354,738 from her mother's trust account to her own personal checking account. On August 27, she transferred $350,000 to her grandparents' account at Pittsford Federal Credit Union in New York. And on August 28, Steve's mother, Jan DeMocker, transferred $250,000 to Osborn Maledon in Phoenix and $100,000 to Sears's office in Prescott.

"So it's all done?" Steve asked his mom on August 29.

"It was done on Friday afternoon. It came through Thursday evening, same day Katie shipped it out," Jan said. "I kept it overnight, hoping to get some interest. Dad and I had a discussion about using it for a vacation in Aruba. I called John to tell him it had arrived."

"Hang on to that information. You'll need it again in mid-October for the second part."

"Yeah, we'll have to do it again," Jan said.

Steve and his mother were referring to the second transfer of funds, due to Charlotte. He'd already set this transaction in motion by having Renee take over for Katie as the personal representative to Carol's trust so Renee, also acting under a parental power of attorney for Charlotte, could move the money from the trust to Charlotte. As soon as Charlotte turned eighteen on October 11, she would make that second transfer of money to Steve's parents, who would then send it to the defense team.

Renee also acted as Steve's spy and advocate in more personal matters, giving him a heads-up on September 15 that Katie had sent Charlotte a letter. As they discussed what the girls might be planning, Steve said they needed to make sure his daughters didn't "try to take anything into their own hands that departs from the commitments that everyone has made."

"Uh-huh," Renee agreed, noting that Charlotte was worried that she wouldn't have enough money to buy a car once her BMW lease ran out.

"Any initiatives outside of, you know, the existing, it's been sort of this interlocking network of commitments, and they need to stick to those," Steve said.

"Uh-huh."

"Do your best and let me know how it goes," he said.

Just then Charlotte showed up, and Renee handed her the phone so Steve could explain his concerns directly. But when Steve tried to find out whether the letter had anything to do with some missing money, Charlotte said her car was running and she had to go to her Young Democrats meeting.

"You know that we're going to replace your car in other ways?" Steve asked rhetorically.

"Yeah, I know," she said. "Can we talk about this later?"

"Well, we can . . . but this is something we have to straighten out," Steve replied, grasping for control.

When Renee got back on the phone, Steve reassured her that all of this movement of money was "proper and has been planned out by the attorneys. It's just that we're trying to make sure that nothing goes anywhere, that the right paper trail is occurring."

He said Charlotte's role and "fulfillment of her part" would occur in about three weeks.

When Renee said she felt "weird" that her name was on Carol's trust account, he assured her that it was entirely appropriate because she had the power of attorney.

"You are the current parent figure," he said. He added that they shouldn't talk about it any further on the recorded line, and directed her to discuss her concerns with John Sears.

Instead, they talked about the other mechanics of his life, such as the size of his legal team, which now encompassed fourteen people all over the country. As such, he'd asked the jail commander for access to a private office at the jail, along with a laptop and an unmonitored phone line, so he could work up to ten hours a day consulting with his attorneys.

But, he said, the commander just laughed, shook his head and said, "We're not going to do any of that. We can't. There's just no way we can do that here for anybody."

Two months later, Steve set the second set of transfers into motion. "You feel like moving three hundred fifty thousand around today?" he asked Renee on October 19.

"Sure, I think I can lift that," she replied.

"The trust matures today, but I assume you and John, or you and Chris [Kottke], or somebody is on it."

That same day Renee moved $350,000 from the trust account to Steve's joint account with Charlotte. And on October 23, Charlotte transferred that money to her grandparents' account in Pittsford, New York. Records indicate that Steve was the "ordering customer," and Charlotte was listed as the "sender's correspondent."

On October 27, Jan DeMocker signed a check payable to Osborn Maledon for $250,000. She also wrote a check to Sears the next day for $100,000.

A timeline and analysis the prosecution compiled of transactions and Steve's recorded phone conversations illustrated the familial friction, even with Charlotte, as Steve continued to try to spend every penny of Carol's trust money on his defense.

Concerning Steve's conversation with Charlotte on November 14, the prosecution's lead investigator Randy Schmidt wrote that Steve *has learned that they owe John Sears an additional $20,000 plus the $5,000 that Katie shorted him. . . . SD tells Char that he is trying to round up all the surplus money from the Kennedy Trust fund so he can give it to Sears. . . . Char refuses to call Katie and tells SD that if he wants to talk to Katie about money, he should call her himself.*

"It was your money, too," Steve told her.

Char says that she never got a say in how the trust money was spent, and she won't call Katie. SD accuses Char of getting pissy with him, Schmidt wrote.

Marlene Appel, the prosecution's expert and trust attorney, characterized the transactions like this:

- Katie, as the PR/trustee, and Renee, as successor trustee, "breached their duties owed to the beneficiaries of Carol Kennedy's trust."
- Attorney Chris Kottke appeared to have "disappeared on the records. To the extent that he knew or participated in the plan to divert the funds, he breached the professional and ethical duties he owed to his fiduciary client."
- Renee, as successor trustee, and also the agent under the parental power of attorney, "breached her duties as well," for the same reasons as Katie.
- The claim by Steve and his attorneys that "the trust funds belonged to Katie and Charlotte and they could do what they wanted with the monies" was a "misstatement of fact and of the law." Those funds belonged to the estate and "were supposed to be

administered by the trustee in accordance with the terms of the trust." Furthermore, "It wouldn't matter what crime Steven DeMocker was charged with or who his alleged victim was. Paying for his criminal defense was not, is not, and could never be a material purpose of Carol Kennedy's trust."

- *The pressure that was put upon these two young women was severe,* Appel wrote. *It would have been very difficult for most people to defy the combined pressure of Steven DeMocker, his attorneys, the probate attorney, Steven's girlfriend and perhaps the grandparents. I believe these two young women were unduly influenced and matters were made worse by the fact that they had no one advising them who was not also working for or in the interests of Steven DeMocker.*

CHAPTER 34

On the evening of May 19, 2009, Steve was reading on his cell bunk when he heard a man call to him through the air vent, which inmates sometimes used to communicate with each other. He didn't know who it was, but he thought he recognized the voice from the dorm.

"Your ex-wife was killed by two guys from Phoenix," the voice said, instructing Steve to get something to write down the details he was about to impart.

Standing on the toilet seat to get closer to the vent, Steve quickly scribbled down notes as the voice talked: Carol Kennedy and Jim Knapp regularly drank wine together in the evening, during which time Jim told her about his illegal drug dealings. These two guys showed up at the house and beat Carol to death with an axe handle because of Jim.

At least that's the account that Steve gave attorney John Sears, a tale that has since been dubbed "the voice-in-the-vent story."

When Steve met with Sears on May 22 to tell him this story, he handed over his four pages of handwritten notes from his conversation with the "voice." Ever since he and Carol had lived in Vermont, he said, they'd kept a splitting-maul handle in their bedroom for protection because Carol didn't want guns in the house. Carol had continued the practice even after they split up.

Before the "voice" story, Steve said he'd heard a similar account about Jim and Carol's murder from a friend in another jail dorm. That friend had heard the story from his cellmate and was asked to pass it on to an inmate in Steve's dorm. The voice said he wasn't allowed to relay the information to Steve until the original source had given him the okay.

At this point Steve was in cell #1 in dorm N at the Camp Verde Jail. Of the fifteen cells in that dorm, only those in certain "pods"—two on the floor above, and two on the ground floor—were connected by air vents. Following that logic, Steve said he thought the voice had to be coming from cell #2, 8 or 9.

On the evening of June 1, Steve called Renee, very intent on having her and Charlotte visit him the next day, saying he'd gotten some information from a fellow inmate. He'd already told Renee about the other inmate's account of the killing some days or weeks earlier.

Steve told Renee to bring Charlotte early so they could get into the first group of visitors. Hopefully, they would be able to visit in a private booth with doors they could close on either side of the glass, rather than one of the more open cubbyholes. He also said he wanted to speak to Charlotte alone first for a few minutes.

As Renee and Charlotte were driving over the next

morning, Steve called to confirm that his daughter had brought a piece of paper and a pencil, as he'd requested.

They were, in fact, able to get a private booth. After waiting outside for a few minutes while Steve talked to Charlotte, Renee went in and saw that they both seemed upset.

Sitting down, Renee looked up at the glass, where Steve was holding up a sheet of paper with tiny handwritten words for her to read. Without her glasses Renee couldn't make out the print very well, and she was also worried that someone might walk by and see them, so she quickly skimmed the note to get the gist of it. While Renee was reading, Charlotte wrote down the note's contents, as Steve had instructed.

The gist was, essentially, that two guys and a woman in a prescription-drug ring had come to Carol's house to "whack" her, because Jim Knapp was involved in illegal drug activities and had shared incriminating information with her.

The note was not only confusing, but the story seemed suspicious, even fabricated, to Renee. When she'd finished reading it, Steve said he wanted to get this information out to the lawyers, where it "could make a difference," but he knew they wouldn't believe the story if it came from him or from the inmate who wouldn't talk because he feared being labeled a "snitch." What he needed, Steve said cryptically, was someone on the outside to write an e-mail and send it to the authorities, to John Sears and to the prosecution.

"Have you told John about this?" Renee asked.

"No," Steve said.

"Well, wouldn't that be the person to tell?"

Renee knew that Steve was really asking her and

Charlotte to do this deed for him, a prospect that made her uncomfortable. She told herself she wasn't going to have anything to do with sending the e-mail, and she could see that Charlotte was struggling with the notion as well.

Still, although it sounded dangerous for Charlotte to do, Renee developed an intricate web of rationalization. She decided that she shouldn't try to stop Charlotte from fulfilling her father's request in case the story really was true, or, at the very least, if it would help create reasonable doubt in the case against him. He'd convinced Charlotte that the prosecution wouldn't believe him if he tried to go to the authorities himself, because he was the only suspect they'd ever investigated. His goal was to get law enforcement to investigate a different suspect, specifically Jim Knapp. Steve was facing a possible death sentence, and Charlotte didn't want to see her father put to death.

"It felt to me like he was up to something. I had the same mixed feelings that I've had the whole way through, which is that my intuitive sense is telling me he made up the story," Renee said later. "This other part of me wanted to believe that there was some hope, that there was some other answer out there that he wasn't guilty, so I wanted to believe that he had gotten that story from someone else."

Although Renee later acknowledged her gut feeling that Steve had totally fabricated the voice story, she said he never admitted that to her.

As Renee and Charlotte left the jail and drove back to the condo, the teenager was teary-eyed, partly because she thought she'd finally learned what had happened to her mother. Not surprisingly, she remained upset for the rest of the day.

Confused, Renee read over the notes Charlotte had taken at the jail. Steve called Renee a couple of hours later to check on his daughter's mood.

"How does she seem to you—okay?"

"Yeah, yeah."

"All right. I just wanted to impress upon her that it's necessary that this project really needs to be you and her."

"She's fairly nervous about it," Renee said.

"Yeah, that's why I just thought it would be best for you and her to have somebody else to talk to about this project."

He also told Charlotte not to talk to anyone else but Renee. "It really needs to be a project for you and Renee, and I wouldn't even trouble Katie with it, and definitely not John [Sears] for right now," he said.

Steve called back a few hours later to check on Charlotte again. "Of course you know that all I can think about is the letter I wrote you and the questions in it," he said. "Do you feel okay about this?"

"Yeah," she said.

"Good, just checking. I don't want to, you know, I was really hoping you'd feel okay about it. . . . It means a lot to me that the trust goes both ways. . . . I'm just asking you to trust my judgment. . . . Finally feels like there's something we can do to fight back."

But Renee—and the investigators who later listened to these taped conversations—believed that neither she nor Charlotte was comfortable with doing what Steve had asked them to do, for which, at that point, there was no real plan to carry out.

Initially Renee was resistant to go any further. "I'm not doing it and I don't think you should do it," she told Charlotte.

Charlotte seemed to believe that her dad's story was

true, and wanted to do whatever she could to help him, even though the whole prospect terrified her. It soon became clear that Charlotte was the one who had to do the deed. She wanted her dad home, and she had her own car. Plus Renee didn't think she could stop the teenager anyway.

"She was sixteen at this time. Why not say to her, 'No, you're not doing that, and here's why'?" Steve's attorney asked Renee in 2011.

"I wish I had," Renee replied. "I wish I had been able to think more clearly and I had been a stronger guide at that time. . . . The fact is, I was in over my head with huge, unbelievable amounts of work that I was doing all by myself. Charlotte was being horrible at home, and, frankly, I thought I wanted her dad home, too. She needs her dad."

And because Renee believed that she couldn't challenge Steve on a taped jail call, she said she also wished that she'd listened to her inner voice, which told her to talk to John Sears about the scheme.

"But the bottom line is, people in Steve's life don't want to disappoint him," she said. "He gets people to work for him."

The specifics of the plan to send the e-mail, which Steve said had to be sent anonymously, developed in the coming days during more cryptic calls.

On June 4, he told Charlotte that he wanted to make her more comfortable with the task at hand, so he'd been doing some research with a new cellmate. "There's a bit of an expert in here," he said. "He's talking all about the technology of it."

Investigators later learned that an inmate who was

serving time for identity theft, fraud and forgery had moved into Steve's cell that day.

As the plan came together, Charlotte and Renee discussed their reservations and how it would work. Charlotte visited the Prescott Public Library to find an Internet café where no one would know her, and from which she could safely send the e-mail. Renee assumed that meant a café in Phoenix or Scottsdale.

Charlotte would take a temporary phone, only for emergencies, but leave her regular cell phone in Prescott, thereby preventing anyone from tracking her whereabouts later through triangulation of the signal from her phone as it pinged off the towers. She also would wear sunglasses to mask her face from any surveillance cameras, and avoid social interaction with anyone who might remember her.

Charlotte and Renee visited Steve on June 9. Four days later, when Steve called his daughter, Charlotte told him, "I'll do anything it takes. . . . Whatever you were talking before . . . I'll do whatever you want."

"I want you to get the message real soon," Steve said. "I sent it to you through Renee, and Renee left it at her house."

After their conversation he called his girlfriend. "Did you get the message to Char?"

"Well, it's imminent," Renee replied.

The next day, Steve assured Renee, "You are going to do something that is pivotal to getting me out."

Steve also told Renee that if she had anything to give him privately, she should come to court and hand it to Sears, who could pass it on to Steve in a stack of legal papers, and vice versa, because no one searched those papers.

On June 18, Renee took Charlotte for another visit.

Afterward, Steve called to thank Renee "for what you did today."

Then he called Charlotte. "You're running some errands tomorrow?"

"Yeah, lots of errands tomorrow," Charlotte confirmed in their not-so-secret code.

"Thanks, sweetheart, you've helped me today."

"Good, I hope so."

When Steve called Charlotte first thing the next morning, she reiterated that she was about "to go do some errands" and expected to be back by six o'clock. He said he would call her then. (Investigators noted that he typically called her all day and night on her cell phone, "with no regard to what she was doing," so the only reason he wouldn't call her that day was so no one could track her phone activity.)

Renee gave Charlotte gas money for the trip. The only time Charlotte used her debit or credit cards that day was to rent a video in town.

A few minutes after hanging up with Charlotte, Steve called Katie. And as they talked about an interview that *48 Hours* had just done for its episode on the case, they joked about *Lithuanian hit men and contract killings, and about Carol being involved in an international drug trafficking ring,* as investigator Randy Schmidt described in his report.

This conversation takes place 4½ hours before the anonymous e-mail is sent to John Sears describing hit teams, contract killings, and international drug trafficking rings, he wrote.

Charlotte turned off her cell phone, then drove that afternoon to the Netlans Internet Café on East Thunderbird Road in Phoenix, the first café that came up in Google

searches for Phoenix and Arizona, and one of the closest
to Prescott. She paid several dollars in cash to use a terminal for an hour, signing in as a "guest" at two o'clock.

Her first task was to set up a Gmail account in the
name of "Anonymous Anonymous," with the address of
anonymousa4b9c4d3@gmail.com.

Next she sent an e-mail to John Sears at the address she
had for him through the state bar association. She spent
about thirty minutes trying to find an e-mail address for
prosecutor Joe Butner, then she attempted to find one for
Deputy County Attorney Mark Ainley or County Attorney
Sheila Polk. Unsuccessful, Charlotte settled on adapting
Sears's bar association address to send the e-mail to Butner,
but it bounced back as undeliverable.

Six minutes later she re-sent the first e-mail anonymously to Sears, asking him to forward it to the prosecutors: *I don't have their email and they need to read it more
than anyone.*

This e-mail later raised eyebrows among prosecution
investigators because few people knew that Butner had
taken over the case from Ainley. The investigators also
could tell that the anonymous sender didn't search for
Sears's e-mail address that day, so he must have already
known it.

The e-mail, into which Charlotte later said she purposely inserted typos and misspellings, read as follows:

> *I can't tell you who I am, but I can tell you what
> really happened the night Kennedy was killed.
> Knapp was running his mouth to Kennedy about a
> prescription drug deal he was in. Two men and one
> woman were sent to do them both. It was going to
> be a home invasion gone bad. Knapp and Kenedy
> used to drink together at night in her house.*

The 2 men would take them if they were together and the woman would be out front. If Knapp was in his apt, one man would take Kenedy and the woman would take Knapp and one man would be out front. the Two men thought Kennedy and knapp were together but when they went into the back bedroom they were wrong. Kennedy was on the phone not talking to Knapp. One man started to leave but they all ran into eachother in the hall outside her bedroom. She tried to run out a side door but one man got her with an asp. She didn't stay down and there was a fight. The 2nd man had an axe handle he from her bedroom instead of his asp. When it was over he threw it over the fence. THey had to leave quickly because she had been on the phone. They couldn't finish arranging the house. They also left behind one guys asp. They tried to go back for it but the cops were already there. 1 man left and the other man and woman stayed waiting for a decision about Knapp. word came to walk away from knapp but they stayed and the next night walked back into the house and got the asp. They also found the axe handle they used and got rid of it. Knapp was not killed by any of the men or woman. This wasn't one crazed man with a golf club. The people you're looking for are major prescription drug suppliers in phx connected to mexico canada and some other off shore operation. That's all I can say.

When Steve called Renee at 5:50 P.M., she was still waiting for Charlotte to come home. When he called again five minutes later, Renee said Charlotte had gone clothes shopping. Asked how things went, Renee told him they'd gone well.

Renee later told investigators that Charlotte returned to the town house feeling exhausted and hot. She told Renee that she'd parked some distance from the café so no one would see her getting out of her car, and it was stifling outside.

Once Charlotte got home, Steve finally reached her on her cell phone at 7:16 P.M. and asked how her day went. Charlotte replied that it was stressful and she'd gotten lost.

"Don't share anything outside the family," he cautioned.

When he called Renee again at 8:42 P.M., she told him that Charlotte was very tired and Jake had gone home early.

The morning after the first jail visit when Steve had told them about this story, Renee had suggested she call Sears to better understand what was going on, but Steve had told her repeatedly to keep this "project" between her and Charlotte. So when Sears asked Renee a day or so after he received the anonymous e-mails if she knew where they'd come from, she feigned ignorance.

John Sears took the bait and called the county attorney's office, saying he wanted to discuss some new information he'd received that pointed to his client's innocence.

On July 7, he met with County Attorney Sheila Polk, her chief deputy, Dennis McGrane, and prosecutor Joe Butner at their office. Sears asked for a waiver before disclosing the information, but the prosecutors refused, so Sears proceeded to disclose details of Steve's voice-in-the-vent story, noting that it dovetailed with, and was corroborated by, the anonymous e-mail.

Expressing concern that the prosecutors wouldn't take

this information seriously, Sears said he thought the stories told by the anonymous e-mailer and the voice at the jail were quite similar, but he believed they were authentic because they seemed to have originated from two different sources.

After the meeting Butner met with his lead investigator, Randy Schmidt, and asked him to look into the communications personally, but to keep it "in house." Butner didn't want anyone accusing them of failing to investigate these claims before the trial started.

Schmidt consulted with a Phoenix Police Department detective at the Arizona Counter Terrorism Information Center. They were able to determine the date and time the e-mail had been sent to the bar association and also that it had come from a Gmail address, but nothing else.

On July 13, Schmidt met with Sears, who gave him copies of the e-mails and the notes Steve said he'd scribbled while the voice was talking. Sears recounted that when he'd first let Steve read the e-mails, Steve became very upset and started to cry.

Sears also recapped Steve's voice story and described Steve's ideas about who that inmate could be. Because Schmidt couldn't read Steve's handwriting and wanted to hear the voice story directly from him, Schmidt and Sears arranged for another meeting on July 21.

From there, Schmidt set out to track down more specific and incriminating information. Through subpoenas and good detective work, he was able to determine many more details about how and where the e-mail account had been set up, along with the sender's browsing and search history.

Schmidt and fellow investigator Mike Sechez also went to the Internet café from which the e-mail had been sent. They talked to the owner, who showed them the actual terminal used, but, unfortunately, no surveillance video was available. And because the sender had paid in cash, he'd successfully left no electronic trail from debit or credit cards.

"We were pretty annoyed," Sechez recalled.

When Schmidt showed Steve the e-mails at the meeting, Steve started to weep. In fact, he became so emotional they had to take a break in the interview.

Steve said he was disturbed that the sender seemed so familiar with the inside of Carol's house, particularly with the axe handle she kept next to her bed. Schmidt agreed. Steve said he had no memory of whether that handle was still in the house when they cleaned it out for sale.

Steve noted that the sender also seemed to know what had gone on in the house before, during and after the murder, but he pointed out that the voice never mentioned a woman being involved in the killing.

As Steve recounted the voice story, he said he didn't want Schmidt or any other investigator to question inmates to try to determine the identity of the voice, because Steve didn't want to go into protective custody.

This surprised Schmidt. *I found it very odd that a person who was facing the death penalty for a capital murder case would not want me to determine who had actually committed the murder, because he did not want to be placed in protective custody,* he wrote in his report.

Steve said he'd talked to Sears about the voice and the e-mail, but not to his daughters, and not even to Renee, saying all he'd "intimated" to them was that investigators were "investigating something."

When Schmidt went back and listened to the recorded calls between Steve, Renee and his daughters from June 1 through June 30, this was an easy lie to detect. Clearly, Schmidt wrote, *[Those conversations] indicated that Mr. DeMocker had spoken to his daughters and to Renee Girard about both the voice in the vent and the "pending" plan to send the anonymous email to the prosecutor.*

Steve told Schmidt that he'd discussed some details from the voice story and e-mail with a few inmates, whom he named. Of the thirty-seven inmates in dorm N, he said, he thought thirteen of them could be the voice. However, investigators checked the ones he named and found they'd been released before the voice reportedly talked to Steve.

As Schmidt set out to prove or disprove Steve's story and the claims by the e-mailer and the voice, he systematically gathered booking photos and release dates for all of these inmates, diagrams of their jail cells, and intel about Steve's relationships with them. He also checked with law enforcement officials in Phoenix about Jim Knapp and the purported drug ring, but none of them, including the Drug Enforcement Agency task force, had heard of either one.

Investigator Mike Sechez was assigned to listen to Steve's jail calls as part of Schmidt's voice probe.

"[Steve] just thought he was so much brighter than the 'stupid' cops, so he would talk in code," Sechez said in 2014. "I've never seen anybody call his family so much. I think at last count it was over two thousand [calls]."

Steve was only allowed to use the pay phone for fifteen minutes at a time, so he would stop a conversation partway through, hang up and call the person back.

During his time in the general population, he was allowed to mingle with others on his pod. And as long as he had credit on his account, he could make calls from eight in the morning until nine at night. At that time he often made a dozen calls a day.

"His ego is so dramatic, it's mind-boggling," Sechez said. "In most cases, even as an investigator, you don't really get to have the total insights into your defendant." But in this case, he said, "I listened to thousands of hours of conversation and so I know this guy."

Renee's friend Reverend Dan Spencer said that as smart as Steve may be, he made major mistakes by creating the voice story and the anonymous e-mail—errors that, in his view, stemmed "from a lack of emotional awareness of how other people will perceive things."

CHAPTER 35

The defense team repeatedly tried to get the five death penalty "aggravators" against Steve dropped for lack of evidence and also to reduce his bail bond, which went as high as $2.5 million. The goal was to get him released with a GPS bracelet so he could help his attorneys prepare for trial.

Carol's killer is still walking free, Steve's parents wrote in a letter to the judge in the fall of 2009.

That November, the prosecution, referred to as "the state," listed the following aggravators, which made him eligible for a death sentence if he was found guilty of murder: *The state presented sufficient evidence to demonstrate probable cause to believe defendant brutally murdered Carol for pecuniary gain and to prevent her from reopening the divorce case and turning him in to the IRS. The state also presented sufficient evidence that the murder was committed in a cruel and depraved manner as well as a cold, calculated manner without pretense of moral or legal justification.*

At a hearing on November 17, Steve's daughters pleaded with the judge to release him on bail until trial.

Charlotte testified that her father wouldn't even kill spiders when she was young, only catch and release them. "If there is one thing I just know, it is that my father is not capable of what he is accused of," she said. "I am certain of my father's innocence and of his nonviolent nature."

It had been "acutely painful" for her to go through the tragic loss of her mother, she said, "but the added loss of my dad was and is unbearable."

Katie testified that both of her parents hated violence, and "despite the fact that I was a stubborn terror of a child sometimes," they didn't even believe in spanking. The last time she was spanked, she was "very, very little," and acting out in the backseat of the car. Carol did the deed and regretted it.

"It affected her and my dad so much that they decided from then on, I would only be given time-outs," she said. "I've never seen my parents, really, or my dad, be violent toward my family or my mom, or anyone. . . . The most he would ever do is yell at me, when I was being . . . the very stubborn child that I definitely had the tendency to [be]."

Katie, who was twenty-two by now, described Steve as her best friend over the last four years, the one she called when she was walking home from class, upset about boys or school. He'd been willing to wake up early, even before 5 A.M. if necessary, to edit a paper she'd just written, "just because he loved being our dad. He liked being there and being part of our lives."

Charlotte was the one who really needed him the most as she prepared to apply for college, Katie said. And although she appreciated the time Renee had been spending with her younger sister, "I don't think anyone can really replace a parent, especially in such discombobulated circumstances that are currently taking place" and that were causing "confusion and instability" in Charlotte's life.

The girls' attorney, Chris Dupont, noted his "bewilderment" when he heard that the judge presiding over Steve's first court appearance in October 2008 had ruled that his daughters were required to waive their victims' rights in order to maintain a relationship with him.

Judge Lindberg agreed. "I thought that was a misinterpretation of the law," he said.

As a result, Dupont said, he was joining the defense's motion to address this problem by asking the court to declare unconstitutional portions of the state Victims' Rights Act. This law had kept the girls from being advised of hearings, from being briefed by prosecutors and from speaking in court over the past year, Dupont said.

The defense also had been prohibited from contacting crime victims such as Ruth Kennedy for interviews unless they chose to talk, he said, and even then, such requests had to go through the county attorney's office. Attorney Anne Chapman explained that the defense team wanted to provide Ruth with information about "the lack of evidence, and about the state's failure to pursue other suspects who may still be out there."

The defense's inability to contact Ruth and Carol's brother, John, was violating Steve's right to a fair trial, they said. Furthermore, all of these factors had strained the relationship between the girls and their grandmother, with whom they'd once been very close.

Prosecutor Joe Butner objected to Dupont's characterization of the issues, contending that state law was not to blame for the girls' strained relationship with their grandmother, but "rather, it's a function of the facts in this case."

Chapman disagreed. "I know that they don't feel like

the information has been free-flowing from that office," she said.

Butner countered that the defense's arguments struck him "as being based upon false premises and concocted from the outset," because he'd tried to reach out to the girls through their attorneys.

Lindberg denied the defense's motion, and Steve remained in jail.

Trying to be supportive of Carol's daughters, Katherine Morris flew out to Los Angeles in advance of the trial and had dinner with Katie. Steve happened to call from jail while Katherine was picking her up.

"He thanked me for looking in on Katie, taking her to dinner, and [said] what a great support I was to her, you know, pleasantries," she recalled recently.

In one of the few conversations where she and Katie discussed the case, Katherine brought up a few points of contention in the evidence and posed some questions.

"What about the Internet searches?" she asked.

Katherine was skeptical of Steve's claims that these searches were done in the course of researching and writing a mystery novel. Looking back, Katherine recalled that she often saw Steve reading a book, but never writing one.

"I never heard that he was writing a book," Katherine said recently. "Never in my life."

But Katie said this was nothing new to her. "My dad always talked about writing a book," she said.

CHAPTER 36

In January 2010, Steve's frustration with his situation could be heard in his calls with Renee and Charlotte as he complained about a recent news report. The prosecution wanted to admit evidence against him relating to the cat-killing incident, a sex addiction and his alleged unethical behavior as a broker—all of which he summed up as "character assassination."

"I am pretty angry," he told Renee and Charlotte on January 8. "I just feel like I am being raped."

"The only thing that they have as true is that you had relationships with other women, and that happens," Charlotte said.

"But Mom did, too," Steve said.

"Mom did, too. They didn't even include that. They put blinders on. Left stuff out."

"They take this man who's never lifted a hand against anyone his whole life, I mean, the only physical violence I ever entered into is roughhousing with my friends and my brothers when I was growing up," Steve said. "I have never even been in a fight. . . . And they take this man who is an impeccable, incredibly ethical businessman, incredibly successful, because his clients trust him, and they accuse him of murder. And then, when that doesn't look like it's going to work, they accuse him of being a sex addict, of killing animals, you know, killing other people's pets."

Charlotte said the prosecution seemed to be "grasping for absolutely anything they can to make people believe that you are somehow this awful guy. They're bringing things up like you killing the neighbor cat, because it attacked our cat, like, eight times. . . . It is disgusting."

"I will come back from this," Steve said. "When this is over, Mom will still be gone. . . . I am horrifically victimized here."

Renee's already troubled relationship with Steve was crumbling under his months of manipulation, the pressures of the upcoming trial, repeated questioning by investigators and her nagging conscience. Bolstered by a grant of immunity from Judge Lindberg, she finally agreed to tell investigators where Steve's getaway bag was hidden.

Renee felt relieved to get this off her chest. She also felt justified that Steve's family wouldn't get angry with her for talking about this, because the investigators had already learned about the bag by listening to the recorded jail calls, not because she had confessed to it proactively.

"In the scheme of things, that bag didn't seem like a big deal to me," she said later. "However, I was not being forthright with the detectives that I knew about it or why it was there. . . . I don't like keeping secrets and I didn't like being dishonest. I'm not proud of myself for having done that. But by the time it came out, it was a relief to talk about it. I started to see the ways in which Steve had put me at risk, or I had allowed myself to be put at risk by Steve, and I was starting to be angry."

On April 9, 2010, Renee and her attorney, John Napper, agreed to meet with prosecutor Joe Butner and investigators at the county attorney's office. Renee told them that Steve had hidden the bag, which contained clothing, cash and supplies he would need to flee the country, near the Hassayampa golf course before his arrest. Knowing their jail calls were being recorded, they subsequently talked about the bag using code words such as "treasure."

Steve had been "all over the map" in terms of escape destinations, including Mexico and a "few wilderness areas," such as one close to the border in Texas, she said. She was going to stay behind, because she still had a son and a grandson living nearby.

"So he was going to take off and leave you," Butner said.

"So be it, his loss," she replied.

But Steve never seemed serious about fleeing, she said. One day he said he was going to retrieve the bag. Another day he discussed putting more money into it. The two of them went back to get it during the summer of 2008, but after rummaging through it, he zipped it back up and decided to leave it there.

Steve called her from jail in April 2009, the month she moved into his town house, while she was walking her dog in the area, and tried to help her find it. She and Charlotte were barely scraping by, and she thought they could use the money in the bag—only she couldn't locate it. She moved out of Steve's town house that September.

By the time she spoke to investigators about the bag in April 2010, she said she was fairly certain it was no longer there, but she agreed to take them to the area and try to help them find it.

That same day Renee led a group of eight, including Lieutenant Dave Rhodes, Commander Scott Mascher and investigator Mike Sechez, to the Hassayampa fitness center parking lot. Confused and having to retrace her steps at times, Renee led them past the eighth hole, looking for an opening near the tee-off area. She wandered off the fairway, down a steep drop to a creek bed, searching for a familiar spot in the tall, thin grass behind some granite boulders, where she thought Steve had hidden the bag.

When Sechez walked west of the trail, where Renee was standing, he spotted something that looked like a black plastic trash bag under a clump of bushes. Pulling the branches aside, he uncovered a deteriorated trash bag, partially wrapped around a blue sports bag. The blue bag, marked *DeMocker,* contained several pieces of clothing, a pair of shoes, a flashlight, a couple of hats and a Samsung flip phone with a Verizon logo, the last of which was wrapped in a clear plastic bag.

As the investigation continued, Detective Sy Ray, a cell phone expert with Gilbert Police Department's Criminal Apprehensive Team, tracked the cell phone towers that Jim Knapp's phone used when he made the seven fifty-eight call to check his voice mail on the night of the murder.

As Ray later testified, the signal pinged off a tower near Ann Saxerud's house—specifically tower 431 by Verde Lane. The call Jim made to Carol's cell phone at 9:37 P.M. from Bridle Path pinged off a different tower, 462. This, Ray said, showed that Jim's phone was not within three miles of Carol's house when she was killed. Ray acknowledged, however, that he could not tell where Jim's phone was between his 7:58 and 9:37 P.M. calls.

Ray also analyzed Steve's cell phone use over the course of a month in 2008, deeming the long period of time that

Steve's cell phone was powered off the night of the murder "irregular and outside the normal pattern seen."

Discounting Steve's trips out of state, the only other time his phone was turned off overnight was June 27, Ray said, when his phone was in the Scottsdale-Phoenix area. Ray also determined that on the night of the murder when Steve turned his phone back on, the signal pinged off the cell tower that was considered his "home tower," in the primary area where he made most of his calls, not near the area where he said he parked his car for the bike ride.

Based on my training and experience, this would be unusual given the late hour and complications reportedly encountered by Mr. DeMocker, Ray wrote in his report.

Looking for outside expert analysis, sheriff's detectives sent a CD of their crime scene photos, featuring the suspected killer's shoe prints, to the FBI in Quantico, Virginia.

In the fall of 2009, Eric Gilkerson, an FBI forensic examiner and shoe print expert, had conducted a search through two databases that catalogued photos of shoe soles by brand, trying to identify one with a pattern that could have made the prints. The first database contained twenty thousand to twenty-five thousand different images; the second database contained fifteen thousand to twenty thousand, with some overlap between the two.

Gilkerson got a hit in the FBI's internal database for the sole pattern—what he described as arrows in a "stair-type design" on the heel, arrows in the toe area, and a "line with a slight curve or circle" at the toe—in a La Sportiva model. Manually scrolling through the database, he found that La Sportiva made a model with that same pattern called the Ultranord. A subsequent search found that the Imogene and the Pikes Peak had that same pattern.

"There were no other shoes in . . . our databases that could have made this impression other than these La Sportiva shoes that are illustrated here," Gilkerson testified later, although he acknowledged that all he could say in court was that a comparison with shoes sent from the manufacturer showed that they "could have made" those prints. Without a flaw or identifying characteristics, he couldn't make a more definitive statement.

Going through Steve's bank records, sheriff's investigators spent days checking to see if he'd used his debit or VISA cards, which he used to make most purchases, to buy any La Sportiva shoes. And bingo.

They found that he'd ordered two pairs of running shoes from his friend Gareth Richards, the owner of an online sporting good business in Denver known as Outdoor Prolink. In early 2010, investigators contacted Gareth, who had been one of Steve's poker buddies and an adventure education instructor at Prescott College during the 1990s.

Gareth described La Sportiva as "probably the best mountaineering, backpacking shoe company in the world." By going through Prolink, which offers outdoor professionals password-protected access to discounts, Steve got a significant deal and paid about half the regular price, which came to a total of $101, including shipping, for the two pairs. While these shoes were not specifically made for use with a mountain bike, Gareth said a person could wear them while riding a bicycle.

Steve purchased the shoes on April 22, 2006, and had them shipped to his UBS office four days later. One model was called the Pikes Peak, a trail running shoe with trademarked FriXion rubber, designed to stick to and grip surfaces. The other, also a trail running shoe, was called the Raja. Each model had a completely different pattern on the sole.

Investigators purchased a pair of each to compare them to the suspect's tracks behind the house at Bridle Path. Asked to do additional analysis, Gilkerson reported back that the tread pattern of the Pikes Peak model could have made the murder suspect's tracks behind the house. The Rajas could not.

Further investigation showed that nearly 8,600 pairs of men's shoes with that pattern had been sold in North America (or were being warehoused) by the day of.the murder. That included 3,800 pairs of the Pikes Peak, only 349 of which were sold in Steve's size. About a third as many women's shoes were sold with that same pattern.

Detectives were never able to find the missing pair of Pikes Peak shoes, and they never asked Steve about them during their interviews with him. But he later told his own attorneys that he generally went through a lot of running shoes; they usually lasted only six months before he donated them to charity or threw them away.

"He has no recollection of that pair of shoes," defense investigator Rich Robertson said later.

However, when investigators went back and examined the photos of Steve's closet more closely, they noticed that the compartment above the pair of Rajas contained only a shoe box, but no shoes. It was this compartment, they speculated, where Steve likely had stored the missing pair of La Sportiva Pikes Peaks.

As prosecutors later pointed out, Steve "was a meticulous, neat man."

In April 2010, detectives also sent Carol's Adidas running shoes to Gilkerson, asking if they could have made the "three Z's" pattern depicted in the photos of the other shoe prints behind her house. He concluded that her shoe print was "similar in design" and "could have made the impression."

But because of "limited detail" and a lack of "sufficient identifying characteristics"—such as a cut, defect or rock stuck in the bottom of the shoe that could be matched to the area where the shoe prints were found—he said he couldn't make a more definitive identification. And because he wasn't sent a casting of the print or photos that had a size scale, he also couldn't match the size of the actual shoe with the impression.

Continuing to look for the murder weapon, volunteers and dive teams from Pima and Yavapai Counties used imaging and radar systems in the lake surrounding the Hassayampa golf course, in Granite Basin and in other Prescott area waterways. But all they found was a muddy right-handed club, apparently thrown into the muck by a frustrated golfer.

CHAPTER 37

With jury selection scheduled to begin in early May, the tensions surrounding the case escalated as hyperbolic accusations flew in every direction—attorney against attorney, the defense against County Attorney Sheila Polk, and the prosecution against Judge Lindberg.

Alleging bias against the state's case and a lack of impartiality by Lindberg, prosecutor Joe Butner asked for a meeting in the judge's chambers, requesting that he recuse himself from the case.

Lindberg granted the meeting on April 2. He restated his previous comments from an in-chambers meeting on March 30, in which he'd said that as part of the state's case in chief he wasn't going to allow the state to bring up Steve's multiple affairs, his use of the HGH injections or the FINRA complaints against him. However, Lindberg had said those elements could be used as evidence in the penalty phase if the case reached that point.

"And you made the comment 'I don't believe we are going to get there,'" Butner said, alleging that this remark showed a clear bias against the state's case.

"I don't think I said that," Lindberg said. "I think I said, 'I am not sure we are going to get to that.'"

The judge had already struck down two death penalty aggravators—allegations that the murder was "cold and calculating" and that Steve killed Carol to prevent her from going back to court to reopen the divorce and from reporting him to the IRS for tax fraud.

But even as he found probable cause to support three others, Lindberg still asked if the state planned to continue to evaluate its overall death penalty allegation. And this worried the prosecution.

"I was really, really concerned that you have, at least to some extent, made up your mind in this case, that you have prejudged the case to some extent, that you are no longer impartial and that you have some bias," Butner said.

Defense attorneys John Sears and Larry Hammond said they didn't remember the comment precisely, but Hammond said he didn't regard it as a prejudgment or it would have stuck in his mind. Because the comment was made in an off-the-record conversation, no transcript existed to check. The meeting had been held in chambers for fear of prejudicing the jury pool with media coverage.

"I don't believe that there is a reason for me to recuse from the case at this point, so I am going to deny the request," Lindberg said, adding that if the state wanted to put this issue on the record, "or do something else, please do."

Butner said he would have to do so, and promptly filed a motion for a change of judge, alleging that Lindberg had shown "favoritism" toward the defendant and an apparent surrender of his "independent judgment." All parties agreed to suspend trial proceedings until a different judge could resolve the issue.

After a short break, during which Lindberg contacted

t was long hair. So I—I guess I am confused, I
"

ued that Jana was not only confused, she also
to connect Steve or his bike to what she saw
d her testimony should be precluded at trial.
against the defense's motion, Butner said Jana
d around during the interview process," after
conducted an "ambush interview" in which
d down the garden path" to make contrary
o what she'd said before.

ss, he said, her testimony still bolstered the
that Steve parked his car across Williamson
, rode his bike to the Glenshandra trailhead,
ed it over the fence, hiked toward Carol's
the bike in some bushes, then hiked the rest
lled Carol and rode his bike back to his car.
ve we are missing things from the homicide
uld have been carried away in a backpack,"
"We also think our killer probably either
with him or her, or . . . took attire away, so
A backpack could have been used for that.
e approximate time of day when the killer
rived."

conceded that the evidence was relevant in
son saw a man riding a bike that day in the
ere detectives found bike tracks and shoe
er, agreeing with the defense that Jana's
d mislead and confuse the jury, he granted
tion to preclude it.

, 2010, Detective John McDormett received
a one-page typed anonymous letter, dated

Judge Robert Brutinel to confirm that he could hear the motion immediately in his courtroom, Hammond said he wanted to put his concerns on the record, too.

"We think this motion is filed in bad faith," he said. "We think it is filed for inappropriate reasons having to do with the state's position in this case. We think it is nothing short of outrageous." And Lindberg, he said, shouldn't be selecting the judge who would hear the state's motion.

Nonetheless, the parties moved into Brutinel's courtroom, where Butner countered for the record that filing his motion was done in good faith, not to delay the trial. "I have never, ever filed a motion like this before," he said.

At this point Judge Brutinel had to put Judge Lindberg under oath to testify about his alleged comment. Butner was allowed to question Lindberg and the defense attorneys about how Lindberg's statement should be characterized, after which the defense attorneys were allowed to cross-examine each other.

With a whole day of motions pending and the trial looming a month ahead, taking time out for this hearing made for quite a bizarre legal scene.

Taking the stand, Lindberg denied any concerns that there was a lack of evidence to support a death penalty allegation, saying he was only trying to ensure that both sides were moving forward "with a diligence that I think is required . . . where the state has asked me for that ultimate sanction."

Brutinel ruled that Lindberg should be allowed to continue on the case. Lindberg admitted this was his first death case, but he said he wasn't morally opposed to imposing this ultimate sanction.

A week later he struck down two of the three remaining death penalty aggravators as a sanction against the state for the late disclosure of evidence the state planned to present at trial. That left only one: murder with the expectation of receiving something of pecuniary value. Meaning, in other words, for financial gain.

As the attorneys continued to debate which witnesses could present testimony at trial, Jana Johnson was called for a hearing on May 26. Jana was the only witness who claimed to have seen a man on a bicycle in Carol's neighborhood on the evening of the murder. Her testimony showed how a person's memory can change over time, can be inexact or even faulty and, when vulnerable to change via suggestions by either side, can be thrown out altogether.

Jana, a homemaker who lived on the 2300 block of West Glenshandra Drive, had worked with police in the past to report license plate numbers related to odd goings-on in a neighborhood park bathroom.

During an interview with detectives in late September 2008, she said she'd been sewing on the afternoon of the murder when she caught a five-second glimpse of a male bicyclist with a similar build as her husband—tall, slender and fit at six-one and 170 pounds.

She didn't see the man's face, but she remembered his hair being short, and his bike tires being fat and wide, not thin like a racing bike, more like a mountain bike. He was wearing blue jeans, a short-sleeved shirt and a backpack. And he was pedaling unusually fast for the neighborhood, "like he was on a mission."

He was pedaling from the direction of Williamson Valley Road—heading west to east—toward the end of Glenshandra, where the detectives later found the bike tracks they

said were consistent with Ste
boy's bike," she said, with a

In 2008, she originally sa
2 and 5 P.M., but by the time
later, she'd expanded the tir
She also said she remember
go down, and that it could ha
or even "eightish" at night. (
tually set at seven forty-six
confusion during her earlie
by detectives questioning h

Defense investigator Ric
her home in May 2010, jus
hearing, and returned the n
son then talked to prosec
again during a visit to his

When she talked to Ro
have been younger—colle
hair flying in the wind. S
tives had never shown he
After seeing photos of S
she didn't remember the

During the hearing
what she actually saw a
by both sides. She ackr
lections had changed a
By this point, she cou
man's hair or whether

"Now you're sayin
member?" defense at

"Well, no," she sai
talked to the detectiv
short hair, right in th

you again,
don't knov
Sears a
wasn't abl
that day, a
Arguing
was "push
the defens
she was "l
statements
Nonethe
state's theo
Valley Roa
where he li
house, reste
of the way, l
"We beli
scene that c
Butner said
brought attir
to speak. . . .
And that is t
would have a
The judge
that Jana Joh
same area wl
prints. Howe
testimony cou
the defense m

On August
in his mailbox

August 16, that read: *On the night of the murder of Carol Kennedy, Steven DeMocker wore a disguise that included dark blue overalls and a long, disheveled gray-haired wig with matted hair just above shoulder length.* The letter was signed: *A concerned citizen.*

CHAPTER 38

When jury selection began on May 4, it proved to be a serious, long and grueling task. The judge and attorneys needed to seat eighteen jurors, including six alternates, who could be objective and willing to vote for a death sentence if Steve was found guilty of murder.

A somewhat intimidating prospect for members of the jury pool, they were called in, one at a time, to sit in the front row and were questioned for hours. The two prosecutors sat at one table, but there were so many men in suits at the defense table that some prospective jurors couldn't tell who was who.

During voir dire one man stopped speaking abruptly, as if he'd just had an epiphany. "Oh, my gosh, I thought you were the defendant," he said to prosecutor Joe Butner.

The jury had yet to be impaneled when the state decided at the last minute to drop the remaining "pecuniary value" death penalty aggravator. The state filed a motion to do so on May 26, which the judge granted that day.

Chief Deputy County Attorney Dennis McGrane told the *Daily Courier* that Carol's "surviving family members opposed the death penalty and prosecutors take victims' view into account."

After the attorneys had spent nearly a month choosing a jury that was going to be able to mete out a death sentence, the defense balked, arguing that "death-qualified" juries were more prone to convict than "non-death-qualified" juries. The judge, however, ruled that the panel they had selected was just fine.

As defense attorney John Sears was delivering his opening statement on June 3, the prosecution team, which had prepared to present 186 witnesses, learned for the first time that Hartford had paid out on Carol's life insurance policies. Detectives were under the impression that Hartford wasn't going to pay on the policies unless and until Steve was cleared of murder, as it had indicated in the five denial letters it sent to Steve rejecting his attempts to collect the money.

Robertson watched as the prosecution's investigators scrambled into action in the courtroom.

"You could see their eyebrows shooting up and they started ducking out," he said. "It was kind of mystifying at first as to what caused that. And, of course, we had no idea that they didn't know that the life insurance had been paid out to the girls. They failed to ask the right questions of the life insurance company. There was no attempt to hide anything. They kept asking whether the proceeds had been paid out to Steve."

* * *

Judge Lindberg was usually prompt in starting the proceedings each day, taking regular breaks at certain times. But on June 16, the eighth day of trial, Lindberg interrupted the testimony of Sergeant Luis Huante to break for lunch fifteen minutes sooner than usual, with fifty-three juror questions pending.

"We're going to take our break a little bit early," he said, prompting the attorneys and investigators to look at each other, wondering what was up.

As the jury was filing out and people were gathering their belongings, Lindberg stood up and walked down the steps that led to his chambers. He sat down in his easy chair and promptly fell onto the floor.

Seeing Lindberg collapse, one of the deputies ran in, helped the judge back into the chair and emerged a minute later. "He's fine," he said. "The judge just fell down."

Startled by this chain of events, defense investigator Rich Robertson now understood what had precipitated the judge's abrupt manner. He wasn't feeling well.

A minute later the judge rose from his chair and collapsed again.

"The judge fell!" the defense team's paralegal shouted, prompting Robertson and Lieutenant Dave Rhodes to run into chambers to help.

Finding the judge flat on his back, Rhodes felt for a pulse and started chest compressions, while Robertson got into position to begin mouth-to-mouth resuscitation. It took only a couple of compressions before the judge took a huge breath and opened his eyes wide, a bewildered and frightened expression spreading over his face.

"Do you have any nitroglycerin?" Robertson asked, thinking that Lindberg had suffered a heart attack. The judge shook his head slightly.

As they let him sit up and gather himself, Lindberg seemed embarrassed at the public spectacle he'd caused.

"At this point we weren't sure exactly what was happening," Robertson said later. "Dave Rhodes concluded he was in full cardiac arrest. But looking back, I'm not so sure."

When the paramedics arrived, Robertson stepped out of the courtroom just in time to see the judge's wife and son, who lived fairly close to the courthouse, running up the stairs.

"This damn case," Lindberg's wife said. "This damn case."

A crowd of onlookers that had gathered watched as paramedics wheeled the judge into the elevator on a gurney and into the ambulance outside. After Lindberg got to the hospital, the doctors "realized fairly quickly this wasn't a heart thing," Robertson said. Diagnosed with a brain tumor, the judge was flown by helicopter that evening to a Phoenix hospital specializing in brain injuries.

Robertson said he didn't remember seeing any signs of the brain tumor before this incident, but he had no doubt that the judge had been "stressed out" about this high-profile case.

"He was very religious, a staunch Catholic, which made it difficult for him sitting on a death penalty case, and I know that added a certain amount of stress to his job," Robertson said. "These were highly litigious attorneys on both sides, so there were a lot of pretrial motions, and they weren't used to this amount of pretrial litigation."

The trial was suspended until a new judge could be assigned, during which time the defense tried again to get a further reduction in Steve's bail, which was now at

$1 million. After a previous attempt to lower it to $250,000 had failed, this time they tried for $350,000, but no deal.

Judge Warren R. Darrow, who was making a name for himself with the highly publicized "sweat lodge" case of so-called "spiritual warrior" and self-help author James Ray, was appointed on July 2. (Ray didn't go to trial until 2011, when he was convicted of negligent homicide. Three people had died and eighteen others were hospitalized after participating in his ritualistic "spiritual cleansing" ceremony near Sedona in 2009.)

The DeMocker trial resumed on July 21, 2010, with Sergeant Huante back on the stand.

But the drama did not end there. More allegations erupted behind the scenes as Judge Darrow held a series of closed hearings on issues filed in sealed briefs, stemming from the state's request to disqualify the defense team after the county attorney's office had opened a separate criminal investigation into the transfer and payment of Carol's insurance money.

By this time the prosecution had learned that the money had been paid to the girls, to Steve's parents and then to Steve's defense attorneys, and the state believed that this was not only improper but criminal. The pleadings and hearing minutes were later unsealed.

John Sears, named as a witness to several notarized filings, including the switch of trustee from Katie to Renee, described the issues that the prosecution had raised concerning the money transfer as "irrelevant" and "unfairly prejudicial" to Steve. He summed them up as an attempt by the state to distract the court from the murder case and to "dirty up" and "smear Mr. DeMocker and his lawyers to the jury."

Joe Butner countered that the nature and details of the money transfer were entirely relevant, saying, "Mr. De-Mocker managed to gain the benefit of those life insurance proceeds after he had killed his ex-wife, and that is something the state is entitled to argue to this jury."

At issue was whether the defense team could continue to represent Steve while a criminal investigation hung over its head. The defense attorneys indicated that they "would not be able to continue with the trial while they are defending themselves."

Judge Darrow initially agreed, saying he believed "that the situation gives rise to an unwaivable conflict of interest." He also said, however, that he didn't agree with the state "that the situation rises to substantiating a criminal offense," meaning "some type of theft." He agreed to suspend the trial while the defense team conferred with its client.

After hearing more of the state's evidence, Darrow found it did not support the prosecution's allegations. He also ruled that the defense had no conflict in proceeding. The state agreed, in turn, to stay the investigation into the defense team, and to refer the matter of any potential criminal involvement by defense attorneys to an agency outside the county attorney's office. That did not stop the prosecution's investigation into Steve's role in the money transfer, however.

The trial started up again with some surprising testimony by Dr. Philip Keen, the county medical examiner.

Keen testified that one evening after the autopsy he'd

transported Carol's body, in a body bag in the back of his pickup truck, to the Forensic Science Center in Phoenix. He was going to Phoenix anyway, so this "just was convenient," he said.

"It was tied down," Keen testified. "I had a little bungee strap. The vinyl bags have handles and I have hooks in the bed of my truck. Just put the bungee strap to the corner so it doesn't go anywhere."

Keen acknowledged that July evening temperatures in Phoenix could rise to "in excess of a hundred degrees."

His goal was to have Dr. Laura Fulginiti, the forensic anthropologist, examine Carol's skull fractures and do a reconstruction. However, she was unable to do the project at that time, so a transport service returned the body to Prescott a few days later.

Keen testified that sheriff's officials brought him a golf club—the exemplar Callaway Big Bertha #7—to see if the shape of the club's head matched up with the margins of Carol's skull fractures. At this point Keen decided to do his own reconstruction to validate his theory that Carol had been beaten with a wooden driver club.

He took a Styrofoam ball, laid some papier-mâché over it, then placed the pieces of her scalp and skull over the paper, taking care not to damage the tissue and bones any further, because he still wanted Fulginiti to do her own reconstruction.

"And you found . . . the golf club and the fracture to be similar?" defense attorney Larry Hammond asked.

"Yes, sir."

Keen acknowledged, however, that he made no notes of this effort, nor did he write up a report until later. He chose to wait until after Fulginiti did her reconstruction, which involved flushing and cleaning the skull pieces, then gluing them back together.

Although he and Fulginiti agreed that some of the fractures were "consistent" with a golf club beating, he said, they "could not specify precisely what instrument caused" the other fractures. They also couldn't rule out the use of multiple instruments or multiple attackers. In the end the golf club was still his "primary explanation" for a weapon, but not Fulginiti's.

On redirect by prosecutor Joe Butner, Keen discussed how he originally settled on the golf club as the most likely murder weapon, after he'd "dismissed a variety of things which you may see in beating-type deaths. The injuries just don't conform to those other kinds of objects."

Keen acknowledged that he'd used unsterilized nail clippers to cut Carol's nails, which he admitted was "not good practice."

Under cross-examination by Hammond, Keen said his assistant tried to identify other autopsies in which those clippers might have been used and potentially contaminated evidence in this case.

"And what she found," Hammond asked, "was that there was no occasion upon which those clippers were used in which there was a reasonable possibility that DNA from someone in a prior autopsy could have been transferred to the body of this woman?"

"I think that's also correct," Keen said.

In September, shortly after his testimony, Keen landed a $205,000-a-year job as chief medical examiner for the state of Oklahoma.

After all, the sixty-seven-year-old had a good résumé:

Keen had been Yavapai County's ME for nearly thirty years, until 2009, and had spent twenty years working for Maricopa County's office, fourteen as chief ME, until 2006. For the six years he was associate chief in Maricopa County, he was working in Yavapai as well. During his career he'd performed twelve thousand autopsies and had spent a year as president of the Arizona Medical Association.

But less than a month after the *Oklahoman* published a story recounting the highlights of Keen's testimony in the DeMocker case, the Oklahoma Board of Medicolegal Investigations withdrew its job offer.

"In retrospect . . . I probably would have done it differently," Keen told the *Oklahoman*. "There was a lot of urgency in this particular case. . . . It was an unusual event."

Although Keen acknowledged that he'd moved eight or ten other bodies in his truck or in a sheriff's vehicle over the past thirty years, he contended that he was not a kook.

"If people think I'm a little bit kooky, they might consider the fact that I'm the only pathologist that's been elected to be the president of the Arizona Medical Association. That's not exactly a credential of a kooky person," he said.

CHAPTER 39

As the trial proceeded in the courtroom, investigators for the prosecution were still pursuing leads in the field that they'd been following for quite some time, working against the clock to nail down evidence to dispute Steve's voice-in-the-vent story before it was too late and the case was sent to the jury.

Over a period of nine months in 2009 and 2010, Randy Schmidt and other investigators had tracked down and interviewed a series of inmates—in and out of jail—who could have been the voice. But none admitted to being the voice or knowing about the e-mail.

One prisoner said the only time he'd heard anything about Jim Knapp was when he overheard Steve telling other inmates that Jim was involved in an OxyContin drug ring. Steve denied making that statement, and the information couldn't be independently traced to anyone else. (Defense investigator Rich Robertson said he could not disclose any details from his own investigation into this alleged drug ring, saying it was proprietary work product.)

Schmidt ultimately determined that Steve had made up both stories from the voice and in the e-mail.

In late May 2010, the state filed a motion to preclude the defense from being able to use the anonymous e-mail as evidence. The defense argued to keep it in, saying, "There are inherent details inside this e-mail that even the investigator conceded that the person had some familiarity with the inside of the victim's home beyond what was available in the public record. There are aspects of the allegations in this e-mail that are consistent with our investigation of the physical injuries suffered by Carol Kennedy."

During a hearing on June 3, prosecutor Joe Butner argued that the e-mail was "clearly a hearsay document," and they still couldn't prove who sent it.

"We investigated Mr. DeMocker's statements of how it may have originated from somebody in the jail that he had conversation with through the jail vents. We were never able to find out that kind of information or validate this e-mail from any source," Butner said.

Asked by the judge how he planned to handle this in court, Sears said he would call prosecution investigator Randy Schmidt to testify about his fifteen-page investigative report, which had traced the e-mail to an Internet café in Phoenix. Butner rightly noted that no one could be cross-examined about the e-mail, though, because they only knew where and when it was sent, not the identity of its author or the truth of its contents.

The judge denied the state's motion.

Riled up, Schmidt and his fellow investigators got back to work, and submitted a supplemental investigative report on September 3, pointing to Steve, Charlotte and Renee as conspirators in sending what amounted to a fraudulent anonymous e-mail.

The sheriff's office, which was doing its own investigation, sent the anonymous e-mails, along with Schmidt's investigative report, to the FBI's Behavioral Analysis Unit (BAU) in Quantico.

Overall, the FBI BAU team indicated that the anonymous email was nonsense and was created specifically to remove suspicion from Steven DeMocker and not direct investigators to the 'real' killers, Schmidt later wrote.

FBI analysts noted that the e-mail described the crime scene staging in a way that was inconsistent with a "hit man" scenario. The analysts noted that killers would only stage a scene if they had ties to the victim, not if they were total strangers. Specifically, the analysts deemed it implausible that a hit team of two men and one woman would come to a house without a weapon and use one they found there. They also didn't believe that the e-mail was written by a male inmate, but rather a female family member or close friend of Steve's, partly because the female member of the hit team was characterized as the heroine. Furthermore, if Jim Knapp was the implied target of this hit team, why kill Carol and leave without killing Jim? This scenario was not only implausible, they said, it was absurd, noting that the fact Carol and Jim drank wine together at night was never publicized.

After gathering all of this information, Schmidt concluded it was either Katie, Charlotte or Renee who had sent the e-mail. He compared the two e-mails sent to John Sears with those Charlotte had sent her mother. And after determining that the second anonymous e-mail was similar in style to the short e-mails Charlotte had sent to Carol just before the murder—starting sentences with lower-case letters and running sentences together, using commas to separate the phrases—Schmidt determined that she was the most likely author.

Around this same time Renee's minister friend Dan Spencer, with whom she'd been discussing her feelings for months, gave investigator Mike Sechez a copy of the notes that Renee had taken from the scribblings Steve had held up to the glass at the jail. The minister also told Sechez that Renee was getting ready to break up with Steve and wanted to tell the truth.

Sechez was skeptical, describing Renee as "a pure follower" and Steve's puppet. Up until this point he and other investigators had interviewed Renee several times, but she'd never been willing to say anything that truly incriminated Steve.

Sechez put a packet together with all the evidence investigators had gathered, pointing to Charlotte as the e-mail's author and to Renee as a willing participant, and gave it to Renee's attorney, John Napper, on Thursday, September 16, 2010.

In court that same day, sheriff's Detective Roger Hoover was on the stand testifying about the various text messages investigators had collected. The jury was excused in the early afternoon to allow the lawyers to argue the admissibility of some other e-mails, and was then dismissed at three-forty while the court dealt with possible juror-misconduct issues that were not publicly disclosed.

Tensions between the lawyers and Judge Darrow were so high that day that the judge actually "stood up, stormed off the bench and went into his chambers, leaving all of us just sitting, staring at each other," defense investigator Rich Robertson recalled. "He came back to the bench twenty minutes later and was still hot, lashing out at all parties."

Those tensions spilled over into discussions the next day, when the jury was not present. The panel wasn't called back until the following week, not knowing that all hell had broken loose behind the scenes.

Now that the prosecution's investigators had figured out who was behind the anonymous e-mail, Renee was finally ready to talk. Facing criminal charges for conspiracy and tampering with evidence if she didn't, Renee agreed to testify as long as she received immunity against any charges.

The prosecution team quickly arranged an interview for that Sunday afternoon, September 19, where Renee came clean about the origins of the anonymous e-mail. Ultimately, Renee's immunity agreement was extended to three issues: one for the getaway bag, one for the insurance money transfers and one for the e-mail. Renee said she had only one more jail-recorded conversation with Steve after this interview.

Asked about attorney John Sears's knowledge of how this e-mail came to be sent to him, Renee said, "My belief has always been that John Sears did not know about this e-mail, about who authored it or who sent it."

Once Renee had revealed these details, the prosecution team arranged for Charlotte to be interviewed on September 25, telling her attorney that Renee had talked, and they now had proof that Charlotte had sent the e-mail. They offered to give her immunity from charges as well, if she would tell the truth about what had happened.

"She was a victim of her dad, too," Mike Sechez said. "We didn't want to hurt her. We just wanted the truth. She's just a young kid, manipulated by her dad."

Charlotte's attorney, Chris Dupont, called the day before the interview to cancel it, saying that based on his advice, his client refused to be questioned. Eventually, though, she had to accept the immunity agreement and agree to testify about the e-mail or face criminal fraud charges.

As it turned out, Detective Hoover was the last witness to testify in this trial. When the jury came back on September 21 and 28, it was dismissed once again as the parties continued to assess the situation behind the scenes.

Although Renee said she'd never discussed this matter with anyone else, Reverend Dan Spencer told the prosecution team that she'd confessed the whole story to him several months earlier.

In his view Renee didn't "buckle" because of pressure from the prosecution. "Renee was conflicted from day one, and this is something the detectives never understood," he said.

She felt a lot of shame and regret about being involved and complicit in the creation and distribution of the anonymous e-mail, he said. She'd felt torn about what to do because she was taking care of Charlotte, who thought her father was innocent, and yet Renee was also worried what might happen to Charlotte if she followed her father's wishes.

"She didn't want to be the first and last woman to say no to Steve," the minister said, "but she was burdened with it, and I knew that she didn't like not being able to cooperate and be more forthcoming about how she felt."

As soon as Renee delivered her confession bombshell, she effectively stopped the trial in its tracks. And once word of this got out, the wheels came off the defense's case.

"It resulted in the attorneys and the legal team trying to

figure out what the implication of all that was, and that was not an easy process," defense investigator Rich Robertson said.

His reaction? "I was clearly disappointed in everybody that was involved" in sending that e-mail, he said.

This series of events set off a flurry of phone calls and meetings, resulting in a superseding grand jury indictment, a whole new conflict-of-interest situation for the defense and a new set of charges being filed against Steve on September 29. In addition to the original first-degree murder and burglary counts, the state added one count of tampering with physical evidence, two of forgery, two of fraudulent schemes and artifices, one of fraudulent schemes and practices, one of conspiracy and one of contributing to the delinquency of a minor.

Yet another indictment, with ten charges against Steve DeMocker, was issued on December 10, 2010. Steve pleaded not guilty and was held on a $2 million bond.

During this time Steve's defense attorneys petitioned the court to withdraw from the case, citing a conflict of interest. This move, which the prosecution opposed in filings under seal, sparked what investigator Rich Robertson described as a "weird transition period."

Not only had the defense team been placed in an immediate ethical quandary over the e-mail and voice-in-the-vent story, but the team still faced the threat of a future criminal investigation into the insurance money transaction that had paid Steve's legal costs.

"I suspect the team could have weathered one or the

other of those," Robertson said, "but the cumulative effects made this extremely difficult for the team going forward."

None of this was made public until some court filings were unsealed later and County Attorney Sheila Polk testified in another matter related to this case in 2013.

Polk testified that she'd contacted the state bar association twice, "seeking guidance," when she felt she needed to report possible criminal conduct and ethics violations by attorney John Sears concerning the insurance money transfer.

"I believe that there was a conflict" by Sears, she testified, adding that she also believed that he'd lied in his opening statement when he indicated that the insurance money was paid out, but not in a way that benefited Steve, when it had, in fact, paid off his defense attorneys.

Polk said she filed a bar complaint "as information was emerging about additional criminal conduct committed by the defendant and the role of Mr. Sears in facilitating, aiding and abetting the conduct." She denied filing the complaint because she was in the "heat of the battle," saying rather that she felt obligated to file it.

The bar investigation was stayed until the DeMocker case was resolved in court, after which Sears was cleared of Polk's allegations by the State Bar of Arizona.

The trial stalled in 2010 because the defense attorneys believed they couldn't continue to represent Steve until the courts decided whether they "could or should continue with this case" after the anonymous e-mail's origins were revealed, Robertson said. This paralysis finally stopped the trial altogether, because Judge Darrow, mired in pleadings and motions, "kind of threw up his hands and said, 'We can't do anything more.'"

Defense attorneys' interests need to be in line with the defendant's and when those interests conflict, "then the attorneys need to withdraw," Robertson said. "That can happen when the client, the defendant, isn't forthright about things, or creates a situation where the attorneys have to defend themselves rather than their client."

Sears declined to comment on these matters or on the DeMocker case in general for this book, saying this was his usual practice, but Steve also didn't give him permission to do so.

The bottom line is this: At the end of the conflict-of-interest skirmish over the anonymous e-mail, which went all the way to the state supreme court in filings under seal, the defense team was allowed to withdraw from the case.

In December 2014, the county attorney's office refused to comment on whether any investigation was still pending against Sears. However, no charges had been filed against him or any other member of the defense team as of that date. A knowledgeable source said the U.S. Attorney's Office had looked at the state's allegations against the defense attorneys, and Sears in particular, and declined to prosecute.

Although defense investigator Rich Robertson denied doing anything wrong in the ethical mess of the anonymous e-mail and voice story, he was sucked in by implication.

In September 2007, a man and his girlfriend were attacked in his home in Williamson Valley, bound with duct tape and robbed of money, a laptop and video games.

The man, who was hit in the head with a crowbar, was seriously injured but recovered.

Prosecutors viewed it as no coincidence that Robertson had requested a copy of the sheriff's investigative report about the incident, and three months later, Steve DeMocker came up with his voice-in-the-vent story.

"It's like a blueprint for the voice in the vent and the anonymous e-mail," prosecutor Jeff Paupore said in early 2014, recalling the chain of events before being appointed to the bench later that year.

This inference became the basis for a defense motion for a mistrial during the second trial, which the judge denied.

Robertson characterized this imbroglio as another ex- ample of the prosecution twisting the facts around to match its wild speculative theories, because he never gave the report to Steve. "There was no reason to," he said, al- though he acknowledged that he did tell Steve about the incident and it also came up during the trial in 2010.

Robertson said he asked for an investigative report on this incident in the Hootenanny Holler neighborhood as part of his own investigation into similar home-invasion crimes in the Williamson Valley area.

The assault victim "was hit in the head with a blunt- force object and left there," he said. "Our point there was . . . whether [the sheriff's detectives] knew where that guy wound up, and where did the guy who was attacked go, because they never arrested anyone."

What infuriated Robertson was that prosecutors left the jury with the inference that he provided the report to Steve "so he could then come up with this information. After I raised hell about it, they came back after a break and said, 'We aren't saying they had anything to do with this, but Steve somehow ended up with this report and used it as the blueprint for the voice-in-the-vent story.' It's absolute bullshit."

Sadly, he said, all of this just hurt the case, and was used against Steve to show that he'd lied about the e-mail.

"Ultimately, it probably was true that people would believe that if he was willing to lie about that, then maybe he's lying about not committing the murder," he said. But, he added, "those things are not mutually exclusive."

Even though Robertson acknowledged that Steve's actions were "not appropriate" and were "not something that we can tolerate, frankly, in the criminal justice system," he said people should consider the context in which they occurred.

"He was facing the death penalty at that time and he was in fear of his life, and I guess people sort of need to look at themselves and say, 'What would [I] do to save [myself]?' Just because he did something in a panic doesn't mean that he killed Carol."

CHAPTER 40

In late October, the Yavapai County Public Defender's Office, which had a conflict in this case, had to find a new defense team to represent Steve, because he'd been declared indigent.

Although this was no longer a death penalty case, it was still a very complex one, so Steve was allowed to have two taxpayer-subsidized lawyers. Craig Williams, a private attorney in Prescott who was the former chief public defender of La Paz County, and was on the county's list of eligible contract attorneys, was designated lead counsel on October 28.

When no other local attorney would agree to be second chair, the public defender had to go outside the county to find Greg Parzych, who worked for the Maricopa County Office of the Legal Defender in Phoenix.

Williams and Parzych did not ask Judge Darrow for a mistrial, but they did say they would need months to get up to speed on the case before they could move forward.

Rich Robertson, who stayed on the team as investigator, now served as the fount of institutional knowledge. His first briefing about the already massive and complicated case—a PowerPoint presentation with photos—lasted eight hours.

That same month Steve was placed in a single "administrative segregation" cell, which spanned seven by eleven feet, at the county jail in Camp Verde. Otherwise known as solitary confinement, that meant Steve was kept in his cell for 23.5 hours a day, with just thirty minutes to shower, exercise or call his family.

According to defense court filings, jail officials said they placed Steve there for his own safety after an inmate reported that Steve was involved in the ordering of a "beat down" of that inmate.

Attorney Craig Williams maintained that this inmate was not credible, and that the inmate's report about Steve's participation in the fight "was simply NOT true."

In a motion to modify Steve's conditions, Williams contended that the defense had interviewed nine of the jurors after the mistrial was declared. Five of them told Rich Robertson that they had been "leaning toward an acquittal," three toward a conviction and one undecided. This was before the state had finished presenting its case and before the defense had even started, but Robertson said the defense took that to mean that the first jury was headed toward a "possible acquittal or, at worst, a hung jury."

And yet, Williams wrote in a sentence that forecasted the defense's subsequent third-party culpability strategy, *[Steve] remained the only suspect, despite the fact that the state documented some truly bizarre behavior by those close to Ms. Kennedy.* Nonetheless, the request to release

Steve on his own recognizance with a GPS bracelet or move him to a jail in Coconino County was rejected again.

In the legal back-and-forth, the defense claimed that the stint in solitary was negatively affecting Steve's mental stability so much that they were concerned whether he would be able to assist in trial preparation.

Despite the state's "hyperbole" that Steve's defenses had been eliminated, attorney Greg Parzych wrote that the DNA under Carol's fingernail was still *not Steve DeMocker's. . . . The most powerful facts remain intact. The state cannot place the defendant at the scene of the crime. . . . Importantly, these facts will never change—no new evidence will surface that will place him at the scene of the crime—because he was not there and did not kill Carol Kennedy.* That *is what is known as a defense.*

Based upon a review of court filings, Steve was apparently still in a single cell as of March 2012. Sheriff's officials cited "security concerns" as the reason.

In response to the defense's claims that these conditions amounted to punishment, prosecutor Jeff Paupore countered that Steve had "continued to break the law even while incarcerated."

Once the ruling came down that the first defense team was entirely off the case, Judge Darrow declared a mistrial on November 12, 2010.

It was an extremely emotional day when the jury was called back to court to be officially dismissed, and Judge Lindberg came to watch.

"He looked awful," Robertson recalled. "He was gaunt, he'd been undergoing chemo and had lost a lot of hair, and he was certainly much thinner and paler. He just looked sickly and weak."

Some of the jurors made some nice, sympathetic comments to Lindberg that day. Some months later, on April 3, 2011, the judge passed away. He was fifty-eight.

CHAPTER 41

As the prosecution team prepared for the second trial, investigators were still working to determine the identity of Mr. 603, whose full DNA profile had been developed from material under Carol's fingernails.

In early 2011, after taking DNA from dozens of people who might have come in contact with Carol at her house, Mike Sechez and Doug Brown were discussing how they could determine, once and for all, where this DNA had come from.

"Why don't we go back to the DNA and look at the men's autopsies preceding hers?" one of them said. "Maybe it was contamination."

Deciding to start with the three autopsies done before Carol's and work backward, they took blood samples from the Yavapai County Medical Examiner's Office and sent them to the DPS crime lab.

In mid-February, Sechez got a call from the lab. "Are you sitting down?"

"Yeah, why?" he said.

"You know that blood you sent up from the ME's? It matches with the blood under the fingernails."

And just like that, the mystery was solved at last: Mr. 603 was Ronald Birman, whose autopsy Dr. Philip Keen had conducted right before Carol's. Birman's body had been found near a puddle of blood in his trailer bathroom in Chino Valley, and because his doctor wouldn't sign the death certificate, his family had asked the ME to do an autopsy. Keen determined that the blood had seeped from an open, bandaged hole over stitches in Birman's chest from recent heart surgery. The death was deemed to be of natural causes from an exsanguinating hemorrhage.

In addition to Birman's DNA, partial DNA from one or possibly two other men was also found under Carol fingernails, but not enough to draw any forensic conclusions other than that the genetic material did not match Steve DeMocker's or Jim Knapp's.

As soon as defense attorney Craig Williams learned of this new development, he went on the warpath, requesting documents to check state and county policies, procedures and crime lab operations, the accreditation of the DNA-testing lab and its personnel, and the chain of custody of biological evidence in this case.

And then came yet another bombshell.

On May 2, 2011, the defense filed a motion to dismiss the case with prejudice—meaning it couldn't be refiled—based on prosecutorial misconduct. The only other option would be to disqualify the county attorney's office as the prosecutor.

The defense accused the county attorney and victim services offices of repeatedly viewing and printing sealed ex parte documents filed by the defense in this case. Ex parte filings are supposed to be available only to the judge and the party filing them. However, in this case, the defense said, employees in these county offices had been viewing these documents on a computer system they shared with the court clerk's office.

This came to light, the defense said, through the state's allegations that the defense had violated state rules of criminal procedure, professional conduct and judicial conduct when filing the indigency and other ex parte motions back in 2010.

These alleged violations, the defense charged, were tantamount to an "illegal investigation" into the defense's case, first by complaining about secret and sealed motions that they weren't supposed to know about, then by alleging violations by the defense. But how could the state even know about the secret pleadings if it wasn't improperly accessing them?

The state illegally viewed and printed ex parte pleadings using the OnBase [court computer] system! the defense wrote, describing this revelation as "the awful truth."

And not just a little. Not by accident. Not inadvertently. No, the state intentionally viewed and printed ex parte pleadings using the OnBase . . . a total of 60 times! . . . This was not a one-time curious peek at forbidden fruit, it was systematic.

In addition, the defense claimed, "sealed documents" were also viewed and printed 104 times by those offices and the sheriff's office.

Put on the defensive, County Attorney Sheila Polk stood up for the honor and integrity of her office, blaming the court clerk for changing the computer system in a way that was out of Polk's control and against her wishes. Characterizing this chain of events as stemming from an innocent computer glitch that amounted to harmless error, Polk claimed she had no malicious intent.

Polk said members of her office regularly—and appropriately—read certain documents that were mislabeled "ex parte," as well as others that were labeled as such but were not appropriate for prosecutors to read. However, she said, the latter category was not read past the basic identifiers unless—and until—a supervisor had deemed it was okay. She also noted that the first defense team never objected to the "ex parte" routing stamp on numerous documents sent to the county attorney's office.

This scandal, which came to be known as "Docugate," resulted in many months of delay, including an eleven-day evidentiary hearing. In court filings fueled by high-octane language, each side accused the other with vitriol, which also spilled into courthouse hallways.

This was all very serious to the participants, of course, but from an outsider's perspective, the whole scandal seemed to be just one more tedious, and albeit very long, chapter of the small-town drama and circus atmosphere that hung over this case.

Steve passed the time that summer by playing chess by phone with his father, using a paper board and pieces made of toilet paper, as the defense filed a mountain of other motions. These included requests for a change of venue and to sever all the new counts from the original murder and burglary charges, arguing that the motive the state attributed to Steve's fraudulent acts was "distinct and different."

Jury selection had been set to start September 7, but the trial date was vacated because of all the pending issues—Docugate, most importantly.

Stepping in for Judge Darrow, who was busy with the time-consuming sweat lodge case and was set to retire soon anyway, Presiding Judge David Mackey tried to get both sides to sit down at a settlement conference and bring an end to this protracted legal battle.

But neither party wanted to participate in any such conference, and only did so after being forced by the court. They were supposed to confer for two days, but the meeting ended after just two hours.

In December, Mackey appointed a new judge, who was then promptly removed. Mackey subsequently recalled into duty a retired judge from Maricopa County, Gary E. Donahoe, known as a "law and order" judge. Donahoe had fought and survived his own political and legal battles, including a complicated and highly publicized dispute with Joe Arpaio, Maricopa's notorious sheriff, and Andrew Thomas, the county attorney.

Donahoe seemed like the perfect judge to take charge of this high-profile and politically sensitive case.

CHAPTER 42

Once Steve's attorneys realized they could no longer use the DNA of the mystery man, Mr. 603, as their line of defense, they shifted their focus to other identifiable third-party suspects, zeroing in primarily on Jim Knapp.

His motive? "Jim Knapp—(a) was not psychologically stable, and (b) he was angry at Carol," said defense investigator Rich Robertson. "He had kind of a romantic interest in her that appeared to be unreciprocated, and (c) he was telling people that she was going to fund his investment in this coffee franchise that he wanted to start and she was going to be his partner and fund it with the money from the divorce. He found out this wasn't going to happen right before she died."

Attorney Craig Williams also came up with a theory to explain away Jim's 7:58 P.M. call from his ex-wife's house: "Just because [Carol's] phone went dead at eight P.M. doesn't mean that's when Carol died," Robertson said. "That just means the phone went dead. She was discovered dead well after ten o'clock, so she was killed sometime between when the phone went dead and the time when she was found, so there was time for Jim Knapp to get out there."

Robertson noted that Jim was involved in a number of get-rich-quick scams, in which he ended up being a victim; he was also lying to people—including Robertson—about his cancer in an effort to get people to give him money.

"He told me that he had stage-four cancer that had been miraculously cured," Robertson said, referring to meetings a week or two after Carol's murder. "He told me that doctors wanted to study him because he'd had this stage-four cancer that had suddenly gone into remission and there must have been something in his genetic makeup."

Another theory being floated, which was more along the lines of the hit man tale and the voice-in-the-vent story, was that Carol had been killed by the drug ring with which Jim had allegedly been involved, but that was not part of the defense's case, Robertson said.

The defense's Jim Knapp theories held no water with Carol's friends. From what Katherine Morris knew, there was nothing romantic between him and Carol.

That said, Katherine wouldn't have been surprised if Jim had been in love with Carol, as Steve told her he suspected. Even so, in her view, Jim had no ill will toward Carol.

"I know he was devastated, absolutely," she said. "He was the one with her in those final days and knew the most about what Steve was doing to her recently. I don't think he had anything to do with her death."

Debbie Wren Hill agreed. "He might have been a little wacky, but they were very, very close friends. He might have had a crush on her, but you don't beat people mercifully if you have a crush on someone. This was a crime of passion. This wasn't someone slipping something into her drink."

The prosecution wasn't bothered by the defense's new strategy, either.

"Once we figured out who Mr. 603 was, they said someone else did it, and it was Jim Knapp," prosecutor Jeff Paupore recalled. "That was a mistake. Because we had cell phone evidence."

Paupore looked at it this way: "The more they go after Jim Knapp, the stronger our case will be, because they've got nothing else. And they didn't."

Nonetheless, the defense's new direction did force investigators for the prosecution to delve deeper into the evidence to prove more definitively that Jim was where he said he'd been and could not physically have been able to commit the murder. As such, they developed a timeline of his activity that day, based mostly on witness interviews and Jim's cell phone records:

By the time Jim got up the day of the murder, Carol was already at work. As was his routine, he went over to her house around noon and let the dogs out to run around. It was unclear when he left the house that afternoon, but he drove to Hastings Entertainment and rented two videos for his younger son at two fifty-three.

From there, he went to a doctor's appointment with Dr. Kent Ward, an osteopath, between 3:15 and 3:44 P.M., during which he turned off his cell phone. The four calls he received from his ex-wife's landline during that time went straight to voice mail. Jim had complained of back discomfort.

At 3:44 P.M., Jim checked his voice mail and returned the calls to his ex-wife's house.

His ex, Ann Saxerud, told investigators that he arrived at her house at five-ten in the evening. She and their older son, Jay, left the house for his hockey practice around six o'clock. She dropped off Jay half an hour later, then went hiking nearby with a friend.

At 7:58 P.M., one minute before Carol's call to her mother was disconnected, Jim checked his voice mail on his cell phone.

While Ann and Jay were gone, Alex said he and his dad watched the movie *Harold & Kumar Go to White Castle,* until Alex got bored and went to play video games on the computer for a while. Alex later testified that his father did not leave the house until Ann returned.

After Jay's hockey practice ended at eight o'clock, Ann and her son left the rink around eight-fifteen, arriving home between eight-thirty and eight-forty. She estimated that Jim left her house at eight forty-five.

Jim put the videos into Hastings' drop box, and headed to Safeway, off Iron Springs and Willow Creek Road, which is six miles and eleven minutes from Carol's house. The security footage showed him entering the store just before 9 P.M. And just as Jim told the deputies, records confirmed that he bought sweet red cherries for $8.46 and a bottle of Freixenet Cordon Negro Brut sparkling wine for $17.96, at 8:58 P.M.

Jim arrived at Bridle Path around 9:15 P.M., after which the deputies ran his driver's license through their database.

Meanwhile, the defense developed an explanation for the searches and files on Steve's computer that he claimed were for book research.

"He liked the idea of writing the book, and the actual writing is hard work, so he had a lot of stuff in that computer that was mentioned that had zero to do with the murder, that seemed to fit that whole spy-novel thing people are talking about," Rich Robertson explained.

For example? "He had some stuff in there for gases. He was researching carbon monoxide. Even the book titles, the ones that seemed to be the most damaging, or portrayed to be the most damaging, or hit man, nothing about the murder fit that. . . . It was 'how to make a homicide look like a suicide.' There was nothing in this scene, if it was staged, that even [given] the state testimony, was staged to look like a suicide."

CHAPTER 43

Within two weeks of being appointed in December 2011, Judge Gary Donahoe got down to business by ruling on the slew of pending motions that had backed up during the months of delays. In so doing, he rejected a defense motion to dismiss the case based on matters raised in the Docugate scandal.

The defense appealed, and three months later, the Arizona Court of Appeals poured water all over Donahoe's ruling. Finding that an intrusion into Steve's attorney-client privilege had been committed, the court ordered Donahoe to conduct a mini trial known as an evidentiary hearing.

Due to appeals and the highly sensitive issues involved, that hearing did not begin until December 12, 2012, and then lasted for several months. The proceedings featured testimony by the very passionate county attorney herself, Sheila Polk, who continued to defend the ethics and integrity of her office.

"I have tried and I believe I have successfully accomplished an office and a culture of ethics, a culture where everyone understands that it's not about some end out there," she testified. "It's about at all times respecting and upholding our obligation of the Constitution to defend and protect the individual rights of citizens and of the defendant as we go through the process."

Admitting that some mistakes by her office "will happen," she also argued that the state had not impaired its ability to provide due process for Steve DeMocker. "If I thought for even an instant that Mr. DeMocker could not get a fair trial from my office, I would conflict off the case," she said. "I have not seen a scintilla of evidence . . . that would deprive Mr. DeMocker of a fair trial."

Aiming to finish the hearing in April, the judge issued a preliminary fifty-three-page ruling in the state's favor in March, which sent Craig Williams into fits once again.

With Donahoe's final ruling in April, the county attorney's office was allowed to move ahead as prosecutor, and the trial process started up again with motions and hearings.

Preparing for the second trial, the prosecution team made a conscious choice to reduce the number of witnesses it had planned to call during the first trial, especially now that there were additional charges to support. The team pared back and simplified its case to rely mostly on evidence and elements of the crime that carried the greatest weight.

"This is a murder trial where we could have gone for weeks on the money part of it," prosecutor Jeff Paupore recalled later. "I made a decision, let's just get enough out there, on these other charges—I care about them, but I really care about getting the conviction on Carol's murder."

CHAPTER 44

The second trial took place in the same courthouse, but in a different courtroom, in which space and sound worked in no one's favor. The first courtroom felt cavernous, which made it easy to move around in; the second one was so cramped that members of the defense team felt as if they were sitting on top of each other.

The acoustics in the second room also frequently made it difficult for people to hear each other talk. Questions had to be repeated and witnesses had to wear microphones. Testimony also had to stop when the old steam radiators banged as they warmed up, and the air-conditioning was often so loud that the judge had to ask for it to be turned off, especially when badly recorded audiotapes were being played. Water dripping from the leaky ceiling had to be caught by pans when it rained.

Jury selection finally began on July 16, 2013, but without the death penalty it only took several days to impanel a jury.

With all the fraud charges at stake, the defense tried to

preclude the state from admitting Steve's conversation with the prosecution team in July 2009 about his voice-in-the-vent story, contending that this had been a "free talk" and couldn't be used against him.

The judge, however, denied the motion, saying that the previous prosecutor and defense attorney admitted under oath that this was an "investigative interview." Steve was no different than an ordinary citizen offering details of what he claimed was a crime committed.

"Of course he hoped it would exonerate him, but there were no promises, no coercion, no quid pro quo," Judge Donahoe said.

When both sides delivered their opening statements on July 19, it had been nearly three years since the first trial ended with Detective Hoover's testimony.

In his ninety-minute opening, Deputy County Attorney Steve Young outlined all the state's evidence that pointed to Steve DeMocker as the killer of his very recent ex-wife, with whom he had been fighting about money up until the day he murdered her.

"The defendant has a financial motive to murder his ex-wife, Carol," Young said, noting that Steve didn't want to pay her $6,000 in alimony monthly for the next eight years, totaling $576,000.

The state would present evidence, he said, of Steve's pattern of overspending, his losses related to the market crash, coupled with his personal and financial split with Barb O'Non, and how he, as the beneficiary, immediately tried to collect on Carol's two life insurance policies that would pay out the $750,000 he ultimately used to pay his first defense team.

Young covered evidence ranging from the staged crime

scene to the blood spatter pattern, shoe prints, bike tracks, computer searches, "dead" cell phone, and golf club head cover that had gone missing by the second search. He noted that the pattern of injuries to Carol's skull was consistent with a left-handed golf club, that Steve was left-handed and he also lacked an alibi. All of this, he said, would persuade the jury beyond a reasonable doubt that Steve murdered Carol on the evening of July 2, 2008.

To support the other charges, he said, the state would illustrate Steve's manipulative and fraudulent moves to persuade his family members to help perpetuate the voice-in-the-vent story, to send the anonymous e-mail and to make the insurance money transfers, which led to the other charges and required his own relatives to obtain immunity before testifying.

And finally, anticipating that the defense was going to point to Jim Knapp as a homicide suspect involved in a prescription drug ring, Young said the state would prove that Jim couldn't have killed Carol.

"The only evidence in this case that's going to suggest that Jim Knapp is a seller of drugs or involved in some nefarious drug ring from Phoenix is the voice-in-the-vent [story] that cannot be corroborated and the anonymous e-mail that was produced by the defendant," he said.

Before the defense made its opening statement, attorney Greg Parzych made one of many mistrial motions he would make, this one based on e-mails and other evidence precluded in previous rulings by other judges. Donahoe said he wasn't bound by these rulings, and he also believed that the e-mails "all seem to go to the financial motive."

After lunch attorney Craig Williams countered the state's position in his brief twelve-minute opening. Williams stated, in essence, that with no physical evidence in Steve's car, house, or washing machine that tied him to the crime scene, he couldn't and shouldn't be found guilty.

"There's no murder weapon, there's no domestic violence in this case, and there's no motive," Williams said in a statement that would come back to haunt him.

Williams faulted the state's investigation for being "conclusion-based" and inadequate, focusing unfairly and prematurely on Steve rather than exploring other leads and suspects, including Jim Knapp. It was sloppy as well, he said, noting that "contamination is the rule"—an allusion to the mystery DNA from Mr. 603, Ronald Birman, under Carol's fingernails.

Once Steve was arrested and in jail, he said, Steve acted out of fear, not guilt. He did the same when he put together his plan to flee, which he never carried out. Caring too much about his daughters, Steve decided to stay and fight the charges.

"We can place somebody in that [Bridle Path] house and we will," Williams said. Asking the jurors to keep an open mind, Williams said the defense would firmly convince them that Steve did not kill Carol.

As the prosecution called its witnesses, Williams pounded them during cross-examination about professional protocol failures with regard to the photographing and preservation of the shoe and bike tracks.

Not allowed to argue until his closing argument, he still managed to put forth his theories, sometimes inserting misstatements of fact, which no one corrected, as he did when Scott Mascher, now the sheriff, took the stand, dressed in full uniform:

"So to recap, Mr. DeMocker, who is a very bright

individual, comes out there. He has these cuts on his arm. He makes no attempt to hide them. He gives financial information. He gives voluntary statements. He talks about his divorce," Williams said. "His alibi is he's across the street, basically riding his bike and he gets a flat, and he gets a very thorough investigation. Mr. Knapp, who says that he was at a hockey game with his kid, doesn't. Am I summing that up right?" (Jim Knapp never said he was at a hockey game; he said he was home babysitting his younger son while his ex-wife took his older son to hockey practice.)

After the jury left and Mascher had stepped down for the day, Donahoe chastised Williams for taking too long with his duplicative and pointless cross-examination, saying that he'd shown Mascher irrelevant photos and asked him too many of the wrong questions.

As Williams explained his line of argument, Donahoe told him to do it faster so as not to waste the jury's time. "That takes two questions. It doesn't take half an hour showing him [crime scene] pictures he doesn't know about. . . . If I see this continuing . . . I'm going to set some time limits. This is the second warning, and that's all the warnings I'm going to give."

Despite the words of caution, Mascher ended up being on the stand for parts of three days.

The prosecution called Dr. Laura Fulginiti to discuss the nature of Carol's various injuries, and she never faltered from her position even when the defense tried to trip her up.

In March 2010, Fulginiti said, she was asked to examine Carol's desk and compare it to the curvilinear skull injuries to determine whether the desk could have caused them, rather than the golf club. As she later testified, "I felt that [the desk] was inconsistent with those patterns."

But there were additional injured areas, she said, such as above Carol's eye on the left side of her forehead, that were apparently caused by an impact with a different object—where "something struck the skull, as opposed to the skull striking something. . . . It's a distinction that's very important."

In this instance, she said, that "something" appeared to be the corner of the desk. (This comment, compounded with other testimony later in the trial, suggests that in addition to beating Carol's skull with a golf club, the killer also likely slammed her forehead into the desk, as opposed to her head passively hitting the desk as she fell to the ground.)

In total, she testified, "I'm saying that her head is impacted seven times minimum."

Under cross-examination by the defense, Fulginiti testified that she wasn't aware that Dr. Keen had first transported Carol's body in the back of his pickup truck. She said she didn't think the trip would have caused further significant damage, although that factor couldn't be ruled out. If anything, the skull "would get jostled and the pieces would separate a little bit more, but I don't think it would create new pieces."

Asked about other possible murder weapons, she said she couldn't rule out the end of a maul or an axe handle.

When Williams questioned why she'd changed her position on this point, Fulginiti went off on him, because she clearly didn't see it that way.

"You lawyers," she said. "Okay, here's the deal. You cannot rule out a golf club, period. You cannot rule it out. So, is that opining that it is a golf club? No. What it is saying is that a golf club has all the characteristics that you need to create any one of those injuries on the skull. And it fits very nicely into one of those injuries."

As a motive for the murder charges, the prosecution focused on Steve's spending habits, his financial troubles and his battles over money with Carol—up to the day she was killed. To support the fraud charges, they presented witnesses to show how Steve manipulated the people closest to him, even his daughters, for his own needs.

Peter Davis, a forensic accountant who examined Steve's financial records, said he issued an "objective" report of Steve's fiscal picture from September 1, 2004, through the day of the murder in July 2008. During this time, Davis said, Steve spent $900,000 more than he earned, and he earned quite a bit.

From 2005 to 2007, Steve's gross earnings went from $315,000 to $525,000, of which he netted $117,000 and $191,000, respectively. And in the first six months of 2008, he grossed $190,000 and netted only $67,000, partially due to the market crash, but also because of tax withholdings due to two forgivable loans totaling $557,000 he'd received when he joined UBS. In addition to his commissions, Steve had spent virtually all of the forgivable loan money by May 2007.

Steve received the first and larger forgivable loan as a sort of signing bonus when he joined the firm in 2004. UBS wrote him a check for $546,938, with no taxes withheld, to spend as he pleased. One-sixth of that amount, considered taxable income, was "forgiven" each year for the next six years. The idea was to help out the broker until he could build a client base.

But that still wasn't enough money to subsidize Steve's luxury tastes. Grabbing money wherever he could, Steve took out second mortgages on his condo *and* on Bridle Path, and borrowed against $129,000 in credit lines on both properties, Davis said. Steve also withdrew $7,000 from his daughters' bank accounts, took out loans against his 401(k), liquidated an IRA and borrowed tens of thousands from his parents, telling Carol it was to "pay *our* bills." At times, his three credit cards were maxed out—on which he historically carried a balance of $70,000—and yet he never seemed to cut back or tighten his belt, even in the face of his ballooning debt.

"I never saw any sort of significant decline in the nature of his spending, even though Mr. DeMocker was overspending on these sorts of items," Davis testified. "It never stopped."

From May 2007 to July 2008, Steve spent a monthly average of $1,500 on clothing, $1,100 on cash withdrawals, $800 on meals out, $600 for the Hassayampa Golf Club, $500 on electronic equipment such as computers, $160 on haircuts, and $120 on spa treatments, Davis said. Steve was also leasing three BMWs for himself and his daughters, purchasing sporting equipment, taking trips and paying alimony to Carol.

At the time of Carol's murder, Davis said, Steve was personally insolvent, meaning that his total assets were less than his liabilities by nearly $400,000.

By Steve's own admission in the affidavits he submitted during the divorce, his personal debt totaled $1.4 million as of March 2007, which he called "crushing." In his February 2008 amended affidavit, he listed his overall monthly expenses at $30,000, more than double his average net monthly paycheck of $12,860.

As a result of Carol's death, Davis said, Steve's financial condition improved dramatically. His worth escalated by $881,000, meaning that his assets were then $485,000 in the red. Of that, there was the nearly $576,000 in alimony he didn't have to pay; and as the beneficiary of Carol's life insurance, he also was set to receive $750,000 in benefits. The only drawback was that he was then obligated to pay for the Bridle Path mortgage.

DeMocker's emails and text messages demonstrated his financial desperation and stress, Davis wrote in his report. *The day before Kennedy's death, DeMocker emails Kennedy that he is unable to float his alimony payment without her payment to him.*

On cross-examination, Craig Williams got Davis to concede that Steve eventually waived his interest in the life insurance.

So on redirect Steve Young made sure to have Davis acknowledge that this waiver "only came after the life insurance company consistently said that they were not going to pay the benefits to Mr. DeMocker because he was suspected of a homicide in this case." Young also got him to underscore Steve's "benefit" of receiving that $750,000, a point crucial to proving the prosecution's case.

"Based on your evaluation, Mr. DeMocker ultimately got the benefit of those life insurance proceeds?" Young asked.

"Correct," Davis testified. "Mr. DeMocker coordinated that the monies from the life insurance company be paid."

The last page of Steve's UBS personnel file shows the firm put him on unpaid administrative leave on October 24, 2008, the day after he was arrested. A "stop draw" was placed on his salary on November 20, apparently ending his relationship with the company. However, his former boss, Jim Van Steenhuyse, testified that Steve wasn't officially terminated by the company until April 24, 2009, when he failed to return from leave. Steve's "book of clients" went to Barb O'Non, with another advisor working as backup.

The prosecution laid out the forensics of Jim Knapp's cell phone calls the night of the murder, based on the cell tower testimony of Detective Sy Ray. The prosecution also presented evidence linking the shoe and bike tracks behind Carol's house to Steve through testimony of witnesses, including FBI forensic examiner Eric Gilkerson.

As Gilkerson had conceded at trial in 2010, he reiterated that the detectives who photographed the shoe prints did not use a ruler to show scale, although some included a flashlight, apparently for that purpose. They also didn't use identifying techniques, such as labeling shots with corresponding evidence numbers to show the tracks traveling in different directions, for example, or adding a date and case number. Gilkerson recommended that castings be made of shoe prints in soil to make three-dimensional impressions because it is difficult to capture uneven surfaces in a photograph.

Holding up a Pikes Peak shoe and photos of the prints left at the crime scene, defense attorney Greg Parzych asked Gilkerson if it was "possible that this shoe created the image" prosecutors said was Steve's shoe print.

"It's possible that a make and model of that shoe could have made the impression, yes," Gilkerson testified.

"But it's also possible that the make and model did not make that impression?"

Yes, Gilkerson said. "The Ultranord and the Imogene could also have made the impression."

* * *

On day nine, forensic analyst Jonathyn Priest, a former major-crimes commander in Denver, testified about Carol's injuries and the corresponding blood spatter patterns at the crime scene.

The two marks on her back, Priest said, were similar to those he'd seen in another murder case in which investigators found a golf club at the scene in 1995. The killer later admitted using the club to beat his victim to death.

Specifically, he said, the elliptical marks, shaped like teardrops, on Carol's back looked like they were made by the hosel, the area where the club shaft joins the head in an inverted *V.* The two parallel linear marks on her forearm, he added, were consistent with the long thin metal shaft, and six of her head injuries were consistent with the head of the club.

Asked whether the injuries could have been caused by an ASP baton, a baseball bat or a maul handle, Priest said he didn't think so, based on the corresponding nature and curvilinear shape of both the club head and Carol's injuries. He said he came to that conclusion independently, not from reading reports from the medical examiner or anyone else.

As for the blood, he said, the "radiating" patterns emanating from Carol's head were typical of blunt-force trauma incidents, while other marks and patterns showed that her body had been moved. That's because some blood spots had dried before others were made, and others were made by transferring blood from one place to another.

"The victim is either moving or being moved or a combination of both," he said, adding that Carol had to be "upright or semi-upright to cause a number of the stain patterns."

Asked for his conclusion about where and how the killer delivered the blows, Priest said the killer was likely standing over Carol, swinging the club from left to right, and pivoting.

In his opinion, Priest testified, six of the seven lacerations on her head were created by a similar object, the golf club, and the last one, over her left eye, "was created by her head striking the corner of the desk."

After the beating, he said, he could tell that the bookcase was moved, because the elliptical stains had a "downward flow appearance," meaning that the bookcase was standing upright during the beating, but was then moved so it was tilting down. The direction of blood flow didn't change because the blood had already dried.

Priest noted that the ladder had no blood on it, but should have, based on the radiating pattern of blood on objects around it.

"So the fact that I have zero evidence of blood on the ladder leads me to the conclusion the ladder was placed there after the bloodletting event," Priest said.

On cross-examination by Williams, Priest conceded that he could have done a more thorough and accurate crime scene analysis if the detectives had taken such procedural steps as measuring how far Carol's body was from the wall, for example. And just because there were left-sided swings, he said, didn't mean the attacker had to be left-handed. He also acknowledged that visiting the original crime scene would have been better than basing his conclusions primarily on photos, which, being two-dimensional, could be deceiving.

"There is a lot you can do at a crime scene that wasn't done here," Priest said. He added, however, that with 1,280 photos, he had enough information to render an opinion.

As a murder weapon, he said, he couldn't rule out rebar, which was found on Carol's property, but "any cylindrical object" could have produced marks similar to those found on her arm, just not the ones on her back.

The attack happened fast, he said, "less than a few minutes," but he saw "no evidence in there of two people" attacking her. He also added that "somebody could move her and not get blood on them," as he had done hundreds of times at homicide scenes.

In the end Priest did not move from his opinion that a golf club was the likeliest murder weapon to have produced most of the injuries on Carol's body.

On day nineteen, Jim Knapp's ex-wife, Ann Saxerud, testified that she'd been concerned about his prescription drug use. On the day of Carol's murder, however, he didn't appear to be under the influence of any drugs when he showed up at her house to spend the evening with their son Alex.

She confirmed that Jim was wearing the same clothes that evening that he was wearing in the Safeway video the prosecution showed her while she was on the stand.

"Did Jim keep his visitation up with Alex and Jay after that time?"

"Yes," she said.

"And was there any real change, as you could see, in his behavior?"

"No."

Under cross-examination by Williams, Ann seemed angry that the defense was pointing fingers at her late ex-husband for Carol's murder. She also acknowledged that she didn't appreciate her privacy being violated by having to testify about her divorce. All of this was hurtful to her and her sons, she said.

"I thought it was inaccurate and inappropriate," she

said. "I don't think Jim has anything to do with Carol's murder."

Williams reminded her that when she first talked to law enforcement, she said she got home between eight and eight-thirty that night, and that Jim had left her house "shortly after that." But after she talked repeatedly with Detective Doug Brown, they moved the times she left and got home to be later and later. She even told Brown that she didn't "remember Jim coming [to her house] that night," Williams said. All of this, he later argued, helped illustrate that she and law enforcement were unfairly trying to reshape their timelines to fit their theory that Steve De-Mocker, not Jim Knapp, had killed Carol.

"I think at the time I didn't understand how far this would go, and didn't put the effort into remembering [the exact times]" Ann countered. "But since then, I've changed my mind." She added that it was "very unclear" to her at the time that she needed to be more precise, because she'd never been involved in a murder investigation before.

When the prosecution called Katie DeMocker to the stand, prosecutor Jeff Paupore created some high drama in the courtroom by playing a recording of the young woman battling with her father over the insurance money transfers in March 2009.

Although it was clear on the recording that she didn't want to go along with the plan, she would not concede to Paupore's implication that Steve had pressured her into accepting the "agreement of how the money was going to be spent," specifically for his defense.

"I wouldn't phrase it like that," she said, contending that she wasn't initially comfortable transferring the money, but she did agree after "lengthy discussions" in which her family provided her with assurances that Charlotte would have enough money for college "and be taken care of, like I was, in that process."

As trustee, Katie testified, she was empowered to move all that money out of Carol's trust, thus exhausting it, even though she was still five years from being twenty-five, as her mother's will dictated. At this point, Judge Donahoe interrupted and told the jury to take a break.

Calling a bench conference, Donahoe, who had spent seven years on the probate bench, told the attorneys that the jury was receiving inaccurate information from the witness.

"I can understand why criminal lawyers don't practice probate, because you've got the law all confused," he said, adding that he wasn't criticizing Katie, but she didn't understand what she was saying.

"Despite what she's saying from the stand, she had no right to dissolve this estate at the age—whenever she wanted to—or the trust. . . . She's mixing the two, and she's telling the jury wrong things."

Donahoe said they needed to find a way to remedy this so the jury got the correct probate law information. Greg Parzych piped up, renewing his motion to sever count three, "fraudulent schemes and artifices."

Donahoe snapped back that this was not the solution. "Don't even bother me with that again. I'm tired of hearing that severance," he retorted, noting that he'd already ruled on it several times.

Back on the record once more, Jeff Paupore restated the wishes in Carol's will to Katie, saying that "it was very clear that there would be no distributions until you reached the age of twenty-five."

Asked if she had discussed that issue with her attorney, Katie said she didn't recall specifically, but it was her understanding that she, as trustee, "was in charge of administering the money as I saw fit . . . that it was mine to do whatever I wanted with."

Saying she "frankly didn't want anything to do with" transferring her half of the insurance money, she came to believe that it was appropriate to hand over her share to her grandparents after a family meeting and getting those written assurances. She then left the other half for Charlotte "in the account until she turned eighteen."

"But you knew that your grandparents were going to use that money for attorneys' fees?"

"That was my understanding," she said. "Some or all of it. I didn't really care at that point."

As Paupore questioned Steve's eighty-three-year-old mother, Jan DeMocker, he played a couple of taped conversations between her and Steve in jail, talking about the money transfers. He also pointed out for the jury that just the day before testifying, she'd received immunity from being charged with a crime.

"Do you know why you were in the middle of this?" he asked.

"I guess I was handy," she said.

Pushing past the flip answer, Paupore asked if she could think of any reason why the girls didn't send all that money directly to Steve's attorneys.

"I don't really know," she said. "There was an issue of quite a bit of money that . . . my husband and I already spent, that they owed us, Steve owed us, probably close to that amount of money." She and her husband had been paying Steve's legal fees for more than a year, she said, so "it allowed them to give us a gift, to pay us back. It gave us the freedom of using that money in whatever way we wanted. Although I think they were very aware at that time that our burning concern was for Steve's safety at that point."

Jan said that Steve *and* Carol owed them that money, which had been spent on their lawyers and lawyers for the girls. "Our output at that point had totaled somewhere between five hundred thousand and seven hundred thousand dollars," she said. "I don't know exactly what it was. My husband was keeping track of accounts."

"Okay, is it your testimony, then, that you decided to take that seven hundred thousand dollars and then pay Steven's attorneys' fees with it?"

"That was a decision my husband and I made with input from other members of the family, yes," she said.

"Was your son Jim part of that discussion?"

"Yes."

After another audiotape was played for the jury, Jan explained that Katie was supposed to transfer the first $355,000, but only transferred $350,000. Jan said the $5,000 difference went to pay the second attorney named Chris—referring to Chris Dupont—to help the girls get their victims' rights back.

On cross-examination, Craig Williams had Jan explain the motivation behind the insurance transfers, painting the transactions as innocent and noting that the planning for them occurred on phone lines they knew were being recorded.

Jan said she wanted to make sure the girls "would be taken care of," in terms of college and future support. "I knew we could support both of them, but I didn't know how long we could do it. And there was always that horrible chance, way out at the end, that, even though we were very positive that Steve was innocent, and we thought there was a ninety-nine percent chance that he would be acquitted, there was still the possibility—he was facing the death penalty then—that he would spend his life in prison or that we could see him executed. And we had to consider that also, what would happen to the girls if their father is never freed. And that's where the family came from. And we had other people in the family say, 'We have your back and we will take over if we need to.'"

After Jan acknowledged that Katie was stubborn, Williams asked, "In your mind, do you think that Steve could get Katie to do something that she didn't want to do?"

"I can imagine he would try," Jan said. "I can't imagine he would succeed."

Moving on, Williams asked Jan the same question he asked several witnesses during the trial: "In the entire time that you were around Steve and Carol, did you ever see any physical violence at all?"

"Absolutely not."

Jan added that she never heard Steve threaten Carol, nor did she ever sense any fear on her part. Carol never came to her to say he'd been violent, either.

Steve's daughter Charlotte was called to the stand next, but her memory still wasn't very clear, despite the prosecution telling her that she needed to be more cooperative than she was during the first trial or she could lose her immunity. Nonetheless, she didn't have much to add.

Barb O'Non testified as well. However, her comments weren't nearly as detailed as they were during her previous interviews with investigators or at the pretrial hearing in 2010.

Renee Girard also testified, going over much of the same

ground about the anonymous e-mail and the insurance money transfers that she'd discussed with investigators.

"I trusted what I was being told [by John Sears and the DeMocker family] . . . that it was legitimate," she said, referring to the money transfers. "I trusted that Steve was not asking me to do something illegal."

Doug Brown, the former lead detective on the case who was back to working as a patrol deputy, was the last of the prosecution's forty-six witnesses. Brown was on the stand for six days—longer than any other witness.

On Brown's second day, September 4, the prosecution tried to introduce into evidence an e-mail that could change the whole landscape of the case. Carol had sent the e-mail, dated May 7, 2007, to Steve. It described a violent incident in which he came into her house while she was on the phone, grabbed it from her hand, threw it against the wall and shoved her.

The defense immediately objected, arguing in a bench conference that the prosecution should have announced this late and surprising disclosure earlier in the trial.

Prosecutor Steve Young countered that the state had properly disclosed the e-mail long ago, but acknowledged that it was part of the case's massive 33,000 pages of discovery. The e-mail, as it turned out, had been part of the prosecution's court filing on August 12, 2012, one of dozens of supplemental evidence disclosures.

"This particular e-mail has been disclosed for over a year, whether he remembers it or not," Young said, referring to Craig Williams.

Williams admitted that he had missed the e-mail, but he argued that the state still should have highlighted the document prior to the trial as evidence it intended to produce.

"I would have approached it a little different if I knew that e-mail was going to be admitted in this trial, an e-mail I didn't even know about, so what we have now is we have an irrevocable tainting in this trial," Williams said, questioning whether the e-mail was even real, given that it never came up during the divorce. "I question the veracity of this e-mail."

Williams complained that the state waited until its last witness to present the document, not while several of Steve's family members were testifying, when the defense could have questioned them in more detail about their knowledge of domestic violence between Carol and Steve. Williams even went so far as to ask for sanctions against the state.

Judge Donahoe, however, pointed out that so far the defense was the only party to have brought up domestic violence by saying there was none in this couple's relationship.

"And this is the voice from the grave saying that isn't true," the judge said. "This is rebutting the defense's assertion that Mr. DeMocker has a peaceful character and that there was no domestic violence."

Young pointed out that the defense had been questioning witnesses all along if they knew of any instances of domestic violence between Steve and Carol, which had opened the door to the e-mail. Furthermore, he said, the state had already notified the defense a week in advance of its plans to introduce the e-mail in court.

Williams referenced a "comeback" e-mail from Steve, saying it "calls her a liar and says that's all incorrect," but the state didn't submit it for admission.

"Is that the one that he's in the shower and thinking about she's coming to kill him, and the one where he admits they shoved each other?" Young asked.

"No," Williams answered curtly.

"That one should be brought up," Young said, underscoring the existence of additional e-mails from Steve to Carol, indicating "that they had shoved each other in arguments before." He said Steve also mentioned in a recorded jail call that "he would have arguments with Carol and they would both end up shaking."

Donahoe noted that there was more at issue here than just the domestic violence. "This almost goes to the murder. Well, almost—it *does* go to the murder, because it's the same thing that happened."

Reading Carol's e-mail aloud, Donahoe said, "'You had Ashley come over to the house and come in against my will, and once you grabbed the phone out of my hands and threw it so violently against the wall.' So when she says, 'Oh, no,' or 'Not again'... the jury could conclude, this is exactly what happened the night of the murder. That he came in unannounced, like she's accusing him of doing before, grabs the phone out of her hand and bludgeons her to death.... It's not only domestic violence, it's what happened on the evening in question."

Calling the e-mail "a dynamite bombshell in this case," Donahoe said he needed some time to do research. He would announce his decision on whether to allow the e-mail the following day.

The next day Judge Donahoe faulted Craig Williams for failing to recognize the importance of this e-mail during his trial preparation, especially when the county was paying for a four-person defense team, which included two attorneys, experts, paralegals and other staff. Williams said he took responsibility for that oversight.

Donahoe said the state shared some fault, too, and should have "fired a shot across the bow" to say, "'If you're going to go down this road, here's what we've got. You might want to change your tactic here.' But again, there's not much I can do to unring the bell. I think the situation the defendant finds himself in at this stage of the trial is entirely the defendant's own making."

Although the judge acknowledged that domestic violence "is generally a very secret matter between couples," and the victim "is often silent because they are embarrassed or intimidated," he wasn't surprised that family members didn't know about this or other incidents.

Nonetheless, Donahoe said, he believed parts of the e-mail were "unfairly prejudicial." The e-mail not only drew "parallels to the circumstances of the murder," but also had Carol talking about being "frightened and concerned about disappearing," and mentioned that Steve owned guns and had some weapons training. Donahoe suggested redacting those parts of the e-mail so it could be admitted.

But as prosecutor Jeff Paupore watched this play out in court, he'd become concerned that he could jeopardize the case on appeal if he pushed the e-mail into evidence at this point. He didn't want to create an opportunity for Steve's appellate attorney to make a claim of ineffective trial counsel.

So, after a long bench conference, both sides agreed to a stipulation: The prosecution would withdraw the e-mail as long as the defense didn't present any more "evidence" or question witnesses about Steve's supposedly nonviolent nature and good character. The defense also wouldn't point to a lack of domestic violence in the marriage, or mention the topic in its closing argument.

* * *

With that defense crisis averted, Williams kept Deputy Brown on the stand with an extended cross-examination that continued to wear on the judge's patience.

"In the bigger picture, is there an end to this endless cross-examination?" Donahoe asked during Brown's fifth day on the stand.

Williams had already run through a long list of people who were asked to give DNA swabs, including three named in the defense's third-party culpability paperwork—David Soule, John Stoler and Barb O'Non—noting that they were never subjected to the same level of interrogation or investigation as Steve. But the list of potential murder suspects seemed to go on ad infinitum.

"How many people committed that murder?" Donahoe asked.

"Well, you know, Judge, you will recall when you told me that I shouldn't put all my ducks in one pond," Williams said.

When Donahoe said he didn't remember saying that, Williams conceded that he might be mixing his colloquialisms. However, he said, he believed he had "to open up the Japanese van here and say there was more than one possibility" of how Carol was murdered.

Prosecutor Steve Young added his objections to the judge's. "There's got to be some reasonable link between third-party culpability so that doesn't open the floodgates to anything and everything," he said.

Donahoe agreed. "I'm getting more and more skeptical as the net widens here on this third-party culpability."

Still, back on cross-examination, Williams continued pounding Brown on this point: "Do you know what tunnel vision is?"

"'Tunnel vision'?" Brown echoed. "Yes."

"The focus had narrowed down on Mr. DeMocker. Would you agree?"

"It did at a certain time, yes."

"I'd say it happened pretty early in this case."

"During the investigation in the early-morning hours of the third [of July], yes."

Williams spent the rest of his time focusing on Jim Knapp, trying to persuade the jury that it was Carol's tenant, not her ex-husband, who had the motive to kill her and could have done the deed.

Numerous times during bench conferences, out of the jury's earshot, the defense attorney detailed his theories extrapolating on how and why this could have happened. In one instance he tried to persuade the judge to let him present evidence of Jim's victimization in several get-rich-quick schemes, while Young argued that it lacked relevancy.

"There's a series of disastrous events in his life and the fact that he's going through one thing after another to get rich," Williams said, referring to the Maui Wowi franchise and Jim's other moneymaking ideas. "And I think it shows state of mind that leads up to the dam burst and he actually killed Carol Kennedy. So I think we have to be able to demonstrate state of mind through disastrous financial decisions."

"I may buy a lottery ticket after this, Judge, and I don't know, I hope that doesn't go to my state of mind," Young quipped.

"Our whole argument is this guy is a con man. He cons a lot of people," Williams said. "He had an ongoing con trying to set up e-mails trying to pay for his fake cancer."

"'Fake cancer'?" Young asked incredulously. "The

autopsy report says he has melanoma. I don't know why you keep saying 'fake cancer.'"

Williams continued during another bench conference: "If you get down to the end where he's telling people in the world that Carol Kennedy was penniless, right, and that Steven DeMocker robbed her of everything, but then we have a deposit slip of one hundred thirty thousand dollars, we have [Jim's] thumbprint on the financial documents that list out how much money she's got. So our theory is that he found out, felt double-crossed, and that's what happened."

"There's no evidence," Jeff Paupore countered. "You asked for the evidence, Your Honor, about Carol Kennedy going into a joint venture [for the Maui Wowi franchise]. . . . There's no evidence that she was going to fund anything. Other than in Knapp's mind, and we've been in there. . . . We know it's an empty shell."

Williams proceeded to hammer his points in front of the jury. While Deputy Brown was still on the stand on September 10, Williams noted that law enforcement admitted to a lack of crucial physical evidence in this case the day before they arrested Steve.

Quoting Brown's search warrant, Williams said: "'We have not been able to locate a murder weapon, the shoes that created the shoe tracks, or any physical evidence tying Steven DeMocker directly to the house . . . from the night of the murder.' Correct?"

"Yes, that's correct," Brown replied, "that's what I wrote."

"And he was arrested the next day, wasn't he?"

"Correct."

"Okay, no more questions."

* * *

As the prosecution finished up with Brown, the deputy countered that he and the other detectives did, in fact, investigate the alibis and whereabouts at the time of the murder of all four suspects Williams suggested in his third-party culpability defense, including Jim Knapp. And that the physical evidence—the staged crime scene, the blood spatter heading out the back door and the nasty e-mail exchanges between Carol and Steve—still pointed to Steve as the killer, who bludgeoned her to death, ran out to his bike in the bushes behind the house and back to his car.

Brown noted that investigators also collected a DNA specimen and fingerprints from Jim Knapp, and had them tested and compared with other evidence at the crime lab. Even though Jim gave inconsistent statements, his memory wasn't good and he offered various theories about how Carol was killed, Brown said he and the other investigators retraced Jim's steps, interviewed his ex-wife and son, examined his bank, cell phone and other records, and, in the end, simply did not see him as the killer. As a result they put together a "Knapp-exonerating timeline," as Young put it.

Brown said he and other detectives did the same type of investigation into Steve's story to try to prove that he, too, was where he said he was. Based on the timing of Carol's last messages to Steve and her handwritten notes on the financial documents in her home office, Brown agreed that it seemed Carol was prepared to talk with Steve that night about the check dispute when he came to collect Katie's car. But even Steve admitted to investigators that he couldn't prove where he was during those missing hours, and he had no alibi.

"'I don't really have proof where I was,'" Brown said, quoting Steve's statement on the night of the murder.

And that was that.

"No further questions," Young said.

During the jury's Q&A with Brown, the former detective touched on his theory on how and when the killer entered the house. Based on the shoe tracks, the timing of Carol's run, her text messages, the phone call with her mom, the unscrewed lightbulbs and the fact that she didn't generally lock the back door while she was out running, he said, "I think it's while she was on a run."

With that, the state rested. The jury was dismissed for lunch and the defense immediately moved for judgment of acquittal for a lack of evidence.

On the murder charge the defense argued once again that there was no evidence of premeditation, because the killer was clearly in a rage. And there was no evidence—"blood, hair, fiber, eyewitness, confession"—tying Steve to the crime scene.

Jeff Paupore countered that Steve showed premeditation as early as February 2008, when he installed the Anonymizer software on his computer to hide his Web-surfing history. But investigators found his incriminating searches anyway.

After the defense went through each count and argued why it should be dismissed, the judge responded by reiterating the state's evidence supporting each count, stating that he believed there was "substantial evidence" to support counts one and two, for first-degree murder and burglary. Curiously, though, Donahoe said he had some doubts about the merits of the state's case on those two primary counts.

"I'm not saying this is the strongest case, and it wouldn't surprise me if there was a not-guilty verdict or a hung jury on count one and count two or both," he said, "but I think there's enough here to go to the jury on both of those counts."

He said he saw enough evidence to support all the other charges, except count six, which he described as "e-mail forgery." For that count he entered a judgment for acquittal, explaining that Charlotte was "the only one that created or committed forgery regarding the e-mail," but she was not charged and had been granted immunity.

CHAPTER 45

The defense began presenting its case after lunch that same day, September 11.

Starting with Carol Walden, the former area developer for the Maui Wowi franchise system, the defense proceeded to put on a parade of witnesses who testified about Jim Knapp's oddities. The franchise executive discussed her correspondence with Jim concerning his interest in buying the Prescott store; his "fiancée," Suzanna Wilson, described the fear she felt after he'd sent her the angry e-mails.

The defense also put on its own financial expert to counter the state's characterization of Steve's finances, as well as witnesses who challenged the state's DNA, shoe print and tire track evidence, including Randy Anglin, a tracker and forensic photographer.

The testimony of Curtis James, the meteorology professor at Embry-Riddle, conflicted with Mascher's definitive remarks about the timing and volume of the rainfall, which the state had argued made it easy to determine that Steve's tracks were fresh.

As defense investigator Rich Robertson summed it up,

"The sheriff said, 'I'm the sheriff, it rained, I have a badge. Believe me, not the academic guy.'"

Forensic accountant Gregg Curry presented a very different picture of Steve's fiscal health, listing a number of points in Davis's report that differed from his own calculations. These included two significant double-counting errors totaling $280,000, he said, which represented about 40 percent of the amount that Davis put toward Steve's excessive spending totals.

Curry's bottom line: "I determined whether Mr. De-Mocker had the ability to pay his debts as they came due with the resources that he had," and concluded that "he had about seventy-four thousand dollars of available liquid assets on July 2, 2008." This wasn't all that far from Davis's calculation, which was $64,000. However, Curry said, Davis also underestimated the retirement savings Steve "could have tapped into."

As the defense tried to undermine Davis's position that Steve was in "financial distress," Curry contended that Steve "was not cash-flow insolvent . . . because he had enough resources to continue to pay his bills up until four or five months later."

He said Steve could have further stretched his resources to seventeen months by reducing his discretionary spending and changing the withholding amount on his paychecks. He also had not maxed out his credit cards, nor was he in any imminent danger of bankruptcy or foreclosure.

But perhaps the most important discrepancy with Davis, Curry said, was that he didn't count the $750,000 in insurance payouts as an asset on his balance sheet, because in his view Steve "didn't actually receive the death benefits."

This statement not only flew in the face of the prosecution's entire case, it also reduced the quantitative improvement in Steve's overall financial picture after Carol's death to just $131,896 for the alimony he wouldn't have to pay over the next eight years. This was a marked contrast to the prosecution's claim that Steve's picture had improved by $576,000 in unpaid alimony *and* the $750,000 in life insurance benefits.

"He had no chance of collecting that as long as he was a suspect and, obviously, he was arrested later," Curry said.

On cross-examination Steve Young confronted the witness with one of Steve's statements. "You don't believe Mr. DeMocker's own words are an appropriate gauge on financial distress?" Young asked, citing Steve's "You get to start clean while I dig out of a staggering hole" e-mail to Carol.

"Not necessarily, no," Curry said.

After Young pointed out several examples of Steve's failure to cut his discretionary spending, Curry said, "I think that's kind of argumentative. I think he's taken some steps."

"So instead of significantly reducing discretionary spending, he's raiding his daughters' investment accounts and borrowing tens of thousands of dollars from his parents?" Young asked.

As the prosecutor went over the options Steve had available for reducing his spending, Curry ultimately had to acknowledge that Steve had taken no action to "avail himself" of any of them after Carol's murder, and continued to borrow money from his parents.

Curry also acknowledged that the suicide provision in Carol's life insurance policies didn't apply because it had been longer than two years since the issue date, which was important in the context of Steve's computer searches.

Referring specifically to the Internet search for "how to make a homicide appear suicide," Young said, "It's fair to assume that he knew in June of 2008 that those life insurance policies would have paid out if Carol's death was ever determined to be a suicide, correct?"

"I don't know what he knew."

In the end Young was able to get Curry to admit, albeit reluctantly, that the insurance checks from Steve's parents to the two law firms ultimately did benefit Steve.

"Well, to the extent that they paid for his lawyers to stay on the case," Curry said.

"Thank you, Mr. Curry," Young said. "Nothing further."

On the morning of September 26, the defense rested its case after eight days of live testimony from seventeen witnesses, and the reading of prior testimony from a law enforcement expert who had since died.

The prosecution's single rebuttal witness was Sean Jeralds, a flight safety professor at Embry-Riddle and the close friend of Jim Knapp's who had checked on him the night he was found dead.

Sean had come forward after reading a news article stating that the defense said Jim was not a pilot and had no license to fly. And having been Jim's flight instructor, Sean wanted to correct the record.

Craig Williams objected to letting him testify, saying it could result in an "endless loop of witnesses," but Donahoe allowed it.

"You've disparaged Mr. Knapp," the judge said. "You've

portrayed him as a murderer to this jury. This is the downside to the third-party culpability defense."

Calling Jim "his brother from another mother," Sean said Jim had earned a commercial pilot's license in 1991. Jeff Paupore then led him through Jim's résumé and the various health, drug-related and behavioral issues that had marked their relationship over the years, ending with Jim's suicide when he believed he was dying.

"That's how he was going to lose his life, cancer," Sean said. "He thought that was a terrible way to go, because he saw what happened to his father and his mother, and so I wasn't surprised he did that."

During the cross-examination Williams produced Jim Knapp's medical records from the Mayo Clinic from February 2008, underscoring the untruths they contained: Jim had written that he was still engaged to Suzanna Wilson, that he was working as a pilot and that he had "no history of recreational drug use."

Under the section asking if he engaged in healing or alternative therapies, Williams noted that Jim had written "meditation and chronic random abuse to strangers." And under the category of significant problems, he wrote in "sociopath."

When Williams asked Sean Jeralds about these "inappropriate" answers on the questionnaire, Sean acknowledged that Jim had never actually worked as a pilot, but he could have if he'd taken and passed a physical.

Sean also said he couldn't "judge the level of appropriateness Knapp had with the folks at Mayo," but he didn't seem surprised by Jim's responses in the medical records. In fact, he said, he laughed when he saw them in Jim's handwriting. "I could hear Jimmy saying that."

Williams then asked if Jim had ever mentioned the

possibility of a sexual relationship with Carol. Sean said yes, they had talked about it.

"He was wondering if that opportunity arose, should he take advantage of that or not," Sean said. "What would that do to the relationship, and should he go down that path or not?"

Although Sean acknowledged that Jim had sent a number of angry e-mails to various people, such as the wealthy donor Steven Udvar-Hazy, Sean told the jury that his friend would not have purposely harmed anybody.

"Is Mr. Hazy still alive today?" Paupore asked.

"Yes, sir."

"Did you ever know Jim Knapp to hurt or cause physical violence to anyone?"

"No, sir."

After the lunch break Greg Parzych renewed his motions for acquittal and to sever the non-murder charges. He also told the judge that Katie DeMocker had e-mailed him, asking that closing arguments be held the following Tuesday, not the next day, so she could be there.

Steve Young said he didn't know why Katie had the erroneous idea that closings would be on Tuesday. Carol's mother, Ruth Kennedy, had already flown in and was ready to be there.

Judge Donahoe ruled again that closings would be the next day, Friday the twenty-seventh.

That night Jeff Paupore woke up at 3 A.M. with an idea. The prosecutor would conduct a dramatic reenactment to illustrate for the jury how Steve had brutally beat his wife to death with a golf club.

He got out of bed, went into the garage, found one of his wife's golf clubs and started smacking a rolled-up rug with it. The thumping woke his son, who "sleeps like a dead person," and came out to see what was going on.

Good. If it wakes him up, I know it's going to work, Paupore thought.

Paupore's wife, on the other hand, slept right through it, but he didn't inform her of his plans. He wanted her to be surprised when she came to court that day to watch the closings. And that she was.

That morning Craig Williams renewed the defense's objection to moving ahead with the closings. He also argued that the prosecution should be precluded from using the words "unique" to describe the shoe prints and "stashed" to refer to the bicycle. Donahoe granted the first request, but he denied the second.

Paupore began his two-hour closing by displaying a photograph of Carol for the jury. As he ran through the slides in his PowerPoint presentation, each representing a fact or puzzle piece of damning evidence in the case, he removed a piece of her portrait and replaced it with a portion of Steve's face.

"This was not a bike ride," Paupore said. "This was an alibi in case something went wrong."

Referring to the anonymous e-mail, which had stated, "This wasn't one crazed man with a golf club," Paupore said, "Oh, yes, it was, ladies and gentlemen. It was the defendant with a golf club. Make no mistake about it."

By the end of his argument, Carol's portrait had been all but transformed by Steve's features, leaving only Carol's eyes.

Paupore told the jurors that he wished he could present

them with every piece of the puzzle, but he couldn't. What he did have, he said, was "a great, huge mountain of strong circumstantial evidence."

"We don't have a hundred percent of the pieces, but through Carol's eyes up on the screen looking at us, you can see her killer," he said, hoping that the jury would get the idea that in her last moments, this was what she saw, too: Steve's face.

Afterward, Paupore's wife told him that she was horrified to see all the dust flying out of their rug as he beat it with abandon.

"If I'd known you were going to do that, I would have vacuumed it," she said.

Craig Williams began his closing argument after lunch, continuing for nearly three hours. Still not finished, he started up again after the weekend, on the following Tuesday, October 1.

Williams spent most of his time laying out every possible alternative scenario to reinterpret the state's evidence, trying to persuade the jury that it was much more likely that Jim Knapp had killed Carol. He spent the rest arguing that the prosecution had made its whole case by twisting the ordinary into the nefarious and the suspicious.

Jim's motive? After snooping in Carol's financial papers, he was angry to learn that she had $130,000 in her bank account, but would not finance his Maui Wowi franchise. To hide his tracks, he tried to frame Steve, repeatedly telling the detectives and anyone else who would listen how and why Steve was to blame.

Williams offered a possible scenario for Carol's last exclamation of "Oh, no." She was heading down the hall after her dogs, who were constantly "peeing and puking in the house," when she inadvertently disconnected her phone as she went to grab the bottle of stain remover to clean up after them.

When the cleaning crew pulled up the rug, he said, there was a stain right where the bottle had been. Following that logic, he said, the murder didn't happen at 7:59 P.M.; it was later than that, because "she was cleaning up the dog pee." This scenario gave Jim more time to drive back, kill her and run off when he saw the lights of Deputy Taintor's cruiser pulling up to the house.

Although the state had dismissed alternative theories as "crazy defenses" to divert attention away from Steve, Williams said, "there really is factual evidence to back" up scenarios where other people, specifically Jim Knapp, could have killed Carol between his 7:58 and 9:37 P.M. cell phone calls.

In fact, when Jim went to Safeway to buy wine and then called Carol in front of the sheriff's deputies, he could have simply been creating a ruse and an alibi, when he knew she couldn't answer the phone.

"Ask yourself this—if Steve had planned this awful, brutal murder, his alibi is to say, 'I'm going to show up at the scene with a bunch of cuts on me and then I'm going to say I was a mile across the road on a bike ride that nobody saw me on?' That's idiotic. It just would not have happened," Williams said. Especially if Steve was such a "criminal mastermind" that he left no DNA or blood evidence at the scene, in his car, office or condo. Steve exhibited a "consciousness of innocence," he said, not of guilt.

The fingerprint on the lightbulb in the laundry room was not Steve's. It was Jim Knapp's fingerprint on the financial documents in the *Body & Soul* magazine, not Steve's. And if Steve was so worried about the golf club head cover, why give it to his attorney rather than get rid of it altogether?

The detectives had "tunnel vision" from the get-go, he said, and conducted a shoddy investigation. They never properly explored Jim's or any other possible suspects' alibis other than half-baked moves, such as obtaining John Stoler's bank records and Barb O'Non's credit card receipt for the night of the murder.

The detectives didn't think anything of flying all over the country to collect Ronald Birman's DNA, Williams said, but they didn't bother to fly to Maine to check out Carol's boyfriend. Why? "Because they had Steve and they don't want to look any further."

Detectives also couldn't "match" the shoes or bike tires with the tracks they found around Glenshandra. "If you can't match them and you're asking somebody to convict somebody of first-degree murder, that's pretty doggone sloppy," he said, reiterating the failure to designate one person to control the crime scene rather than let an army of sheriff's investigators "tromp" all over it.

The prosecution had no photos or evidence that Steve laid his bike down in the bushes behind Carol's house, he said. And none of Steve's computer searches, or the reportedly incriminating files in his "Book Research" folder, had anything to do with how Carol was actually killed.

Referring to Paupore's "connect the dots" closing, Williams said it was not the jury's constitutional duty to do that. Based on the severe injuries to Carol's head, the killer had an emotional, not a financial, motive.

"Yeah, [Steve] spent some cash, but he's not a murderer," Williams said, repeatedly comparing the prosecution's case to a board game of Clue. "It's Mr. Plum in the study with a left-handed golf club," he said, referring to the Clue character Professor Plum.

"I don't have to prove [Knapp] guilty and I don't have to tell you who absolutely murdered her, but there's way more here on Jim Knapp, and it's not a crazy defense theory," he said. "It's facts, way more than they had against Steve DeMocker."

As for evidence to support the fraud charges related to the insurance money transfer, Williams said, there was none. Steve, just like his other family members, simply relied on their attorneys' advice, which they discussed on recorded phone lines, with nothing to hide. And as Katie and Charlotte testified, no one forced them to put that money toward Steve's defense.

"They can't put him in the house because he wasn't there," Williams summed up for the jury. "You know why? Because he did not kill her. You've got to find him not guilty."

The prosecution always gets to do its closing argument first and speak last with a rebuttal argument, because it has the burden of proof and defendants are presumed innocent until proven guilty. Prosecutor Steve Young followed up Williams's closing with a nearly hour-long statement, which went until 10:32 A.M.

Young disputed many of Williams's points, starting by dismissing John Stoler, David Soule and Barb O'Non as viable murder suspects, along with Jim Knapp, whom the defense "hung their hat on," and who, because he committed suicide, couldn't be in court to refute or defend himself against evidence presented by the defense.

Jim Knapp, he said, had no motive to kill Carol. The Maui Wowi deal was dead in February, months before the murder; and even if he did know that Carol had money, he had no way to get it from her or her estate or her life insurance policies once she was dead.

"The defense cannot point to any credible evidence that has been presented in court to show by any stretch of the reasonable imagination that Jim Knapp had any reason whatsoever to kill Carol Kennedy," he said, shrugging off Williams's scenarios as "rank speculation" that stretched the timeline of events to fit the defense's theory.

The stains on the carpet? There were many of them, and no way to measure their age. The rimless glasses on Carol's desk that the defense claimed were Jim's? Even one of the defense's own exhibit photos, taken in the guesthouse on July 3, showed two pairs of rimless glasses. "Those are his glasses. They're in his guesthouse," Young said, adding that surely Jim would have retrieved the blood-specked pair from Carol's desk if they were his.

If Carol's landline was disconnected as Williams described, why didn't Carol answer when Ruth called back? Because she was already dead, and it was Steve who killed her.

Steve was the one who had a motive—financial gain— and "750,000 reasons" to kill Carol, so he didn't have to pay alimony and so he could collect on the life insurance policies, of which he was the owner and beneficiary, Young said.

Steve also had an emotional motive, which was clear from the disputes in the e-mails and texts between them, Young said. Steve had no alibi. His phone was mysteriously turned off, and he uncharacteristically didn't answer his calls or texts.

Why, if he was bleeding from cuts on his arm and leg, would his bike and car be free of blood? "Doesn't that prove to you that the defendant took measures both before and after the murder not to get any blood in his vehicle, and if there was any blood, to clean it up? . . . He had gloves on. He took measures that he wasn't going to leave anything behind."

Steve gave inconsistent accounts about where he was that night and what had happened with his cell phone—he turned it off; there was no signal; he had a dead battery.

Who had a reason to stage the crime scene? "The defendant, who did research on how to kill and collect on life insurance," he said.

Steve's behavior after the murder only served to further implicate him, Young said, noting that the defendant fabricated evidence with the voice-in-the-vent story and the anonymous e-mail, which was completely contrary to the defense's "consciousness of innocence" claim.

"Hold Steven DeMocker responsible," Young said. "Find him guilty of the murder of Carol Kennedy so justice can finally be done in this case."

The jurors took a twenty-minute break and listened to their instructions. After the five remaining alternates were chosen by lot, the rest of the jury began deliberating at 11 A.M.

By this time counts six and seven, relating to the forgery charges, and count eight, involving the willful concealment of fraudulent schemes to defraud, had been dismissed.

After deliberating for the next three days, the jury reached a verdict late on the third day. Ruth Kennedy, who had stayed in town to hear the verdict, got the call just as she was heading out for her evening meal. However, the judge decided to hold off on announcing it until first thing the next morning at nine o'clock.

* * *

Before the proceedings began promptly on the morning of October 4, Charlotte and Katie made sure to hug and kiss their grandmother, who sat behind the prosecution table. Ruth felt numb, not knowing what to expect, as she waited with a box of tissues in her lap.

"I love you," Charlotte whispered to Ruth before taking a seat with the rest of the DeMocker family on the opposite side of the gallery, where Steve sat stoically at the defense table.

As the clerk read the verdicts, count by count, the courtroom was packed and yet silent:

"'We the jury, duly impaneled and sworn in the above-entitled action and upon our oaths, do find the defendant, Steven DeMocker, on the charge of first-degree murder on July 2, 2008, as the result of the death of Virginia Carol Kennedy as follows: Guilty.'"

Hearing this, Katie and Charlotte immediately burst into tears. One of the court officers leaned over to Ruth, grabbed a handful of tissues from the box in her lap and handed them to the girls.

Ruth was in shock. She had waited so long to hear those words. Five long years of waiting and hoping that Steve would be found guilty. As the clerk recited the verdicts for the other counts—guilty, guilty and guilty—Ruth sat back as a wave of relief settled over her.

Sentencing was set for November 13. After the reading was over, and everyone was walking out of the courtroom, Jan DeMocker grabbed Ruth's hand.

"I'll never believe that Steve killed Carol," Jan said, handing Ruth a medallion with the word "peace" on it.

Ruth didn't agree, of course, but as a mother, she

thought she might feel the same way if she were in a similar situation. Steve was Jan's firstborn, after all. But Ruth didn't utter a peep in response. What was there to say? She was just glad she could finally put this horrible ordeal behind her and move on.

It's over, Ruth thought. *Thank the Lord for small things.*

CHAPTER 46

The defense filed the usual motion for a new trial and a separate motion for acquittal, which Judge Donahoe denied.

And, as people are apt to do in a small town, the residents of Prescott talked about the case and whether the verdict was a just one. Although some had strong opinions, others still weren't sure what to think.

Some said that if Steve was guilty, he really was a heinous person, because the crime scene was so bloody. And if he did kill Carol, then the prosecutor's office really messed up the case because it had to take the death penalty off the table after making so many screwups, not the least of which was the Docugate scandal.

For some folks this was also a story about the hubris of County Attorney Sheila Polk, and her ambitions to make her career on this case, only for her office to mishandle it. Steve DeMocker, they said, was a former high-ranking college administrator before becoming a broker. He was a well-respected and moral financial advisor. And Carol Kennedy wasn't a very nice person, dragging out the divorce and milking him.

But there were others, including Carol's friends, who believed that Steve got exactly what was coming to him. After all those years of adulterous affairs, which were known around town, he still managed to get women to sleep with him and continued to torture poor Carol's psyche. He fought with her over finances, spent far more than he earned, then committed this horrible murder. He got what he deserved.

Still, most everyone saw it as a tragedy all around. As gallery co-owner Joanne Frerking put it: "It just seemed like such a lovely family, and behind it all was this horror story, and just deep sadness."

But no matter how they felt about the trial's outcome, the end of this long roller-coaster ride to justice couldn't end soon enough for most residents, especially when it had cost the taxpayers in this small county so much money.

Dean Trebesch, Yavapai County's public defender, told the *Daily Courier* that the defense's case for the second trial alone cost taxpayers $1.3 million, half of which went to the attorneys, the other half to expert witnesses and staff. Additional money, also paid by taxpayers, went to outside experts and investigators for the first trial, because Steve was declared indigent.

In a memo dated April 2010, before the first trial even began, Trebesch stated that the DeMocker case had dealt the county "a major financial blow" from the "tremendously burdensome expenses." *Because of its unique and high-profile circumstances, the expenses have been frightful.*

But, of course, this case couldn't end without some more drama.

In mid-October, Dave Rhodes, now a sheriff's captain, pulled Steve from his cell to talk to him without an attorney present, which created a flap that ultimately delayed the sentencing hearing. The defense turned this kerfuffle into yet another reason to ask for a new trial and to disqualify the Yavapai County Attorney's Office from the case.

The state noted, however, that the defense didn't make much, if any, mention of Steve's conversation with Detention Officer Steve Chavez on October 1, immediately after the closing arguments, in which Steve reportedly blamed his attorney for the insurance fraud charges.

"I can't believe that I am being charged with fraud when it was my lawyer's idea," he told Chavez, adding that this was the reason John Sears and his first defense team had to quit the case.

At an evidentiary hearing on January 8, 2014, Craig Williams called his client to the stand for the first time to give his version of what happened.

Steve DeMocker testified that after the verdict on October 4 he was moved to the infirmary for three days, where he was placed on suicide watch in an observation cell, then was sent back to the general population. The following is Steve's version of events with regard to that meeting with Rhodes.

On October 14, Steve said, he was pulled out of his dorm while he was playing chess with the other inmates, and was told that Rhodes, the jail commander, wanted to talk to him. A detention officer put restraints on him, after which he shuffled to a small room equipped with a camera and monitor, where inmates can talk to judges. Rhodes came in and told the officer to wait outside.

Alone with Steve, Rhodes brought up the interview requests from producers for *Dateline* and *48 Hours,* saying he wanted to hear from Steve—not his attorneys—whether he truly wanted to do the interviews. When Steve said yes, Rhodes asked if he was feeling pressured, because other people, not just the networks and their sponsors, would benefit from the publicity. Steve took that to mean that his attorneys would benefit as well.

Switching gears to the insurance policies, Rhodes said he didn't feel it was right that Steve's daughters didn't get any of their intended inheritance, and that it all went to attorneys who didn't even finish the case.

"They let you take all the blame for it," Rhodes said.

Steve told Rhodes that he was still represented by attorneys and wasn't sure what, if anything, he should say other than his lawyers thought the money transfer was legal, and that no one was to blame.

"We didn't think any of us did anything wrong," Steve said.

"We know you were only acting on your attorneys' advice," Rhodes replied.

"But I was the one you charged," Steve said.

"This is your chance to get some money back for your daughters," Rhodes said, adding that the TV networks had the resources to make restitution to Katie and Charlotte, and now Steve had an "opportunity" to make that happen.

Steve testified that he felt manipulated by this exchange, as if the state and Sheila Polk were asking him to help them recover this money. "My feeling was then, as it had been all along, that my attorney—my daughters—did what they wanted to do with their money as adults," he said.

When Steve told Rhodes that he needed to discuss the matter with his attorneys, the captain replied, "We're just putting it out there" as something for Steve to think about.

"There's no rush. Nothing is going to happen until after the sentencing."

By this point, Steve testified, he was feeling pretty anxious. The life insurance money would likely be a "live issue" at some point, probably as soon as the sentencing hearing. And his gut instinct and experience told him that without an attorney present, he shouldn't make any statement to a law enforcement officer "who is asking me about something that had been alleged to be a crime."

"If you want to talk to me again, just put in a kite," Rhodes said, referring to an inmate request form.

"I can contact you through my attorneys, can't I?"

"Yes, of course, you can do that, too."

With that, Rhodes nodded to the officer through the glass to open the door, then left.

As soon as Steve was back on the cell block, he immediately called his attorney's office. Investigators noted later that he also called his sister Sharon, telling her that the jail captain had pulled him out of his cell "just to confirm that I indeed did want to do these interviews with [NBC and CBS] before they went ahead and tried to figure out how to do them. . . . I guess he just wanted to make sure I wasn't being pressured by my publicity-hungry attorneys. He didn't say that, but that was the implication."

Steve later learned that the TV networks' requests to interview him had been denied. Rhodes had determined that they couldn't accommodate that many people in the secure part of the jail.

When it came time for prosecutor Steve Young to cross-examine Steve DeMocker at the hearing, Young queried the judge if he could ask questions about the murder.

Judge Donahoe said any issues raised in the defense's motion for a new trial were fair game.

However, a few questions into Young's cross-examination, in which he focused on the defendant's "inconsistent answers" during statements to detectives in the hours after the murder, Craig Williams invoked Steve's right to remain silent.

Williams accused the state of inappropriately attempting to retry the case, arguing that the cross should be limited to whether Rhodes had violated Steve's Sixth Amendment right to appeal his conviction.

Donahoe didn't see it that way, saying that Steve's entire testimony would be stricken if he wouldn't agree to be cross-examined.

After a ten-minute recess, Williams objected to the judge's move to strike the testimony, noting that Steve had chosen not to testify during the trial. This, Williams said, could just force Steve into "wide-open cross-examination" of all trial evidence, postconviction and at a time when his appeal was pending.

Although the judge did not support the defense's position, Donahoe made several more curious statements about the strength of the state's case.

"I'm not saying that I wouldn't have been surprised if there was a not-guilty verdict, but I thought there was sufficient evidence viewed in a particular way that you could find beyond-a-reasonable-doubt guilt on all those counts, and that's why I let it go to the jury," he said.

"I think this was a close case and it turned on credibility determinations," Donahoe said, but the jury was attentive and showed no bias or misconduct. "Based on the totality of what went on for those thirty-seven days, I think Mr. DeMocker got a fair trial."

As such, the judge denied the defense's motion for a

new trial. He also rejected the request to disqualify the county attorney's office.

Williams tried unsuccessfully to seal a prosecution investigator's report about Steve's jail calls with family after the verdict, calling it "editorializing," "incendiary" and "highly prejudicial."

Written by Randy Schmidt, the report summarized 113 of Steve's 140 calls that weren't protected under attorney-client privilege. The report lends some interesting insight into Steve's and his family's perspectives on their own intellects and their place, power and influence in the world around them.

Judge Donahoe said he didn't see anything "unusual or inflammatory" in the report, to which he wasn't going to give any weight at sentencing anyway.

During those calls Steve blamed the judge, Craig Williams, the jury and even the clerk of the court for the guilty verdict. Steve repeatedly described the judge and jury as biased, corrupt and stupid, often characterizing the jurors as idiots with low IQs. Acknowledging that the calls were being recorded, Steve contended that no one could get in trouble for complaining about the jury's vote.

Steve said numerous times that Williams was incompetent, refused to listen to members of the defense team and was too insecure to admit his own inability to provide a good defense. *Steve . . . agreed with his daughter, Katie . . . that it was "shitty lawyering" for Craig . . . to use the third-party culpability defense and to blame Jim Knapp for the murder, when that entire concept was too difficult for a jury with a ninth grade education to grasp and comprehend,* the report stated. *Steve . . . not only agreed with*

Katie, but he told her that he *didn't even believe that Jim Knapp had killed Carol.*

On the day of the verdict, Steve told his mother that it was the worst day of his life. "Tell the girls that I am so sorry it turned out this way, but I'm okay," he said.

"This was not fair," Jan DeMocker said. "I hope we get a better judge next time."

Steve agreed. "This guy was a nightmare," he said. "He crammed that jury down our throats and the closing statements—the judge made biased and prejudicial statements."

Talking to his dad, Steve said, "The judge really hurt us, and that was not a very sophisticated jury." The next time, he added, he hoped he'd have a better defense team as well.

Steve told Charlotte that he'd been worried about the jurors because five of them had law enforcement officers in their families. "It was just the wrong jury."

The next night Steve reiterated to Katie what he'd already told Charlotte: "I didn't take Mom from you. I didn't do that." He also told Katie that the domestic-violence blockbuster e-mail had no basis in truth, contending that Carol had made up the story for a guy she was dating in Las Vegas.

On October 6, Steve told his mom that his relationship with Carol had been misrepresented during the trial. Regardless of the tension from the financial negotiations, he said, they still loved each other.

Never mentioning that Carol was murdered, Steve's calls were all about Steve. "Everything done to me and to my family is just huge," he told Charlotte on October 7.

During the three days he was on suicide watch, Steve constantly complained that he was being mistreated, forced to wear only a blanket designed to prevent self-harm. He urged his family members to inform the media of these wrongs as a way to influence public opinion, news coverage and the Arizona Court of Appeals.

"I'm being tortured," he told his mother on October 7. "It's clear what's happening. There is no other way to put it."

Schmidt's analysis was that Steve wanted to *create a groundswell of dismay and outrage to cause the news magazines and news media to alter their story lines*.

Steve DeMocker and his family seemed to be holding out hope for a third trial, which they strongly believed would take place sometime in the future.

CHAPTER 47

After persuading my editor that this compelling case was bookworthy, I drove to Prescott on a research trip the week of the sentencing hearing, hoping to meet in person Carol's daughters, members of the extended DeMocker family and other key players.

I sat in the second row on the left side of the courtroom, thinking I'd be behind the prosecution table. That's where I usually sit in California courtrooms because it gives me the best vantage point to watch the speakers and to see the defendant's face from the side, rather than the back of his head.

As people started filling in the row in front of me, I realized, however, that I was sitting behind the defense table and Steve's family—his mother, his daughters, two of his sisters and two of his brothers. At the time, the only ones I recognized from reading the *Courier* online were Charlotte and Katie. I initially mistook Steve's mother for Carol's, because they're both small, white-haired women, and I figured Ruth would be there to watch.

Watching the DeMockers interact before the hearing, my first impression was that their faces—Charlotte's and

Katie's in particular—looked oddly devoid of emotion. As I'd never talked to them, I couldn't tell whether their blank expressions stemmed from a heightened awareness that they were being observed, a general numbness because they knew what was coming or a desire to hide their feelings from the cameras.

Many times a convicted killer's family members look raw, vulnerable and red-eyed at times like these, and I didn't see any of that. But like I said, I didn't know them yet; I had only just started looking into this story.

The county had recently spent $1 million to put a new roof on the one-hundred-year-old courthouse and replace the air-conditioning system. I was told later that the acoustics had been bad in the courtroom before, but the new cooling system only worsened matters. As soon as the air switched on, people sitting in the gallery couldn't hear much of what was being said by speakers facing the judge, with their backs to the gallery. Even the *Courier* reporter, who was sitting closer to the action than I was, seemed to be straining to hear. The couple behind me got up and left in the middle of the sentencing, muttering that they couldn't hear anything.

The hearing began with arguments for and against the defense's motion to delay sentencing based on new information Steve's attorneys believed could vacate the judgment against him.

"We're getting new information every day," attorney Greg Parzych said.

The defense contended that it had discovered information indicating that Captain Dave Rhodes had lied. The prosecution should have disclosed these details, Parzych said, which the defense would have used to discredit Rhodes's testimony at trial. At issue were his actions during an investigation into a fight among members of a motorcycle club of law enforcement officers known as the Iron Brotherhood. Mark Boan, the deputy who had been assigned to babysit Jim Knapp for four hours on the night of the murder, had lost his job after thirteen years because of his affiliation with this club.

Judge Donahoe denied the motion, saying he would have had to call witnesses from the Iron Brotherhood, which "would have confused the jury and wasted a bunch of time." The defense had ample time to cross-examine Rhodes, he said.

"There's nothing new here," Donahoe said. "It's all collateral. I wouldn't have let it in anyway."

As the judge listed the seven counts against Steve for sentencing purposes, Charlotte smiled a little as the judge read the last one: "contributing to the delinquency of a minor." I wasn't sure why she would smile at that, and I never got a chance to ask her because, despite repeated requests to interview Steve's family members, including his daughters, I was told no, they weren't interested.

Carol's friend Debbie Wren Hill wrote a letter to the judge that included a "very likely" diagnosis of narcissistic personality disorder for Steve, whom she described as "a dangerous man" and a sex addict who exhibited a "sociopathic behavior pattern."

I am thankful beyond measure that the jury found Steven DeMocker guilty of murdering my friend, Debbie wrote, noting that she supported a life sentence for him. *I am grateful that Carol's precious mother lived to see this day in court.*

Craig Williams asked to strike the letter, objecting to

Debbie's offering a psychological diagnosis of Steve without being a "neuropsychologist" and "without ever talking to" Steve. Perhaps Williams didn't realize that Steve had known this woman since he and Carol were first dating. And although Debbie wasn't hired to examine Steve in an official capacity in the case, she is, as she stated in her letter, "a mental health clinician."

Donahoe, however, saw no reason to grant Williams's request. "I usually don't give much weight to these types of personal opinions," he said.

Prosecutor Jeff Paupore noted that Carol's mother was not at the hearing, but she'd requested that her letter be read into the record and that a photo of Carol be displayed. As such, Paupore put a blowup of Carol on an easel so she could be remembered during the hearing.

Over Williams's objection Paupore then read Ruth's letter aloud. "I think it's something that the defendant needs to hear," he said.

Ruth's letter was short and emotional, saying, in essence, that Carol's death had "left a hole in [her] heart and a vacant place in [her] life." The loss of Carol was incalculable to everyone who loved her, including Charlotte and Katie, she said.

All that can be done now is to seek to bring justice to the man who so violently, selfishly, and senselessly took her from us, Ruth wrote. She asked that Steve's punishment fit his crime, and given that he'd robbed Carol's life, she hoped the judge would give him a sentence in kind. Because she didn't approve of the death penalty, she asked for a sentence of life without parole. Anything less would be neither appropriate nor reflective of his actions.

Because Carol's side of the family was not in the courtroom—other than her daughters—and Steve's was there in force, Paupore made a point of reminding everyone that this case was not just about Steve DeMocker, it was about the victim, Carol Kennedy, and "the brutal murder of a very beautiful woman. She had a thirst for life and beautiful things. . . . Carol had a beautiful smile that still radiates today. She loved her art, her friends, Katie and Charlotte, and the moments daily when she could talk to her mother."

This case had been long, he said, as were the trial proceedings. Five years was "a long time to wait for justice."

Based on Carol's work at women's shelters and as a therapist, she was very familiar with domestic violence. She understood what it could do to someone's ego and self-esteem. But Carol likely never considered that it would take her life in a way that no one deserved, he said, a way that "defines domestic violence at its extreme."

Although Carol battled with Steve till the end "over money, honesty and his fidelity," he said, she'd finally found the strength to let go of the love of her life. She made it clear to her newly divorced ex-husband over coffee that last Sunday that their relationship was over and that she was moving on.

Based on the text messages they exchanged in those last days and hours, he said, the evidence showed that Carol thought Steve was coming over to exchange checks the night she was murdered.

"He set her up," he said, noting that the violence that occurred in Carol's home office "was fueled by hatred and rage," and the nature of the crime was "overkill." He couldn't even describe what that experience must have been like for her.

But as if that weren't enough, he said, Steve then went

after her trust account. By manipulating others, he took control of her estate.

"He invaded Carol's spirit, her will," Paupore said, knowing that she'd wanted that money to go toward maintaining her daughters' health, education and welfare. Never in the hundreds of cases he'd prosecuted had he seen the victim victimized again in her grave like this.

"This case is about money, and it always has been."

Turning around to face the defense table, he looked directly at Steve and called him a "murdering, lying thief." If the punishment was set to fit the crime, he said, Steve deserved the maximum sentence allowed.

Paupore asked the judge to hand down a sentence that would keep Steve in prison for the rest of his natural life for the murder, compounded with consecutive five-year sentences for each of the four counts relating to the anonymous e-mail and insurance money transfers. He also asked for a consecutive six-month term in jail for the misdemeanor delinquency charge, and that the credit for time served be applied only to the life sentence.

In addition, the prosecutor asked that Steve be forced to pay $756,628 in restitution for $700,000 in insurance payouts that "unjustly enriched the lawyers," the $6,000 in alimony that he didn't pay in July 2008, the more than $20,000 in car insurance money he received after Charlotte totaled Carol's Acura and the $28,500 he was reimbursed for cleanup of "the mess he made" at the house on Bridle Path.

"Justice really cannot be served unless that money is put back into Carol's trust," he said.

When the judge asked if any other victims wished to speak to the state's case, Paupore said no. Till the end the Arizona law that prevented Charlotte and Katie from being called victims in this case still seemed very odd to me. I wondered if, in the end, that roadblock had helped inspire Katie to graduate magna cum laude and Phi Beta Kappa from Occidental, to enter Boalt Law School at the University of California, Berkeley, my alma mater, and to attain a clerkship at the U.S. Attorney's Office in San Francisco.

Speaking for the defense, the DeMocker clan made a series of statements, starting with Steve's mother, whose quiet voice did not carry well back to the gallery. The gist of Jan's long statement, which she sent me several months later, was that she wanted to tell the judge and reinforce for Steve that he'd done many positive things in his life. Turning around to face her son, she directed her preamble to him before speaking to the judge once again.

Describing Carol as "an inspiring teacher," Jan acknowledged that Carol had been repeatedly described as a victim who had finally done what she told her battered clients to do, which was to walk away.

Carol and Steve met when both were starting grad school, she said. They lived in a house on his parents' property in New York and interacted with his parents quite a bit. The couple had a lot in common, she said, including a love of being outside. Writing their own wedding vows, they promised to support and nurture each other.

"Both of them really, really wanted to make a difference," she said.

Jan proceeded to tell stories of how Steve had saved the lives of the rock climber and the kayaker, and had served as a leader among his siblings and others with his heroic, larger-than-life deeds.

During the time she and Steve's father spent with Carol

and Steve every year, she said, she never saw any sign of their disagreements turning physical.

"There isn't any possibility of justice," she said, which would be to see Carol sitting with her daughters in the courtroom.

Because Carol lived her life with fairness and compassion, Jan said, she thought that even Carol "might very well be here with me asking for leniency and hoping for a sentence that would allow her grandchildren to have a chance to visit and to play with their grandfather sometime in the far future, when he was a free man again."

As Jan slipped along the front row of the gallery to return to her seat, Katie hugged her.

Next up was Michael DeMocker, Steve's youngest brother, who at forty-eight was twelve years younger.

Saying he'd met Carol when he was a teenager, he recalled being so upset one day that she pulled the car over in the middle of Boston traffic to hug and comfort him. She had also posed for photo portraits, and he felt he owed her for encouraging him to pursue the avocation that ultimately became his career.

Michael described Steve as even-tempered, noting that on a scuba-diving trip to Belize with all four DeMocker brothers, they headed out to sea with a group of strangers and lost their boat while the waves were high. Even though Steve was not a terribly experienced diver, "he kept his head," and his first instinct was to save the lives of others, not his own.

As a "very loving father," Steve was a good role model for him and had made a positive impact on so many lives, Michael said. Steve and Carol had passed on their "strength, love and resiliency" to their daughters.

Steve's sister Mary, a self-described "stay-at-home

mother," related how she and her family had moved to Prescott in 1998. They used to play tag outside the courthouse, but never went inside until this case began.

When Carol was killed, she said, "I lost a sister, I lost a friend, and I lost a mothering mentor. . . . I miss her. I miss her terribly."

Mary said she didn't understand why the rules within the courthouse had been so different during this case than they were in the community at large, where mothers taught their kids to play fair and not to lie. Turning around to face the prosecution table, her voice dripping with disdain, she said that in this case she saw "an investigation seeking not truth, but the conviction at any cost of someone close to me. It succeeded."

"My question is, why are we here at all?"

The scenario simply didn't fit with the evidence, she said, or who her brother had been for the past fifty-three years of her life.

"I haven't even seen one thing showing he was even on Carol's property," she said, adding that she rejected the guilty verdict.

She, too, asked the judge to show leniency, to give Steve some hope he could do the things he loved before he died and to "take the least unjust action that you can take today in an utterly unjust situation."

Sharon DeMocker, the physician, spoke less animatedly than her sister, as she described Steve as a "natural born leader" and "the creator of games, adventures and sometimes misadventures." He'd taught his siblings how to play fair and take care of each other, opened up a world of possibilities and helped boost her confidence while climbing and kayaking. She had put her life in his hands before, and if she could, she would do so again.

She and Steve had talked about traveling with medical teams to Third World countries, which obviously wasn't going to happen now, but Steve had already helped keep "many people alive," she said.

Switching to Carol, whom she described as a sister, confidante and "joyful, loving presence," Sharon said her sister-in-law had inspired the big, close-knit DeMocker family.

"There's a giant hole that was ripped in our hearts more than five years ago with Carol's murder," she said. The justice system only added to the injury when it not only failed Carol but her family and theirs by convicting the wrong man.

As Sharon walked back to her seat, she turned to Steve and mouthed, "I love you."

After Craig Williams asked to take a break, Steve's daughters made their statements. Katie went first, describing her family home growing up as "balanced, beautiful and overwhelmingly loving."

Her father skied down the most advanced slopes, carrying her as a two-year-old on his back, and her mother tucked her into bed. Their family danced together to loud music. Her mom worked in the garden and sprayed her with the hose; her dad bounced her and her sister on the trampoline. They all sat around the table after dinner and laughed till it hurt—memories that today are "both beautiful and sad."

Her parents balanced each other out, she said. Describing Carol as "unconditional loving, openhearted, open-armed and open-minded," she said Carol brought light into the room. She "loved people to a fault" and "forgave easily, sometimes too easily." Saying she was a better person for knowing her mother, Katie's voice started breaking.

Describing Steve as a kind and "deeply devoted father" who taught her how to climb rocks, ski, and kayak, Katie said he also showed her how to value herself as a woman, to be strong and confident and to believe "that I was as good as any boy."

As she acknowledged that this same man was accused of killing her mother, Katie said that, as a daughter of both the accused and the victim, she would rather talk about "healing and forgiveness," because that's how she was raised. Noting that the judge had the ability to grant her father the possibility of parole in twenty-five years, she asked Donahoe to do so.

As she and Charlotte passed each other in the aisle, Katie kissed her younger sister.

Taking the family's final turn at the podium, Charlotte spoke of her "self-destructive path" during her parents' divorce. She described her father as "my protector, my teacher and my greatest advocate," who gave her ice cream as an adolescent when she was feeling anxious. "He still remains someone I deeply respect and admire."

Her mother's death has been "absolutely devastating," she said. "I miss her joyful spirit." And the fact that neither her father nor her mother would see her get married or watch her children being born constituted an "excruciating punishment." In a soft voice she asked the judge not to "force the permanent loss of a second loved one."

Finally, Steve DeMocker stood to make his own statement, shuffling up to the podium in his ankle and waist chains, flanked by his two attorneys. Firmly, strongly and yet calmly, he declared his innocence to the judge in a low, monotone voice.

"I did not kill Carol," he said. "We loved each other for more than twenty years. Our marriage was over, but not our affection for each other. . . . I'm incapable of violence against her."

To believe that he killed Carol was to doubt *her* judgment, he said. They were still a family, and still as "fiercely protective of our children as any parents. I would no more have harmed her than I would harm my daughters by taking her from them."

He told the judge he had nothing more to ask than his siblings and daughters had been asking since the night of Carol's murder. Justice for her would not be accomplished by putting a falsely accused man in prison forever, he said, contending that the injustice to Carol was only compounded by taking him away from their children.

Steve turned to face his family, with his back to the court reporter, and thanked them for the faith they'd shown him. He told his daughters how proud he was of them, and "of the strength and the grace" they'd displayed when faced with the loss of both parents.

At that point the air-conditioning went on and the court reporter said she couldn't hear him, so Steve gave up and returned to the table. Katie started crying as she, Charlotte, Sharon and Mary circled their arms around each other for strength.

After another break Craig Williams gave a brief statement, noting that when he first started working on this case, the hefty files filled two giant trucks that had to be unloaded.

"I can tell you one thing for certain. It's not just that

Steve DeMocker is not guilty. It's that Steve DeMocker is innocent of killing Carol Kennedy. This is a wrongly convicted man."

Judge Donahoe started his comments by disagreeing with the family members who had dismissed the verdict and the justice system as unfair.

"It was a just verdict," he declared.

The outcome, he said, could have been different depending on how the trier of fact determined the credibility of the witnesses and weight of the evidence, for which he had considered "some residual doubt." But, he added, "The thing that I can't get past is this horrific crime scene. I saw these pictures, and I'm not sure I'm ever going to be able to erase those photos from my mind."

"This was a premeditated murder," he said. "It was a brutal murder. And from all appearances, the motive was money." As a result the circumstances of the murder outweighed the call for a lenient sentence.

Noting that Steve had already spent 1,919 days in jail, the judge fulfilled most of the prosecution's requests for sentencing, making sure that Steve DeMocker would spend every last day he had in prison, plus twenty-one years for the other counts.

Donahoe also ordered that Steve pay restitution to Carol's trust—$150,000 with an additional eighty-four percent surcharge, as well as the $700,000 in the insurance payments. The monthly amount, to be determined by state corrections officials, should be paid to the court and then to an interest-bearing account.

"Mr. DeMocker, good luck to you, sir," he said.

With that, the bailiffs walked Steve, whose expression remained stoic and unemotional, out of the courtroom with little fanfare.

* * *

I'd already called Craig Williams's office before the hearing to introduce myself. Now I approached him to ask if he would agree to an interview with me at some point. He said, rather abruptly, that he would have to get permission from his client, then promptly started talking to a couple of local reporters. I shrugged it off as a small-town snub.

To put someone in prison for life when detectives couldn't even put him at the crime scene "ought to shock the conscience," Williams said. "The investigation in this case is unbelievable."

Yes, what was done to Carol was terrible, he said, but "that doesn't mean that it's Steve. You can luminol the whole planet," he said, and you still wouldn't be able to put Steve at the scene.

After months of subsequent calls and e-mails to Williams with no definitive response, I sent a three-page letter to Steve in prison describing my attempts and my reasons for wanting to interview him, his defense team and his family, all of whom had stonewalled me so far.

Steve responded to me once via an e-mail from his sister Sharon, saying he needed to consult with his attorneys before doing so. When I received no further response, I e-mailed Sharon to follow up. She politely replied that she was sure Steve would contact me if he was interested in talking. He never did.

During the hearing the DeMocker clan looked like a bunch of angry, wounded and wronged soldiers, banding together for the battle of a lifetime. With him being the firstborn of nine kids, how could they not look up to him? Their worlds must have felt like they were falling apart, especially the youngest siblings.

Just as I'd thought at the start, the whole hugging ritual after each victim impact statement looked choreographed, as if they were thinking, *The world is watching. Let's show them how together we are—that we are a force to contend with.*

Months later, after reading Randy Schmidt's report about Steve's postverdict calls with his family, in which they discussed ways to influence the media, I'm guessing that my first impressions weren't too far-off.

But it's also possible that this resulted from being watched and filmed for the past five years, as *Dateline, 48 Hours, 20/20* and now *Inside Edition* covered this story for episodes that wouldn't run until after the sentencing. Somehow this story from this tiny mountain town had shown up on the national media radar.

After the sentencing the DeMockers appeared more exhausted than anything. Looking out the window in the hallway outside the courtroom, they huddled to discuss whether to make a statement and, if so, what to say to the few media, including the *Inside Edition* crew, standing outside with a TV camera.

Outside the courthouse the crew blocked the sidewalk, so Michael DeMocker, who, as a staff photographer for the New Orleans *Times-Picayune,* apparently felt more comfortable with the media than his siblings, stepped forward to make a statement.

"The family is obviously as disappointed in the sentence as they were in the verdict," he said. "Steve has a lot of appeals available to him. We're just going to stand by him while he does." In the meantime, he said, "we will wrap our arms around his daughters."

"It was the wrong verdict and the wrong sentence," Sharon DeMocker added.

Jan DeMocker said she'd been back in Prescott for weeks at a time, and expressed her thanks to the people who had been good to her and who, even after a "horrible, long five years," still seemed to believe in her son's innocence.

The *Inside Edition* crew shouted out questions and followed the family members as they walked to their respective cars. To me this overly aggressive behavior seemed predatory and big-city insensitive. It was also the talk of the family's lunch afterward.

CHAPTER 48

Craig Williams filed a notice of appeal on February 3, 2014, after which attorney David Goldberg, of Fort Collins, Colorado, was appointed by the Yavapai County Public Defender's Office to represent Steve through the appellate process. Because this was designated a complex case, Goldberg got an extension on the filing deadline.

The appeal was filed a little more than a year later, in March 2015. Goldberg cited multiple grounds for requesting to vacate Steve's convictions and dismiss the case with prejudice. Short of that, he requested a new trial—with a different prosecutorial agency—as "the only way to erase the appearance of impropriety that surrounds this case."

Before he'd even read it, defense investigator Rich Robertson said he believed the appeal had a good chance of producing a new trial. "When cases get as screwed up as this one did—for all the twists and turns and sideshow stuff that happened—it's almost inevitable that there was some mistake that occurs," he said.

But Mike Sechez, the retired prosecution investigator, said justice had already been served.

"I don't *think* Steve DeMocker did it and was convicted,"

he said, "I *know* one hundred percent in my mind that he did it. So his standing up there and saying, 'I didn't do it,' is him still hoping that his sentence will be overturned. He will never admit that he killed his ex-wife as long as his daughters are alive."

The Arizona State Bar investigation into Sheila Polk's allegations against John Sears, Steve's first lead defense counsel, was delayed until after Steve was convicted. It was finally completed in January 2015, resulting in dismissal of the bar charge against Sears.

The State Bar does not believe that we have the "clear and convincing evidence" necessary to prove the alleged misconduct, Craig Henley, senior bar counsel, wrote in a letter to Polk.

While Sears did notarize the documents in which Steve disclaimed the insurance proceeds, Henley wrote, it was a different law firm that negotiated those details with Hartford and secured the proceeds. Similarly, it was another attorney who represented Charlotte and Katie DeMocker concerning the transfer of money to Carol's estate, and also in the girls' decision to give that money to their grandparents and ultimately to fund Steve's defense. Although Henley described the nature, timing and ultimate use of those money transfers as "suspicious," he said Steve's daughters' testimony about these issues supported Sears's account of the events.

As the ultimate recipients of the proceeds, Katie and Charlotte were authorized to use the insurance proceeds as they wanted, Henley wrote.

Finally, Henley stated, although Sears did make an "incomplete" statement about the insurance payout during his opening statement, it didn't "appear to have been a knowingly false statement." During the investigation, Henley said, Sears argued in his own defense that his statement was "technically 'correct,'" noting that the parties were about to craft a stipulation about these issues when Judge Lindberg had to step down.

Jim Knapp's friends were upset by how he was portrayed by Steve's attorneys at the second trial, in the local newspaper and also on the *Dateline* episode, all of which painted Jim as an "odd duck," said Ken Korn, Jim's childhood friend.

"He wasn't that odd. He was a great guy," Ken said. "And I just get kind of annoyed that he was being portrayed as some kind of weirdo."

Like Ann Saxerud, Ken was also irritated that the defense went after Jim, saying he was obsessed with Carol, when he couldn't defend himself.

"I don't think he was," he said. "I think he just relied on her friendship. I think they had a natural bond that way."

The Jim Knapp whom Ken Korn once knew was not violent and would never have hurt Carol. In fact, Ken laughed when asked whether he'd ever seen Jim do anything physically violent.

"No, not at all. . . . There's no way. He's just not a violent guy. That's not part of his [makeup], especially to a woman."

When Ken heard the theories that Jim was killed because he was part of a drug ring that came after him and killed Carol, or that perhaps Jim had killed Carol himself, Ken couldn't believe any of it. He knew Jim was taking prescription drugs for his medical issues, "but to say the 'prescription drug ring,' I mean, c'mon."

"He got passionate, whatever he was into," Ken said.

"He was like all of us, searching. I know what he was, I know the truth. Whatever happened to him, it's just really sad. My wife and I, we just said, 'Poor Jim.'"

For Carol's friend Debbie Wren Hill, it was obvious that her murder was a crime of passion, as if the killer was saying, *"I'm mad about this, and take this! I don't want to give you six thousand dollars, and I didn't want you to leave!"*

"It all added up," she said, citing the cuts on Steve's legs and the long hours that he admitted to biking near Carol's house while his phone was off. "It didn't take rocket science to convict this man."

Sometime after the sentencing, Ruth Kennedy asked Debbie if she thought Steve had convinced himself that he didn't murder Carol. "Do you think that's how he keeps this up?" she asked.

Debbie didn't know how to answer that question. "Clinically, it's possible that he's deluded, that he really has convinced himself that he didn't do this," she said. "More likely is that he knows he did it and just doesn't want to come clean."

When Debbie asked how this whole tragedy hadn't destroyed Ruth, Carol's mother replied that she would forgive Steve if he asked her; she couldn't live out the rest of her life if she didn't.

"I have prayed for him this whole time and it's helped me a lot more than it's helped him," she said.

"You are an incredible inspiration for me because I don't know if I could do this, as her mother," Debbie told her.

"I felt kind of sorry for him," Ruth said.

In the end, Debbie said, "I deemed this as such a tragedy for everyone, including Steve. I mean, Steve, where was your impulse control when you did that? What I think is that he just flipped out and went into a rage and lost the ability to consider what the ramifications of his actions were going to be."

While I was researching this book, I learned from Katherine Morris and Joanne Frerking that Carol had told them about Steve coming to the house a couple of nights before she was killed, trying to get her to reconcile with him. When I told Ruth about this, she said the tone she heard in Carol's last two words, "Oh, no," matched that scenario.

Katherine said she was positive about the timing of his visit. She said she never mentioned it to investigators because they never asked; she just answered the questions they posed, and this never came up. But even if she and Joanne were confused, Steve had shown up at the house recently, unannounced, to drop off the artwork the day that Jim stopped him from coming inside. Carol had also told friends that Steve had come into the house unexpectedly with Thai food, and that she thought he'd been entering when she wasn't home and hacking into her e-mail.

Ruth said this scenario made it "even more logical that Carol said, 'Oh, no,'" as in, *"Oh, no, you're not showing up inside my house again"* or *"Oh, no, you're not coming here again to try to get me to get back together with you."*

Sturgis Robinson said he believes Steve carried out the murder wearing a full rain suit, which he discarded somewhere in the hills afterward.

For him, Steve's motivation grew out of a confluence of

factors. First, he was completely stunned that Carol actually went through with the divorce, then refused to reconcile. "It was the one constant that he could always count on in his life, that he could have Carol under his thumb," Sturgis said.

Second, the divorce carried severe financial ramifications for him, which were worsened by the stock market crash and his growing debt. This, coupled with Barb's simultaneous move to break free of his control, financially and personally, was just too much for him to bear.

"I'm sorry that there's not more direct evidence that it was him, but I cannot imagine any other scenarios where it wasn't him," he said. "Nothing was stolen and [Carol] wasn't raped."

Looking back, Sturgis said he now believes that the entire community of Prescott was complicit in what amounted to Steve's domestic abuse of Carol by letting him get away with his "deviant behavior" and womanizing for so many years.

"Steve wasn't ostracized" and no one rose up in indignation when he slept with the midwife, he said. "We failed Carol in a domestic-dispute situation. We should have recognized it as being abusive."

Sturgis started writing a book about this case, but gave up after putting several chapters together and facing the harsh reality that his friendship with Steve was never what he'd thought it was.

My friendship with Steve began over a woman, Sturgis wrote. *Over the next twenty years we would share others. We would revel in our narcissism, our physicality and our good fortune. What handsome boys we were. How badly we behaved. I would share my deepest feelings with him. I would find employment for him. I would stick up for him*

*when he mistreated others and I allowed him to tryst with
his lovers in my house. I lied to Carol for him.*

*Like a lover, I never questioned my passion. I called it
loyalty and friendship. I loved him right up to the moment
he [took] . . . millions of dollars [in client accounts from
me] and then coldly denied it in the face of incontrovert-
ible evidence. By the time he emerged as the primary
suspect in the murder of Carol Kennedy a few years after
our estrangement, I had come to believe, to fervently wish,
that the man I had chosen as my best friend was not merely
a shallow narcissist and a damaged man-child like myself,
but a sociopath, a changeling, beautiful, beguiling and
monstrous. That would explain all of it and I would not be
such a heart-broken fool.*

Charlotte DeMocker graduated from Arizona State
University with a finance degree in May 2014, with
neither parent there to watch her accept her diploma.

Carol's friend Katherine Morris came as their proxy,
while Ruth Kennedy sat at home in Nashville, sad to be
missing her granddaughter's important rite of passage.

"I'm eighty-nine, and that trip for the closing arguments
just about did me in. It was pretty grueling," Ruth said. "I
don't know, the older you get the harder it is to do something like that. But I do have the lines of communication
open. We do talk, sporadically, not as much as I'd like. I did
talk to Charlotte the day she graduated. Katie called me on
Mother's Day."

Two days after Charlotte's graduation ceremony, the De-
Mocker family had its first contact visit with Steve in five
years at the state prison in Florence, Arizona, where,
unless he wins his appeal, he will be spending the rest of
his days.

* * *

In the beginning Katherine couldn't believe that Steve had killed Carol. Sure, she thought, he was having affairs, but he wasn't a premeditated killer.

But now that she's come to believe that Steve was responsible, she "mindfully chooses" to think of him the way he was when they first met.

"At his core authentic self, he's good people. He really was a good father and a good provider, and illness and addiction took over. His addiction is what contributed to her death. They say in the big book for AA that sex and love addicts end up in jail or dead. He used and abused women to fill himself up, and when he couldn't have her anymore, he killed her."

Although she stays in close touch with Katie and Charlotte, she said they purposely steer away from this painful topic.

"Katie and Charlotte are strong, strong, strong women," she said. "They're becoming more clear as they are getting older, in setting boundaries" for themselves.

In some of the taped calls from prison, those boundaries came across in their tone of voice, as the young women told their father that they hadn't answered his previous calls because they were trying to study, pass tests and get jobs. They needed to focus on themselves.

"They are obviously very dear to me, and we don't talk about [the case]. Plain and simple," Katherine said. "They know my stance. They know what I think. They know what I feel. They've known that from the beginning."

Katherine was initially hesitant to do an on-camera interview with *Dateline* for its two-hour episode. But after discussing this with others close to Carol, they decided that someone needed to represent her, so Katherine agreed.

When the episode aired, it included a segment from a video taken on Whidbey Island, featuring a recent interview with Carol about Touch Drawing and the work she did during these meditative sessions. I obtained the full video from Deborah Koff-Chapin, and as I watched it, I almost felt as if Carol were speaking presciently to this case.

As her curly hair blew softly in the breeze, Carol sat smiling, exuding earnestness and calm as she looked into the camera. I could see why people saw her as a guru. Asked what message she wanted to deliver to whoever might be watching, she spoke as if she had a spiritual wisdom and knowingness about her.

Carol said she hoped that people could appreciate the "sense of wonder" and "mystery" that live in the "quiet stillness" of their hearts, where they could "drop down in and tell the truth. At any moment any one of us can make a choice, but it's a choice that has to be made, that I'm going to stop doing this other thing that I've been doing, and I'm going to choose to tell the truth now," she said.

I was so struck by that last sentence that I posted it on my website.

Carol went on to suggest that some folks may tell "malicious falsehoods to get ahead," but even when they try to live right and authentically, they can still "betray" something deeper in themselves.

Some might say these were apt messages for Steve, the man she called her soul mate, to get in touch with his "authentic" self, the one she'd fallen in love with so many years before. To finally stop with all the stories, such as the voice-in-the-vent tale and the anonymous e-mail, all the manipulation and all the lies. To tell the truth about what happened.

Katherine believes that if Carol could weigh in on this

situation today, she would do so in the same manner in which she lived her whole life: with kindness and absolution.

"Whoever did this she would have had a great compassion for. She absolutely would have. I know that sounds absolutely insane to most people, but that's who she was, and I don't feel it's my place or anybody else's to judge that. Carol would forgive him. That sounds crazy, but I felt that from the start."

AUTHOR'S NOTE AND ACKNOWLEDGMENTS

With all its legal twists and turns, this case was one of the most complex stories I've ever encountered as an author. Sometimes I felt like it was a bear I had to wrestle to the ground. But this story really got to me on a personal level as well, not just because of the facts of the case, but because it brought up some ghosts from my own past. As a result, researching and writing this story was at times an emotionally gut-wrenching and intellectually challenging journey.

At the outset I wondered how someone could murder such a peaceful, loving and spiritual being like Carol and in such a horribly violent way. I wondered how and why, as someone who had counseled battered women and women in recovery, she stayed with Steve for so long. I could almost feel the "self-torture" she described, the pain of loving someone who had hurt and manipulated her for so many years, and I empathized with her when Charlotte sided with Steve in the divorce battle.

By the same token I was also amazed at how Steve could keep so many women on the line, even his own family members, thinking he was such a good, sensitive guy, and yet treat Carol the way he did. I wondered how he could spend and borrow so much money and cheat with so many women, and yet not be willing or able to rein himself in. Was it compulsiveness, narcissism, entitlement, greed or addiction?

I did not judge. I just dug in and searched for the answers to these psychological questions so I could illustrate and explain the dynamics of Steve and Carol's very textured and complicated lives. Along the way I felt I got to know Carol Kennedy better than most murder victims I've written about, and wanted to pay her and her story the utmost respect.

When I learned that Carol had told the newspaper reporter in New York that she wanted to write a book about domestic violence someday, I felt I had her blessing. When Katherine told me about a dream in which she described me to Carol, who then said, "She sounds wonderful," I felt happy, as if I were really on the right track. And then, when I listened to the video and heard Carol express that prescient gem of a quote with which I ended the last chapter, I almost felt like she was talking to me from wherever her spirit had gone.

I was also drawn in by the crisp beauty and dark corners of Prescott, a small town that still seems to hold on to remnants of the Wild West and allowed Steve to womanize without consequences for so long. I was intrigued by the messiness of this ever-evolving criminal investigation, the scattershot methods used, and also the detectives' dedication to pin down leads in the end. The endless court filings and legal hyperbole. The kooky medical examiner who transported Carol's body in his truck and sent investigators on such a wild-goose chase to find Mr. 603. The ethical allegations flying in every direction, the anonymous e-mail, the voice in the vent, and the insurance money transfers. The judge with the brain tumor and the judge from the "sweat lodge" case. The Docugate scandal and the bombshell e-mail that got thrown out on this roller-coaster ride to justice. Suffice it to say, I came to empathize with the attorneys in this case, because there was so much information it became a challenge to decide what to include and what to leave out.

Because the second defense team made Jim Knapp such a major part of its case, I went more into his background, his role in this case and his death than I would have otherwise. I tried repeatedly to reach his brother, Bobby, through Jim's friends, but he didn't want to talk to me. Understanding his desire for privacy, I drew much of the information I used to craft those chapters from trial transcripts, court exhibits, witness interviews by law enforcement and my own.

Having had an alcoholic husband who committed suicide—and acted very strangely when he took narcotic painkillers and even more so when he mixed them with alcohol—I think I can safely say that Jim Knapp did the same. Yes, his life and the condo where his body was found were full of oddities, but that's what happens when addicts relapse amid depression, fear and addled thinking. To them, their lives seem hopeless and helpless, and they see no other way out. Jim's friends said he was a prankster, and they believed, as did police, that he might have staged the scene at the condo to look like something more nefarious happened, perhaps not as a joke in this case, but to protect his two young sons from the harsh truth that their father had taken his own life.

My late husband was found with a bag of crushed lightbulbs in his hotel room in Mexico, which I was told he might have been planning to eat if he wasn't successful in killing himself there by his chosen method. I can't even imagine what it must be like to be in such a depressed, inebriated haze to think that way. But in the end, suicidal people typically are not acting or thinking rationally.

One of the unusual aspects of telling this story was that I had to rely more than I typically do on document research and court transcripts than my own interviews with human beings. That's because neither the sheriff's office nor the county attorney's office would agree to talk, citing "legal and ethical rules" and the pending appeal. That said, Jeff Paupore spoke to me briefly and the prosecution was very cooperative with releasing as public records the trial exhibits, crime scene photos and thousands of pages of investigative reports, witness interviews, and audiotapes and transcripts of Steve's many recorded jailhouse calls. I also had access to five years of court filings and transcripts from both trials. Any minor editing of testimony or witness interviews was done for storytelling purposes, mostly by deletion or for clarity or ease of reading. Any errors are unintentional.

As I mentioned, I tried to get interviews with Steve's daughters, but my attempts to do so were unanswered or rebuffed, so I respected the girls' obvious wish to be left alone. I tried to tell their side of the story through their own words when I could, or through those close to Carol who knew them well.

As I also mentioned, my efforts to speak with Steve De-Mocker, his parents and siblings were rebuffed as well. Defense investigator Rich Robertson told me that because they believe he was wrongly convicted, they saw no reason to talk to me for this book. That said, I think Steve's and his family's comments at the sentencing, as well as the emotions they expressed in the postverdict jail calls, are indicative of what they likely would have said to me. Luckily, I found others who were more than willing to talk about him and what makes him tick.

When I asked for interviews with John Sears and Craig

Williams, the lead attorneys from Steve's two defense teams, neither one agreed. Nor would they provide me with any "released" defense exhibits or investigative reports that I couldn't get through the courts.

When the county attorney's office wouldn't let me publish the evidence photos it had released to me as public records, Robertson kindly gave me permission to publish his, and I thank him for that. He was also the only person from the defense team who was willing to answer my questions and help me fact-check, which proved invaluable. Although I'm not required to give a "balanced" version of a case in a book, as news outlets are supposed to do, I also don't like to write one-sided stories quoting only those people who think the convicted killer was a bad person and did the deed. I'm grateful that Robertson made himself available to me so there was least one voice representing Steve's and the defense's perspective. I just wanted to state for the record that it wasn't for lack of trying on my part.

I don't believe that anyone—even a convicted killer—is all bad, any more than I think crime victims or their family members are all good. People are human and flawed. In this case Carol and Steve were victims of love, obsession and addiction, as well as a desire to make their relationship work and last, despite numerous red flags along the way telling them to stop. This is a tragedy all around, especially for their daughters, who have now effectively lost both parents.

It felt very rewarding to get such an extraordinary degree of cooperation from Carol's family and close friends. I am especially grateful to Katherine Morris, Debbie Wren Hill and Ruth Kennedy for giving me the backstory of Carol and Steve's relationship, and for helping me illustrate how its dynamics—and Steve's personality—evolved as he earned and spent more money, up until the day she was murdered. Like me, they wanted Carol and her spirit to be remembered in a case that has been so centered on Steve. I know that rehashing some of this was difficult for them, and I am thankful that they helped me capture her and her words. I also am grateful for the contributions of Sturgis Robinson, who gave me some crucial insights into Steve's character. The conversations and events these folks re-created for me were approximated from memory, which I cross-checked with official sources wherever possible.

I want to thank all the other people who gave me interviews or helped me gather photos, documents and information. I send a special nod to Sue Willoughby, who first sent me news articles informing me of this fascinating case, then later took some photos for the book. She'd originally contacted me after reading my book *Dead Reckoning,* which features two other murder victims from Prescott: Tom and Jackie Hawks. A retired Yavapai County probation officer, Tom owned Matt's Saloon, a bar on Whiskey Row near Van Gogh's Ear and across the street from the courthouse, where I had a drink in the Hawkses' memory during my research trip for this book.

Because Prescott is such a small town and the college was such a microcosm, privacy was a concern for some of the people I interviewed, as well as some interviewed by law enforcement, so I used a number of pseudonyms in this book, which are noted in the text.

Big thanks also go to: Les Stukenberg, Michelle Madigan Herman, Jakob Trierweiler, Tina Fenton, Shelly Bacon, Penny Cramer, Sheila Polk, Mike Sechez, Jeff Paupore, Sally and Casey Ober, Sandy Moss, Joanne Frerking, John Lutes, Clayton Heath, Ken Morley, Dan Spencer, Julie Bull, Bonnie Manko, Rick Debruhl,

Deborah Koff-Chapin, Ken Korn, Jack Nathan, Janice DeMocker, Carole and Chris Scott, Sharon Whitley Larson and Géza Keller.

Also much thanks to my agent, Peter Rubie, as well as to Michaela Hamilton and Karen Auerbach at Kensington, and to photographer Joel Ortiz.